THE GREAT QUEST

THE GREAT QUEST

FIFTY US STATE HIGH POINTS AND MORE

MATTHEW GILBERTSON AND ERIC GILBERTSON

KEITH GILBERTSON, EDITOR

authorHOUSE®

AuthorHouse™ LLC
1663 Liberty Drive
Bloomington, IN 47403
www.authorhouse.com
Phone: 1-800-839-8640

Published by AuthorHouse   07/17/2013

ISBN: 978-1-4817-7670-7 (sc)
ISBN: 978-1-4817-7669-1 (e)

Any people depicted in stock imagery provided by Thinkstock are models, and such images are being used for illustrative purposes only.
Certain stock imagery © Thinkstock.

This book is printed on acid-free paper.

Because of the dynamic nature of the Internet, any web addresses or links contained in this book may have changed since publication and may no longer be valid. The views expressed in this work are solely those of the author and do not necessarily reflect the views of the publisher, and the publisher hereby disclaims any responsibility for them.

TABLE OF CONTENTS

Fifty states in chronological order with altitude and date of first ascent

Extra Credit

Next Project: Country Highpoints
Included is one country highpoint report from each continent
(Except Antarctica)

Patch designed by Amanda Morris

Available for purchase from matthewg@alum.mit.edu

Fig 1: A collection of pictures from each state highpoint.

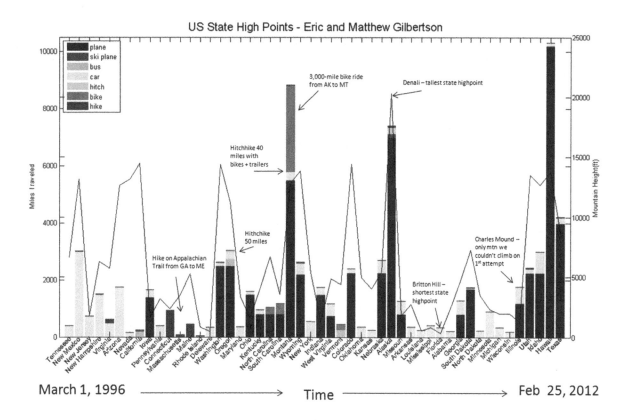

Fig 2: An effort graph, showing the different modes of transportation we used to reach each of the state high points. Each color represents a different mode of transportation. On the X-axis is state and time (increasing from L-R). On the left Y-axis is the miles traveled for each mode of transportation, while the right Y-axis measures the mountain height in feet, depicted by the thin black line.

INTRODUCTION

Why the state high points?

In calculus, the Extreme Value Theorem states that if F(x, y) is a continuous function in some closed, bounded set D in R2, then there are points in D, (x_1, y_1) and (x_2, y_2) so that $F(x_1, y_1)$ is the absolute maximum and $F(x_2, y_2)$ is the absolute minimum of the function F(x, y) in D. If you consider F(x, y) to be elevation above sea level, the region D to be a state, and apply the theorem to each of the 50 states, this means that every state has a highest point. Some states might use a different term such as mountain, peak, hill, butte, mesa, mound, mauna, or dome rather than "point," but the fact is that every state has a maximum elevation. That means that every state is worth visiting.

Our quest for the fifty state high points has taken us to the most spectacular places in the country. From the golden wheat fields of Nebraska to the glistening glaciers of Alaska to the dusty deserts of western Nevada the quest has introduced us to parts of the USA that we wouldn't have visited otherwise. You see, on the state high points list, all states have equal importance. Although Alaska's Mount McKinley and Delaware's Ebright Azimuth differ vastly in terms of difficulty, if you're working on "The List," sooner or later you're going to have to climb both of them. As we've learned over the past fifteen years, and you'll find out through our stories here, there's beauty to be discovered in every state, and State Highpointing takes you on the grandest tour through all fifty of them.

For us, the quest began gradually and intensified exponentially. First, a family trip to Clingmans Dome in Tennessee with our parents and brother Jacob. A few years later, a climb up New Mexico's Wheeler Peak with Dad and Jacob. A few more years go by. Then High Point in New Jersey. School starts at MIT. We get involved in the MIT Outing Club (MITOC) and meet other outdoor aficionados. More hiking, more trips up Mt. Washington in New Hampshire. Gradually we begin to build up some momentum. Pretty soon we get into mountaineering. Then the hard mountains begin to fall. Granite Peak (MT)—check, Gannet Peak (WY)—check. Now we've contracted high point mania. We start grad school and can afford to rent cars. Colorado, Oklahoma, Kansas, and Nebraska in one weekend. Then Alaska, the crux. By the time we realize that someday we'll actually finish, we're already at number thirty-four. Now we're spending hours on Google Maps, optimizing driving routes with Matlab, and days monitoring ticket prices on Kayak, saving up as much as we can, focusing our efforts on the great quest . . .

Along the way, we've (somehow) managed to write a trip report about each and every state. Most of the time there is a certain sense of satisfaction in pouring out our experiences and trip highlights onto virtual paper, relieving our minds of the need to remember all the details. But occasionally it has been a little painful. We'll get back from an action-packed weekend on Sunday evening, absolutely exhausted and reluctant to fire up our computers, fearful that our email inboxes will explode from a weekend or longer of our absence. We want to eat and get straight to bed.

But we know that our Dad is waiting. He's waiting to hear about Jerimoth Hill or Borah Peak or whatever mountain we just climbed. The posting of our trip report onto the MITOC Photo Gallery webpage is his indication that we're OK, and he'll tell Mom (so she doesn't have to get worried

Matthew Gilbertson and Eric Gilbertson

by reading the report herself). We know that tomorrow, his English-as-a-Second-Language (ESL) students will be reading, analyzing, and acting out our stories. We know we've got to provide them with fresh reading material. We also know that if we don't write everything down soon, many details from the trip will be forgotten over time. Lastly, we want to share our stories with fellow adventurers, hoping that our own trip reports will inspire others as much as others' trip reports have inspired us. Writing a trip report gives us a sense of relief, a feeling that we've tied a bow around the trip and that we can finally relax and start planning the next adventure.

So, we postpone a few hours of sleep, rewind, and mentally play back the adventure, outlining in our minds the salient points from the trip, the noteworthy experiences, the challenges, the problems solved, the people we met, the boulders we scaled, the snow we tasted, and begin to write the trip report . . .

ABOUT THIS BOOK

When you climb a mountain, you don't acquire anything tangible. You gain an experience which you can express via a trip report. This book is a collection of our trip reports, favorite stories, and photos from our climbs to the summits of all fifty state high points. This book, therefore, is the tangible manifestation of our quest.

Through this book, our goal is to inspire others in the same way that others have inspired us. As we'll discuss in a moment, over the past fifteen years we've made many good friends, particularly through the MIT Outing Club, who have given us something to aim for. "I've climbed X," someone might say. "That's cool, we've juggled on top of Y," we respond. "Well I've glissaded from the top of Z," another person would counter . . . *silence*, as we gape with amazement . . . . And thus the seeds of inspiration for a new adventure are planted in the back of our minds. In this book we hope to give back to the community of adventurers who have challenged and motivated us. Let these trip reports serve you, the reader, as inspirations for your own epic adventures.

The reader might also be interested in another book we published a few years ago, titled "Mountain Adventures: Whites, West, and the Appalachian Trail." The 231-page book features trip reports from our hikes on the Appalachian Trail, a 3000 mile bicycle ride from Deadhorse, Alaska to Great Falls, Montana, and other adventures from the Rockies to the White Mountains. Ordering details: *www.emadventures8.blogspot/ also available at all online book outlets including Amazon, Barnes and Noble and many more.*

The book is organized chronologically from state high point #1 to #50 with a few bonus reports sprinkled in at the end. We've taken turns writing the reports so pay attention to the text at very beginning of a report to know whom "I" refers to. In some cases we've climbed a high point multiple times or Eric has summitted on a different day than Matthew. In that case, we've included our favorite trip report(s).

Why climb?

Over the years a common question has come up: why do you climb? It has been asked by our friends, fellow hikers, even our Dad's ESL students. Occasionally we might even ask ourselves. It's tough to articulate our motivation for climbing the state high points, but here are a few reasons that come to mind:

Problem solving opportunities. Each mountain presents a new problem to solve. How do I get to the mountain? What is the best mode of transportation, hiking, biking, driving, flying, or hitchhiking? What gear should I bring? What's my backup plan if things don't go smoothly? How do I fit the trip into the available time? As mechanical engineers, we're always figuring out how to design a system within a set of constraints and limited resources, and climbing gives us the opportunity to apply our problem solving skills to our adventures.

The physical challenge. Sometimes in school it feels like we spend too much time indoors, sitting down, looking at a computer screen or reading. Or course, there's nothing wrong with giving ourselves a mental challenge, but we think that in order to be healthy we need to challenge ourselves physically too.

The sense of accomplishment from working on and completing a project. As engineering students we're used to working on projects with fixed milestones and Gantt charts monitoring our progress. Maybe we need to design a solar trough actuation system, and part of the design process is to brainstorm ten ideas, then make sketch models of the top five ideas, then prototype the best one. It gives a sense of fulfillment to check off milestones accomplished and track progress towards the end goal. The same holds for climbing mountains, where the end goal is all 50 US State highpoints, and each state is a milestone along the way.

Seeing new places. Highpoints are rarely in easily-accessible locations, and just getting to the start of a climb usually entails travelling through areas we would possibly never visit otherwise.

ABOUT THE AUTHORS

ERIC GILBERTSON
AND
MATTHEW GILBERTSON

According to the USA State Highpointers club, we are the first twins to climb all fifty state highpoints and the second team to climb all of them unguided. As of 2012 there are fewer than 250 people who have climbed all fifty state highpoints, so there's still plenty of room for other firsts.

We were born in Berea, KY in 1986 and started hiking with our Dad in the nearby hills and hollers of Kentucky as soon as we could walk. Before that, our parents carried us on their backs. As we grew older we became faster, and started hiking and backpacking at the Pigg House, the Pinnacle, and Anglin Falls near Berea. Twice a year we would go backpacking for several days in the Smoky Mountains of Tennessee and North Carolina. Then we went to Philmont Boy Scout Ranch near Cimarron, New Mexico, where we learned how to pack light and survive for days out in the wilderness.

We started college in the fall of 2004 at the Massachusetts Institute of Technology (MIT) in Cambridge, Mass, and there we discovered the MIT Outing Club, which has shown us a whole new world of adventure. The MIT Outing Club (MITOC) has offered us an avenue for adventure, a way to make friends and meet other outdoor enthusiasts, and has helped us to escape the stresses of MIT and energize us for the next week of problem sets, hard work, and little sleep. MITOC is a group of more than 1,400 students and staff from the Boston area who share a passion for outdoor adventure. Through organized trips called "Circuses" we soon made friends and started going on more extreme hikes deep into the White Mountains of New Hampshire.

MITOC's Winter School program dramatically changed our perspective on hiking. Our first Winter School in January 2005 introduced us to a small sample of the endless opportunities provided by snow. We learned from experienced winter adventurers how to snowshoe, ice climb, cross-country ski, build snow shelters, hike above tree line, and survive in the winter. These skills would prove invaluable in our future highpointing adventures.

We graduated from MIT in the spring of 2008, each with degrees in Mechanical Engineering, and took a summer break from studying to travel and climb mountains. We flew up to Prudhoe Bay, Alaska and bicycled 3000 miles south to Great Falls, Montana, climbing the Montana and Wyoming state highpoints, Granite and Gannett Peak, at the end of the trip.

In the fall of 2008 we settled down again back at MIT to work on masters degrees in Mechanical Engineering, developing a handheld force-controlled ultrasound probe (Matthew), and a thermally-actuated deep-sea oil well safety valve (Eric). By then we were trip leaders for Winter

School and MITOC Circuses, and could start passing down our knowledge to the next generation of mountaineers.

We finished our masters degrees after a year and a half and both decided to stay on for PhDs in mechanical engineering, but not before another adventure break. We negotiated with our advisors to have a summer off before continuing our studies, and within 12 hours of handing in our final theses we were both on a plane to Alaska. Our first trip of the summer was to climb Alaska's state highpoint, Denali, which would require the culmination of all our MITOC Winter School skills. Next on the agenda was another 3000-mile bicycle tour, this time in Europe to hit the country highpoints of Iceland, Finland, Sweden, Norway, Denmark, Netherlands, Belgium, Luxembourg, Germany, and Liechtenstein.

Since the fall of 2010 we've been back at MIT working on our mechanical engineering PhDs and squeezing in state highpoints whenever we can. Our dad and grandpa accompanied us for a weeklong road trip to finish off the mid-west highpoints, and we finished off Idaho and Utah during an intense weekend trip out west. While studying for our doctoral qualifying exams in January 2011 we took another week-long road trip with our dad to climb all the southern state highpoints. Our dad drove while we studied in the back seats, taking breaks to go out and hike up the highpoints. We both passed the exams, so we can now say highpointing contributed to our degrees.

In February 2012 we finished our final state highpoint—Guadalupe Peak in Texas—with a quick weekend flight down to El Paso. Now we're busy trying to finish our PhD degrees: Matthew is designing an improved handheld force-controlled ultrasound probe and Eric is working with autonomous kayaks.

ADVENTURE FUNDING

We're often asked, "How in the world do you guys have enough money to do all that traveling?" The answer is comprised of three parts: 1) graduate student stipend, 2) frugality, and 3) stealth camping. We try to live in the cheapest apartment, don't own a car, don't eat out often, and repair our own gear in order to devote the rest of our stipend to adventure. The stipend might not seem too big, but with frugal daily living we've been able to stretch it pretty far.

Another important factor is stealth camping. By "stealth," we mean camping in places where camping might not necessarily be "approved." Over the years we've discovered that as long as you keep a low profile and nobody finds you, there are almost unlimited stealth camping opportunities throughout the USA and world. The stories throughout this book will further flesh out that definition.

By stealth camping we avoid staying in hotels. Back in 2006 we spent $200 on our tent that we've slept in for about 300 nights. That's just 67 cents/night, a few orders of magnitude below the price of a hotel stay. By shopping at grocery stores during our adventures we avoid eating at restaurants. This lifestyle enables us to save money that we can dedicate to other adventures. Plus, we've always found that a night of stealth camping in Hawaii, for example, is usually a lot more memorable (and thus better trip report material) than a night in a hotel.

Another tough question often posed to us by fellow adventurers is, "so now that you're done with the state high points, what's next?" The next logical step is of course the country high points (we're up to 51 of those so far). And maybe the Canadian Provincial high points too. We're open to suggestions. The blessing of topography is that every region has a highest point, so there are always more mountains to climb.

ACKNOWLEDGEMENTS

Along the way, our family, friends, and highpointing colleagues have motivated, inspired, energized us, and provided companionship.

With our family trip to Clingman's Dome trip back in 1996, our Dad helped launch us on the quest. Dad has always supported us, eager to hear about our adventures, encouraging us to write about our experiences, and putting together blogs so our grandparents can vicariously hike the Appalachian Trail or bike through Alaska or Norway with us. He's the first to read the trip report, the first to plot our progress on the map, and the first to ask us "which mountain is next?" He's always given us the verbal "wow" of approval which motivates us to keep exploring. This book and the stories it contains exist because of our Dad.

We'd like to thank our Mom for keeping us safe. She's the voice of reason that keeps us on the right side of the safety vs. danger line. I don't know too many moms who tolerate their sons spending sleep-deprived nights driving through the Sahara desert, weeks on an Alaskan glacier, or months camping in Canadian grizzly country, without worrying too much. We thank our mom for her thoughts and prayers which have helped keep us safe on these adventures.

Our brother Jacob has given us a model of toughness to live up to. No matter the temperature, the weight on his back, the miles to hike, or the mountain to climb, we've never heard a single complaint from Jacob. With us, he's shirtlessly summitted Mt Washington, Mt Greylock, and Newfoundland's Cabox (that's for another book) and sets an unmatchable high bar for stamina and hardiness.

Our family has often provided that extra push of motivation it has sometimes taken to get the trip reports written. Grandma Wright was an avid reader of "Mountain Adventures," our first book. I think she always took a certain amount of satisfaction in telling everyone about the latest place her grandsons had been to. Grandpa Gilbertson has the most complete collection of our postcards—he always asks about our adventures and where we're headed to next. Eric and I are always working to provide Grandpa with new talking material for morning coffee at Valentino's.

And, of course, Matthew would especially like to thank his wife Amanda (*we were married June 15, 2013*) for her unwavering/faithful support of and dedication to our goal. Amanda's commitment to our highpointing quest stretches all the way back to one of our first days together: during a hike to the highest mountain on Santa Cruz Island in the Galapagos Islands back in Spring Break of 2005. Since then, whether it has meant a road trip dedicated to Spruce Knob or Ebright Azimuth or Point Reno, stretching out an already packed road trip to include Cerro de Punta or Backbone Mountain, or standing around in a bathing suit on a frigid day atop Mt Washington for the webcam photo, Amanda has always been committed to helping us achieve our goal. In fact, Amanda actually accepted Matthew's marriage proposal in the midst of a raging hurricane at the trailhead for Montanha do Pico—the highest point in Portugal.

Amanda is the ultimate authority on our whereabouts, our plans, and our progress. She's the last person I call before we plunge into the wilderness and the first to know when we're back safely. And when we're on a summit I'll do whatever it takes to call or text to let her share in the excitement.

Whether it means tip-toeing out to a precarious ledge for optimal cell phone coverage or peeling off my mittens during a blizzard on Mt Washington to fire up the cell phone, that last joule of energy in the cell phone battery and last bit of feeling in my fingers is reserved for one simple text message: "hey Amanda—made it to the top—hope ur having a good day—love matthew." Her voice is the sound I look forward to most at the end of every adventure.

We'd also like to thank Mrs. Morris (Amanda's mom) for her logistical support and for making the quest so much more enjoyable. An exquisitely-prepared home-cooked feast to celebrate climbing Spruce Knob; an amazing post-hike dinner at the beautiful Mt Washington Hotel; a few days of R&R with a real bed at the half-way point of the Appalachian Trail—Amanda's mom treats us like sons. Switzerland, China, Peru, Barbados . . . I can't help but smile when I think back to all the nice places we've experienced and local cuisine we've enjoyed thanks to Amanda's Mom. I'm looking forward to the next adventure with my mother-in-law.

A big thanks goes to our friends Jake Osterberg and Garrett Marino. Since we met Jake—a native Minnesotan—during freshman pre-orientation in 2005, he's shown us the endless engineering and adrenaline opportunities that snow provides. With Jake we've built snow shelters and countless gigantic snowmen on MIT's Briggs Field, biked through blizzards, explored the alpine backcountry of the Whites by sled, and played pond hockey just below treeline on Mt Lafayette. When the snow starts falling and most people seek shelter inside, Jake puts on his gloves, picks up his snow shovel, and marches into the storm to see what fun can be had. Jake's affinity for snow is contagious; he has inspired us to enjoy the snow—and seek it.

And thanks to Señor Garrett Marino, our expert weather consultant. I remember one time, during a hike across New Hampshire in January, Eric and I had been holed up in our tent for 20 hours, waiting out a freezing rainstorm. "Garrett, how much longer do you think this'll last?" I asked over the phone from inside my sleeping bag. "We're about five miles east of Hanover." "Well, you've got another four hours, then it'll clear out," Garrett answered, "a high pressure system is coming in this afternoon and it'll be clear and cool the rest of the week." And sure enough, Garrett's forecast turned out to be dead-on. Garrett, a professional meteorologist, can craft personalized, pinpoint weather forecasts so accurate they put to shame weather.com, weather.gov, and weather dot anything else. His forecasts remain a vital component to our success.

Thanks to Bill Vannah, for always asking about and appreciating what we've been up to over the past weekend. Motivated by Bill's encouragement, Eric and I have begun to seek new opportunities for adventure in cold bodies of water such as the Hudson Bay, Labrador, Newfoundland, Iceland, and glacial pools in New Zealand. Thanks to budding highpointers Adam Rosenfield and Doug Powell for our adventures across the frozen tundra of the Northeast in search of highpointing glory.

And we'll never forget the friends we've made, and continue to make, through our eight years (and counting) with the MIT Outing Club. There's our all-star team from Denali: Woody Hoburg—fearless skier, handstander, and MIT 5.0'er; Darren Verploegen—fearless climber, highest and bravest leaker in the state of Montana; and Dan Walker—fearless teacher, jokester, and possessor of the ability to make everyone smile. There's Philip Kreycik, architect of the most ridiculous trips, including a one-day bicycle ride + climb of Mt Washington from Cambridge, and a 56-mile/19-hour

Hut Traverse. And Bilal Zia, our inspiration to start running marathons and colleague on Mount Rainier and the Four State Challenge.

And thanks to a few other friends with whom we've had the privilege of hiking: Chris Glazner, Mike Kokko, Greg Wallace, Jason Katz-Brown, Jon Hanselman, Ian Reese, Adam Rosenfield, Elliott Fray, John Romanishin, Kapil Singh, MinWah Leung, and Nadine Mueller-Dittman.

—Matthew and Eric Gilbertson, December 2012.

1 CLINGMANS DOME

TENNESSEE

6,643ft

Dates climbed: 1996; March 1999; June 14, 2006

Author: Matthew

Accompanying climbers: Keith Gilbertson, Jacob Gilbertson

Our quest for the state high points began in 1996 with Clingmans Dome. For this reason it holds an extra special place in my state high points collection. Since then we've summitted it two other times.

It also has what I believe to be the coolest state high point name. It's too cool for a "mount" or "peak" or "hill"—only "dome" is worthy of it. The coolness of its name is potentially rivaled only by Delaware's "Ebright Azimuth."

1st Ascent: 1996. Unfortunately the records for this early ascent are scarce. I remember there being a lot of snow though. We were on our way to Myrtle Beach, South Carolina.

2nd Ascent: March 1999. Sometime in middle school we started backpacking the Smokies with our dad. With the money we had earned from digging and selling ginseng in Kentucky we were able to purchase some nice backpacking equipment which we put to the test in the Smokies.

A critical turning point in our backpacking career came when we visited the Philmont Boy Scout Ranch in northeastern New Mexico in 2000. We went on a 60-mile trek and learned the essentials of what gear and food to take, how to pack, and how to be bear-safe. After being empowered by Philmont we started visiting the Smokies twice a year for four-day treks with our Dad and Jacob: once during Spring Break and once during Fall Break.

In the Smokies we learned how to deal with rain. We became pros at navigating creek crossings. During one four-day hike I remember we got about six inches of rain and at one stream crossing we actually had to throw logs into the creek to build our own bridge. A few miles later we had to take a different trail because the creek crossing we were planning on taking had turned into a raging, muddy river. Hiking in the Smokies toughened us up.

Back to Clingmans Dome. We climbed to the summit for the second time in March 1999 during a Spring Break hike with our Dad and Jacob. It was nice because it was still early enough in the season that the road was closed, which meant that we had the summit all to ourselves and wouldn't have to deal with all the tourists.

Afterwards we hiked a few miles down the road and descended on a trail into the valley. That night an epic rainstorm struck. By the morning the creek we had planned to ford turned into the Amazon River and entire trees floated by. Luckily we found another trail and made it back to the car after some hitchhiking.

3rd Ascent: We climbed Clingmans Dome for the third time while we were hiking the Appalachian Trail. Up to that point we had enjoyed relative solitude on the 150 miles of trail we had hiked since Springer Mountain in Georgia. But as we emerged from the "Green Tunnel" into the visitor's complex at Clingmans Dome we were astounded by the number of people. We hadn't seen that many people for a couple of weeks. While walking to the summit on the asphalt road we even had to wait behind a couple of wheelchairs and senior citizens in high heels. That was probably the most crowded section of the A.T

2 Wheeler Peak

New Mexico

13,161ft

Date climbed: June 2000

Author: Matthew

(Report Written February 2011)

Accompanying climbers: Keith Gilbertson, Jacob Gilbertson

It can be tough to remember experiences from eleven years ago. A lot of mountains can be climbed in eleven years and they may all start to blend together. But New Mexico's Wheeler Peak is not one of those mountains. It is not one of those fuzzy memories. I still remember vividly from Wheeler—our 2nd state high point—my first very encounter with altitude sickness. I also remember the thrill of snow in June. It was the first big Rocky Mountain that we climbed, and helped to ignite our interest in mountaineering.

Our destination that summer was the Holiest Land in all of Boy Scouting—Philmont. We were on a pilgrimage to the large Boy Scout Ranch in Northeastern New Mexico to learn the art of backpacking from the kung fu masters who had trained generations of scouts. Our Dad had visited Philmont several times on Boy Scout trips when he was a kid and got hooked. He worked there for a few summers too, teaching scouts how to pan for gold, fly-fish, and how to keep from getting eaten by bears. Now it was our turn to follow in his footsteps. The plan was to climb Mt Wheeler before heading a few miles over to Philmont.

I would say that Islam is to Mecca as Boy Scouting is to Philmont. All self-respecting Boy Scouts must at some point in their lives complete a trek at Philmont. More than once Eric and I have been hiking somewhere in the country and met another hiker who proclaimed they were an Eagle Scout. Eric and I would momentarily pause with respect to acknowledge their notable achievement. Then, to level the playing field, we would reply that we have been to Philmont, and we soon became equals with the other hiker again.

Our plan that summer was to drive from Kentucky to Philmont, then embark on a five-day trek and drive back, for a total of about 3 weeks. But things became complicated when we signed up for a calculus class at Berea College that summer. We really wanted to take the class but doubted it would be acceptable to miss three whole weeks of class. We presented our dilemma to our professor, Prof. Schmidt. Surprisingly, he said it would be all right to miss that much class, but to make up for it we needed to do every odd-numbered problem in the first half of the textbook. Every odd-numbered problem. Ouch. We said we'd do it. We brought the textbook in the van with us and started driving west.

The route from Berea, KY to the summit of New Mexico's Wheeler Peak is long indeed. It took us through Tennessee, Arkansas, and then Texas. We stopped in El Paso to cross into the country of Mexico at Ciudad Juárez. The quick hour-long visit made us appreciate our US citizenship. Next we headed over to White Sands National Monument in New Mexico for some awesome dune jumping. We visited our friends Bob and Jane Fistori in Deming and then drove north.

The main trailhead for Wheeler Peak begins in Taos ('tauss'—one syllable), the home of a big ski resort. As we drove in we looked up at the mountains and couldn't believe the snow we were seeing. It's June, for goodness sake, what's snow doing around here in June?

The place was deserted but there was some kind of a German festival going on and for some reason that meant we got a good rate on the room. We stayed the night in the lodge and headed out the next morning. Our mom would manage base camp (9,400ft) while we pushed on for the summit (13,161ft).

We headed up the Bull of the Woods trail early that morning. We planned to stay overnight at the Bull of the Woods Meadow campsite to make things more interesting. We climbed through the trees up to about 12,000ft and starting running into our first snow. We just couldn't believe how much snow there was for June. Some of the drifts were three feet high in the trees. For us it was unbelievable. We had only seen summer snow one other time, in the Big Horn Mountains of Montana.

Luckily we found a clear spot amongst the trees and pitched the tent. I remember feeling awful that evening. I couldn't eat anything. I couldn't even force down the Ramen noodles. I didn't know it at the time, but I was suffering from AMS (acute mountain sickness). For some reason I was the only one affected. Jacob, Eric, and our Dad were fine. We just assumed that I was sick and would get over it in the morning.

I think I bounced back a little in the morning, probably because I had acclimated a little overnight. We kept climbing and soon emerged onto the biggest snowfield I had ever seen. I couldn't believe it. Here it was, June, and we were standing on top of a fifteen foot deep pile of snow the area of a couple of football fields. At that time I didn't know that was possible. It certainly didn't happen in Berea, KY. Our hiking horizons were beginning to expand.

After following some footprints in the snow we soon made it to the top of Wheeler Peak, the summit of the Land of Enchantment. I don't remember much of the view but from the pictures it looks like it was spectacular. I was feeling awful from altitude sickness, but at the time I just thought it was something I had eaten. Nowadays we know better than to hike when you've got that pounding headache and feel like you're going to throw up.

We tried to open the summit register, which was a steel pipe cemented to the ground with a cap at one end. But the cap was on too tight. So this is the only written record that we actually made it to the summit.

Wheeler Peak was our second high point. The following week we learned the art of backpacking at Philmont during a five day trek. I really believe that these two experiences ignited the flame of our mountaineering careers.

3 High Point

New Jersey

1,803ft

Dates climbed: June 22, 2003, July 18, 2006, and February11, 2012

Author: Matthew

Accompanying climbers: Amanda Morris, Doug Powell, Adam Rosenfield

In our quest for the 50 state high points, New Jersey's highest point (called "High Point") has proven to be surprisingly elusive. Our first summit of High Point was with our family in June 2003, while driving from KY to Maine. Our dad took a picture at the top but unfortunately the film got exposed and the pictures were ruined.

We tried again on July 18, 2006 while we were hiking through on the Appalachian Trail. Luckily the A.T. goes almost right over the summit. We met a Guatemalan family at the top and they were amazed that we had hiked here all the way from Georgia. The patriarch, Manuel, in particular was incredulous. He gave us each a nice cold bottle of water and $10. We thanked the family immensely for their generosity. (That's what we refer to as "Trail Magic.")

That hot July day in 2006 we departed the summit with a sense of relief that we had finally recovered the "lost" photo from 2003. We had finally made this summit "official." But in a cruel twist of fate, during a brutal rainstorm a few miles up the trail the memory card in Eric's digital camera, which contained the only photo of both of us on the summit, was corrupted, ruining the photo. Repeated attempts to recover the precious photo months later using advanced software proved fruitless. Although we had been to the summit twice, it felt that something was missing; something was unofficial, because we didn't have proof that both of us had been there, only a photo of Eric with the Guatemalan family.

Years went by, and our memories and agony from the lost NJ photos slowly faded. But as we climbed higher up the list of high points and realized that we could actually finish them, the anguish was reignited. If we actually ended up climbing the highest point in every state, by gosh, there should be photographic proof of all 50 of them, we thought. So it became an unspoken mission, a mission to someday revisit the New Jersey high point and bring back indisputable proof that we had been there.

The time for that mission came in February 2012. By then, our threshold for the number of miles that you can reasonably drive in a weekend had increased enough to put a day's trip to High Point, New Jersey within the realm of possibilities. On one trip we had driven 16 hours one-way to Nova Scotia's White Hill and 17 hours one-way on another trip to Ontario's Ishpatina Ridge both in long weekends, so a 5-hour drive to High Point seemed no sweat. We were surprised we hadn't thought of it before. Since the route would take us near to Connecticut's Mount Frissell we figured we'd add that one on too.

Next it was time to assemble a team. Through earlier adventures we had met fellow Highpointers Adam and Doug, who were working their way up the list of state high points and were fired up to tag Frissell and High Point. We set a date for Feb 11. Shortly before setting out from Boston we welcomed a late addition to the team: Amanda. She was going to be in town anyway to check out some medical schools and wanted to add some more mountains to her high point résumé. Due to some time constraints we needed to pack everything into a single day. 12 hours of driving and a few hours of hiking in one day would be ambitious but not unreasonable.

As soon as Amanda landed at Logan at 9am we picked her up, packed into Doug's car, and headed west onto the Mass Pike. First stop would be Connecticut's Mount Frissell (2,380ft), a rather unique state high point. It's unique because the high point isn't actually the top of a hill or even a local maximum; it's actually on the side of a mountain whose peak is in Massachusetts.

Even though we had visited Frissell five years earlier on the Appalachian Trail, we wanted to visit it again because we had some unfinished business: we needed a small rock from the summit. Somewhere around state highpoint #30 we decided it would be cool to have a little stone from the top of each state high point. So now we've got a stone from highpoints #30-#50 but need to revisit some of #1-#29, including Frissell and High Point. It might seem ridiculous to embark on a 12-hr road trip for just one photo and two rocks, but when you get close to high point #50 you want to make things as official as possible.

Even though Connecticut's highest point isn't a local maximum that doesn't mean it's a cakewalk to climb. In summer it involves driving a few miles on dirt roads and hiking a mile or so to the top, but with snow on the ground things become trickier. Earlier that week I had emailed the street department of the nearby city of Mt Washington, MA and learned that even though the roads aren't plowed the roads are still passable since there's "no snow in the area." Today, however, the area had just received an inch or so of snow and the roads were slick. But thanks to Doug's expert Cleveland-trained snow driving we made it to the trailhead without too much swerving around.

As it turned out, we had chosen to climb Mount Frissell in quite possibly the most treacherous conditions that the area ever experiences—a thick layer of ice covered everything we stepped on. Without crampons the steep rocks became especially perilous. But after grabbing on to some well-placed tree branches on the uphills and doing the old butt-slide on the downhills we made it to Mt Frissell's Massachusetts summit without incident. Even though the true Connecticut High Point was still a few hundred feet farther away on a side trail, the peak was marked with summit register which we diligently signed.

Since the previous visit to Mt Frissell we had acquired a long list of high point rituals. By now we had a full-blown high point routine. First, there was the standard photo of me and Eric, then the photo of Eric juggling, then the photo of me jumping. But this day was extra-special: we also captured a shirtless summit photo along with a photo of me holding Amanda up with one hand. Adam's highpointing career was just beginning, but he had already decided that his high point ritual would be to solve a Rubik's cube on top of every state high point. Accordingly, he whipped out his Rubik's cube, scrambled it up, then solved it in just a few minutes. Eric and I congratulated him on his skill and creativity.

But now it was time to turn our attention to the day's primary objective (for me and Eric at least): High Point. After a cautious descent over the steep, icy rocks it was onward to New Jersey. We headed south and after a few hours of driving we exited I-84 at Port Jervis, the northernmost town in NJ and the staging point for High Point summit attempts. We wound our way up the mountain to High Point state park and recognized the spot where we had crossed the highway five years earlier while hiking the Appalachian Trail. We could taste the summit.

The pride that New Jersey has for its highest point makes High Point an interesting place to visit. Christening the 1,803ft summit is a giant 197ft-tall obelisk, making the top of the Garden State exactly 2,000ft. Unfortunately the monument doors are locked, but at least it's nice to see the Jersey pride. There's also a really nice little state park in the High Point vicinity. Additionally, there are numerous road signs proclaiming this hill to be the highest point in the state. Contrast that with nearby Delaware's Ebright Azimuth which, at the time we climbed it, was totally unmarked and tricky to find.

We rounded the corner and soon the huge monument towered into view. We parked the car and walked the final 100 yards to the top. With a sense of relief we climbed the final stairs and we were once again at the familiar spot that had proven elusive to photograph during the previous two visits. This time we weren't taking any chances—we took photos with three different cameras.

There was just enough snow to remember that it was still winter, but not enough to make things difficult. From the summit platform we had a surprisingly good view of the NY/PA/NJ tri-state area. I bet on a clear day you could even see New York City. I remembered the last time we were here, when it was in the mid-90s. According to Garrett Marino, our expert meteorologist, on that particular day in 2006 the *low* at NYC's LaGuardia airport was 91F! Today it was a much more refreshing 35F, but still not too cold for the shirts-off summit photo.

Even though this time we had driven almost the whole way to the top, the fact that it would end up taking five hours of driving meant that we had "earned it." With a big sense of relief we returned to the car for the long drive back to Boston. As soon as we were back at our computers we immediately uploaded the summit photos so that the evidence was safe. Now we can finally feel at peace with New Jersey's highest point.

4 MOUNT WASHINGTON

NEW HAMPSHIRE

6,288ft

Dates climbed (more than 30 successful ascents): June 27, 2003, Feb 5, 2005, April 9, 2005, Sep 24, 2005, Oct 29, 2005, Oct 14, 2006, Jan 18, 2007 . . .

Author: Eric

Accompanying climbers for this report: Jon Hanselman

What better way to celebrate President's Day than to climb every mountain in the presidential range of New Hampshire? I read on the internet that a winter Presi traverse is supposedly "one of the most difficult winter mountaineering challenges in the Eastern United States", but Matthew, Jon, and I felt up for the challenge. We knew we could handle the distance (~22 miles) and elevation gain (~9000ft); we just had to get lucky with the weather. On Saturday there had been 100mph winds on Washington with fog reducing the visibility to nil, and it would have been suicidal to attempt the 11-mile above-treeline section of the traverse in those conditions. But the forecast for Presidents Day was only mostly cloudy with possible snow flurries, winds around 30mph and temps in the single digits. We figured we could handle that.

We rode up Sunday night with Aaron Yahr, who was doing a half-Presi traverse the next day with Matt Boynton, and got to the Appalachia trailhead around 10pm. Matthew and I had done this traverse in February about four years ago and it took us 16 hours, so we knew we should get an early start. Sunset was around 6pm so we figured to start at 2am and hopefully get done by sunset.

Now between the hours of 10pm and 2am there's no chance anyone would be hiking, and the only compacted, flat area of snow that isn't a road or a snowmobiler's path is the trail, so we all three threw out our sleeping bags on the trail a few minutes in from the trailhead and went to bed.

Our alarms went off angrily at 1:45am and we were off hiking by 2:15. Unfortunately this sleeping-at-the-trailhead plan would force us to each carry our big −15F sleeping bags and pads over the whole ridge, but that was better than stashing them at the trailhead and having to drive all the way back up north at the end of a long day.

I was surprisingly alert for that hour, after putting 10 hours in the sleep bank the previous two nights in anticipation of this trip, though I'm not sure I can say the same about Jon and Matthew. We hit treeline around 4am and it was obviously still dark, but not too windy or cold. Our first president, Madison, was a half-mile hike to the north (but in the opposite direction of our traverse), so we dropped our packs and ran up to tag the summit. That's probably not winter-school-approved behavior but Matthew and I had been up there so many times we could probably do it with our eyes closed.

By the time we got back down the moon was up. It provided almost enough light through the clouds to not need our headlamps, but not quite. Matthew took over the lead here and we made our way to president number two—Adams. It was still pretty dark on this climb and in those conditions a snow-covered rock looks a lot like a snow-covered cairn from a distance. Not surprisingly we got a little bit lost once, but Matthew whipped out the GPS and got us successfully to the summit, where we knew there would be more cairns.

It was civil twilight by then and the alpenglow was a red line on the horizon. The clouds even cleared out momentarily for us to catch a view of most of Washington (except the summit, which was still in the clouds as usual).

We finally got to turn off our headlamps around 6am after two hours of above-treeline night hiking. For the next few hours we had pretty limited visibility with clouds above and around us, and we could probably see just a couple cairns ahead at any time. However, by the time we reached

Jefferson we were greeted with a phenomenon I've only experienced once before in the Whites—undercast. It was amazing. The cloud level was at 5000 ft and we were above it. It was like we had just finished scuba diving and swam back up to an island sticking out of the water. There were more islands too: Clay, Washington, Monroe, and even Franconia ridge in the distance were all poking out of the clouds.

We snapped a bunch of pictures and headed on to Washington, reaching the summit just minutes after the last pesky little cloud rolled away at 9:30. As if the undercast scenery weren't spectacular enough, there was virtually no wind at all on the summit. The little anemometer on the observation tower which usually spins like a helicopter blade was actually going slow enough to count the three wind cups. We estimated the wind to be five mph max, maybe gusting to ten. Later I would read the observer comments that the day was probably the best-weather day so far this winter. That's pretty lucky.

We took the obligatory shirts-off summit photo and posed for the webcam photo too. The temperature might have been in the upper single digits, but with the sun glaring down and almost no wind, we actually walked around for about fifteen minutes without our shirts on and didn't get all that cold.

The original plan had been to meet up approximately at the Washington summit with Aaron and Matt who had started from Pinkham that morning, but after spending an hour at the top we decided to just keep going and meet them at the end.

It felt to me like the traverse was almost over at this point, even though we still had over ten miles to go. The southern Presidentials are so much easier than the northerns, though, and we had already done most of our elevation gain for the day. We descended down to Lakes of the Clouds and on the way passed our first group of hikers for the day. The exchange was something like this:

Them: "So, you hiked up Ammonoosuc this morning?"
Us: "Well, actually we started at Appalachia"
Pause to recall where Appalachia is,
Them: "What!? Are you crazy?"

We hiked on to Monroe and sadly that was our last island in the clouds. One of our plans had been to build a snowman on the summit to signal to Matt and Aaron that we had made it there, but that's easier said than done with 10-degree windswept snow and rocks. We called and left a message on their phone instead.

By noon we were on to Eisenhower and met another group of hikers. This time when we told them where we started they responded something like "oh, that's nice". Obviously they had no clue where the Appalachia trailhead was.

Shortly after Eisenhower we welcomed the protection of the trees again before hitting our last official president, Pierce. It was only 1:30pm on the summit and we all agreed it would be lame to just end it there, so we pushed on to tag a final (unofficial) president—Jackson. (Apparently the mountain was named after a geologist, not the president, but at least the name sounds presidential).

The trail down to Crawford Notch offered awesome glissading practice and we finished the last three miles in just 45 minutes, ending in 14 hours total.

We thought the day couldn't end any better, until we found a buffet of free chips and meatballs at the Highland Center while waiting for Aaron and Matt to finish. If anyone at the Highland Center is reading this we thank them for their generosity to us hungry hikers.

5 Mount Rogers

Virginia

5,729ft

Date climbed: June 2004

Author: Matthew

We climbed Virginia's highest mountain near the beginning of our highpointing career, at #5. As I write this, eight years later, I can start to put Mount Rogers in perspective. In 2004 we weren't consciously working on any kind of high points list; we were just hungry for mountains. Growing up we had gone hiking all over Kentucky, from the Pinnacle, the Pigg House, and Anglin Falls—our favorite spots near Berea—to Mammoth Cave and Natural Bridge, to the Smoky Mountains in TN/NC. The big eye-opening experience for us came in 2000 when we went hiking at Philmont, the Boy Scout ranch in New Mexico.

At Philmont we realized that there are other mountains in the world. There are treeless mountains, desert mountains, mountains that have snow in the summertime, and mountains that are so high that it's hard to breathe at the top. We were hooked. Ever since we had learned the art of backpacking at Philmont we were hungry for more mountains.

On family hikes down in the Smoky Mountains we began to get intrigued by the Appalachian Trail. The thought that there could be a trail so long that it took months to hike and brought you all the way from Georgia to Maine fascinated us. On backpacking trips in the springtime we'd often see thru-hikers at the shelters in the Smokies and hear their stories around the campfire. Then, in 2003, a friend of ours named Ian Rees quit high school to pursue his dream of hiking the Trail. While he hiked we were always checking his blog, hiking the trail vicariously through him. We began to get the idea that someday we'd hike the Great Trail too.

Right after graduating high school we wanted to get a little taste for the trail before starting college. We knew we'd be at MIT for the next four years (well make that ten) and also knew we'd be pretty busy. We didn't know when we'd ever get a chance to hike the entire trail. So we wanted to hike a little section of the trail before going away to Massachusetts. We had a few weeks in between graduation and the first day of the Canada/USA Math camp we were going to in Maine for the summer, so we decided to spend a week on the AT. We figured that you couldn't carry more than a week of food in you backpack anyway so seven days would be a reasonable goal.

We had already hiked a section of the AT (from Davenport Gap –> Roan Mountain) over Spring Break and hoped that our one week of hiking in June would be a little less challenging than that week in March. During that March hike, I remember starting out in a t-shirt and shorts with temps in the 80s. But by the end of that week we were postholing through two feet of slushy snow! I still vividly remember the moment when our Dad picked us up: we were wrapped up in our sleeping bags, huddled and shivering next to a big snow bank, our cotton clothes completely saturated, when finally, to our huge relief, we spotted our Dad in the big green van coming around the corner . . . But that's a story for a different trip report; this story is about Mount Rogers.

One hot June day in 2004, after a 4.5 hour drive from Berea we arrived at the Appalachian Trailhead in Damascus, Virginia. Our Dad bid us farewell and we disappeared into the woods. It was a hot one, but from growing up in KY we were used to it. Twenty miles and one day later we were at the junction for the Mount Rogers Trail and a sign that read "Mt Rogers 0.5 mi."

"You mean the trail doesn't go over the top?" I complained to Eric. "A half mile side trail? We're already hiking a hundred miles this week. It's a shame we've got to add one more mile to that."

"Well it's just one mile, I bet the view will be good too," Eric answered. At that moment we had reached a decision we'd have to make many more times in the future: do we take a side trail to a cool feature? Or do we keep hiking because we've got a lot more miles to hike and we've already seen enough cool features?

We decided to go for it, because after all it was the tallest mountain in the entire state of Virginia. Ten minutes later we arrived at a little clearing with a large rock outcropping. We were on top of the "Old Dominion" State!

"Well there isn't a view but at least there's a big rock to sit on," Eric said.

Next came the big dilemma: the summit photo. We wanted to get a picture with the both of us in it, but our cameras didn't have a time delay or remote trigger so we would have to get two separate photos: one of me, one of Eric. These were the early days and we each had one disposable camera. Twenty-four photos for me, twenty-four for Eric. We had just forty-eight photos for an entire week of hiking. Do we burn up two photos right now and risk running out of photos farther down the trail? What if there are bears or toads or turtles in the next few days? What it there's some epic stream to cross or some awesome rock formation that we need to document? Is it worth it to devote two pictures to this viewless mountain?

Then I came up with an idea. We'd use a long stick to push down the trigger so both of us could be in the photo. There weren't any long ones around so we'd have to make our own long stick. We grabbed our hiking sticks and scrounged around for some other branches. I cursed myself for not bringing any duct tape, but at least I had a bunch of rope from hanging bear bags. I lashed some sticks together and carefully balanced the camera on a rock. I advanced the film and cautiously rested another rock on top to hold the camera down. We retreated to the actual summit rock and I extended the stick towards the camera.

"Dang it, it's hard to hit the button," I said, "This stick is too flimsy."
"Here, let me do it," said Eric.
"No, I got it."
"Just give me the stick—" CLICK!

We saw the flash go off so we knew the picture had taken, we just couldn't be sure that it was a decent photo. But we didn't know what excitement awaited us farther down the trail so we decided to take our chances and assume that this one summit photo would be good enough. As I think about this eight years later, I'm sure glad that the summit photo was a good one, because otherwise that'd mean another trip to Mount Rogers. I've got to laugh when I see that photo because in it I'm wearing a nerdy cotton math t-shirt; I guess we wanted all the other hikers we met to know we were math geeks.

We looked around for a while, trying to admire the view, but came to the realization that the view was much better from atop the balds and fields back on the AT. Mount Rogers is situated in Grayson Highlands State Park, which in some places reminds me of hiking out west. There are high alpine meadows, cool rock formations, rugged hills, and not to mention the wild ponies!

They say not to feed the ponies, which is good considering that our food rations were already pretty slim.

Another cool fun fact about Mount Rogers is that it was actually named after the founder of MIT, William Barton Rogers, back in the 1800s. Just like us, I guess ol' Mr. Rogers split his nerdiness between science and hiking.

6 Humphrey's Peak

Arizona

12,633ft

Date climbed: May 30, 2005

Author: Matthew

If you've ever been on Mount Washington in the middle of January, then you have a good idea of the weather atop Humphrey's Peak. During this trip, our impressions of Arizona drastically changed.

We camped at the Arizona Snow Bowl ski resort at the base of the mountain and got an Alpine start at 2:30am. Even though it was already late May, Humphrey's Peak and adjacent mountains were still heavily snow-capped. We navigated by headlamp, but it was very difficult to stay on the trail, for it was buried under five feet of snow and there were no tracks to follow. So we were constantly studying all of the trees, looking for any sign of a cut branch or missing bark. It was very slow going and eventually around 5am we reached a dead end. We could no longer find any sign of a trail at all, so we retraced our steps and finally got back on track.

Soon a few rays of sunlight hit the tops of the evergreens and we could finally see where we were going. At that point, we decided to completely abandon our search for the trail and instead we headed straight up the mountain. Temperatures were still in the mid 20s, so we had a tough time ascending the icy slope without crampons. At about 8am, we finally reached the edge of the trees and stepped onto the ridge. I've never experienced wind like that before. As soon as we stepped onto the crest, we were blasted by gale force winds, blowing from the east at over 50mph. We started following a vaguely-defined user trail through the talus, but decided to duck below the ridge to avoid the brunt of the wind. But the worst was yet to come.

We continued our ascent via the southeast ridge and soon suited up in our serious above-treeline gear: windproof pants, fleece, shell, balaclava and goggles. We never expected we'd need this gear in May, least of all in Arizona, but without one of these articles I don't think we could have made it. We took one step onto the crest of the ridge and it felt like we were stepping into a wall. The wind was so fierce that we could barely keep our balance. A couple of times just for fun we jumped straight up into the air and landed two feet away. I could feel the straps on my pack slapping me in the face and all of my loose clothing flapped violently like a flag in the breeze. I shivered as the frigid wind pierced through my "windproof" rain jacket and three other layers of synthetic clothing.

Just when we thought that the wind couldn't get any stronger, we were literally knocked to our feet by a tremendous gust. On our final approach to the summit I experienced the strongest wind I've ever seen in my life. We couldn't even stay on the trail anymore. The raging wind forced us to the west and finally, just 50ft from the summit, we could no longer stay on our feet. I will never forget that final climb to the top. We actually had to crawl on our hands and knees to avoid being knocked over. At the risk of being blown off the mountain, I used one hand to hold the camera as I recorded Eric trying to crawl up the snow on the final ascent. I could feel the wind being ripped from my lungs as it blew across my bare face and a few times my ears popped from the pressure difference.

The general rule of thumb is that a wind gust (in mph) that is half of your weight (in lbs) can knock you over. Just below the summit we were completely unable to stand up, so we calculated that the wind must have been sustained at over 80mph. The gusts were near 100mph.

If we couldn't have seen the top, we might very well have turned back. We faced a thousand foot vertical drop to the west and the wind was threatening to blow us over the edge. But we pushed on—or rather crawled on—to the summit. Thankfully previous generations of hikers had built a pretty large rock wall at the top to provide shelter from the wind and we took full advantage of it. We hunkered down inside the structure and enjoyed a quick reprieve from the hurricane-force winds. Then I decided to reenact the famed Mount Washington experiment, except I had a Nalgene full of water instead of milk and Wheaties. Eric recorded with the camera as I emptied the Nalgene into the air. The wind drove the water horizontally and it vanished into a cloud of spray before it ever reached the ground. Good times.

It was amazing to look north into the Arizona desert, 8,000 feet below, where it was perhaps already 80 degrees, and at the same time we were standing in snow with wind chills well below zero. We quickly cooled off and started our hike down the mountain at about 10am. It was almost too dangerous to glissade, as the snow was still frozen solid and you could lose control easily. But we made it down safely and certainly had quite a story to tell.

7 BOUNDARY PEAK

NEVADA

13,140ft

Date climbed: June 27, 2005

Author: Eric

Accompanying climber: Greg

Matthew and I were working on a trail crew in the Sierra Nevada for the summer based out of Mammoth Lakes, California, which put us within easy striking distance of the roof of Nevada. Boundary Peak, as the name implies, is right on the Nevada-California border and just a few hours from Mammoth.

On one of our weekends off from trail crew we convinced another trailcrew volunteer, Greg, to drive over to Boundary Peak for a dayhike. This peak doesn't officially have a trail, but since it's mostly above treeline anyway, route finding wouldn't be that much of a problem.

We drove down from the alpine, forested city of Mammoth Lakes and as we got closer to Nevada the scenery got more and more desolate until it was complete desert—not a sign of life anywhere. We had to cross over into Nevada to approach the mountain from the East. The roads got worse and worse as we approached the trailhead, eventually turning into dirt washboard that shook the whole car for half an hour.

Finally at the trailhead we found a few trees and undergrowth, and followed a user trail to the edge of treeline. (A user trail is unmaintained, and only exists from people following the same route until a path is worn). From here we could see the summit—it was still mostly covered in snow even in late June! This was quite a contrast to the blistering heat in the desert we had just driven through. We picked our own path through the rock field up toward the summit and about 500 ft from the top were forced to cross a weird-looking snowfield. The snow had formed what looked like stalagmites pointing up at the sun, like the penitentes of the Andes. None of the snow on the other side of the valley in the Sierra Nevada had looked like this, and we speculated somehow the sun must be more intense over in Nevada and had melted the common sun cups deep enough until they looked like penitentes.

These penitentes posed no real obstacle and by mid afternoon we reached the summit. Most people would be feeling some effects of altitude here above 13,000 ft, but we had all been on trail crew jobs based at 10,000ft so were already well acclimated.

Curiously, Matthew found some bones at the top. We joked that they were the remains of the last person to summit Boundary Peak, but in reality they were probably some cow bones someone had brought up for fun.

After a quick break came the best part of the day—glissading back to the car! On our way up we had spied a few snow chutes on the eastern side of the mountain that made it almost down to the trailhead. From our month on trailcrew playing around on snow after work, Matthew and I had become expert boot-glissaders, being able to basically ski down mountain slopes doing turns and all with nothing more than our boots.

Greg decided to take the hiking way down (he wasn't as confident in glissading), while Matthew and I went down in style. At one point Matthew duct-taped a camera to his head to get a video of the descent.

After several thousand feet of vertical descent in about 15 minutes we reached the end of the snow and were forced to earn our way back to the car. We fooled around for a little while climbing trees to wait for Greg to catch up, then all returned to the car together. We made it back to Mammoth in time for dinner and started planning our next adventures.

8 MOUNT WHITNEY

CALIFORNIA

14,494ft

Date climbed: July 24, 2005

Author: Eric

We called this trip one of our four biathlons of the summer, involving as much biking as mountaineering. As poor volunteer trailcrew workers that summer we didn't have a car, but luckily a bus took us (and bikes) to the town of Lone Pine, (elevation 3500 ft) 13 miles from the trailhead (elevation 8,300ft). With a 50-lb pack each and 5-speed, yard-sale bikes, we took off up the road.

Matthew started out with a prominent "Mount Whitney" sign hanging from his pack, hoping a friendly truck-driver would pass by and offer us a ride, but after a couple miles we both agreed that we couldn't be that lazy to accept a ride, so we toughed it out for the whole 4000ft+ climb.

Now, the hardest part of getting up Mount Whitney must be figuring out how the permit system works and somehow getting one for the day you want to hike. Unfortunately, we couldn't get a permit (there's some lottery in February that we didn't enter). However, I discovered a sort of loop-hole that if you climb the mountaineer's route in a day, you don't need a permit. This is not a trail, and the rangers who told me about it laughed at me, saying "no one does that in a day". It's a class 3 route marked intermittently with cairns and vague user-paths and can get pretty sketchy in places. Next year you'll need a permit to do it in a day (the rangers have finally found the loop-hole), but that didn't affect us.

We got to the trailhead on a Saturday afternoon and were greeted with hordes of tourists and a campground with a fat $16-per-night fee. Staying two nights there would have cost 4 days food wages for us poor volunteers, so we instead snuck into the woods and found our own asphalt-free campsite.

We were pretty tired from all that biking, so we slept in til 4:30 the next morning and started our climb at 5am. I was excited about the route, since we had encountered a few people the other day that had to turn back and warned us we would have trouble. The only problem we found at the beginning of the route was that there wasn't enough sunlight. We had to zigzag up some steep ledges (called the Ebersbacher ledges) that were several inches wide in some places next to a 300ft drop, but that posed no difficulties.

After the ledges we skirted an alpine lake, scrambled over a talus field, and made it to Upper Boy Scout Lake in time for a water break. I was surprised to catch up to a group of five Indian hikers trudging slowly up from the lake, obviously not acclimated and having a tough time. They said they had left that morning (that must have been a serious alpine start) and were planning on doing the route in a day. I gave them 1 in 10 odds of succeeding.

As it turned out, that was the only group of hikers we saw on the whole ascent, which really surprised me considering that hundreds of people take the main trail every day, especially on a weekend. We continued up perhaps another thousand feet until we reached Iceberg Lake and our first good look at Whitney (it's pretty deep in the Sierra range, hidden by a bunch of other peaks). From our view it was basically a vertical face with no obvious way up. By then we had started hearing "Off Belay!" about every 10 minutes and saw a group of rock climbers about 1/3 the way up on some class 5 route. Luckily, we knew there was a safer way.

To the right of the face there was a really steep couloir, half-covered in snow, but with decent handholds in the rock. This was the place where we'd heard we might need helmets, in case careless climbers above us dislodged rocks in an area of scree, but since we beat everyone else to the couloir it would only be them worrying about our rocks. We ditched our hiking poles and ascended about a thousand feet, trying to stay on the rocks but eventually pushing through the soft snow.

At the top of the couloir we gazed west at the last stretch of the climb—a 500 ft snowfield traverse wrapping around to the summit. This was the place where one mountaineer died several years ago after slipping on the snow, and it was definitely a no-fall zone. Unfortunately, we didn't have any ice axes (in hindsight MITOC would have been a good source for them), so we decided to climb some class 4 rocks instead to get around the snow/ice. Perhaps that wasn't so wise, since the rocks were icy too, but it worked out.

By then it was about 9:30 in the morning and we were just about at the top. We had about halved the ascent time predicted by my internet guide printout, and we were ready for an awesome view. We climbed up the last boulder and were met with a big cloud bank to the east and about 15 other hikers posing for pictures (Mount Washingtonesque for sure).

I thought we would be some of the first climbers up there, but in the summit register I counted at least 40 other names—and more people kept pouring in! They must have camped about 2 miles from the top.

After taking the obligatory shirtless summit photos and 1.5 hours of relishing the fact that we were the tallest objects in the lower 48 states, we finally headed down the main trail. We'd found out that in our circumstances we could descend the 11-mile trail permit-less since descending the mountaineer's route was rather dangerous.

I noticed on the map that there happened to be another 14er (Mt. Muir) near the trail, so we decided we might as well bag it too. The rest of the descent was really easy—we boot-skied down snow when we could find it, and otherwise passed about 50 people also descending.

The next day we finally got our reward for the trip—4,000ft+ vertical feet of descent over 13 miles of road by bike. We didn't even touch the pedals. It was the long-awaited downhill stage of Le Tour de Whitney.

9 Hawkeye Point

Iowa

1,670ft

Dates climbed: Aug 24, 2005 and Dec 22, 2011

Author: Eric

Accompanying climbers: Keith Gilbertson, Jacob Gilbertson, Mary Kay Gilbertson

Hawkeye Point—the roof of Iowa—should be one of the easiest state highpoints to reach: it's only a few hundred feet from a paved road, is on public property so has no access restrictions, is at low altitude, and is easy to find. But throw in some Christmas holiday travel chaos and it becomes considerably more difficult.

I had just finished my last final exam on December 21 and the plan was to fly to Louisville, KY that night, meet up with Matthew, Dad, Jacob, and Mom, and drive through the night up to Grandpa Gilbertson's house in Minnesota, stopping at Hawkeye Point along the way. The first leg of my flight from Boston to Cleveland went without a hitch, but every flight out of Cleveland seemed to be delayed. My Louisville flight was supposed to leave at 9:00pm, but was posted to leave at 10:45pm. I waited around a few minutes, and then it changed to 11:20pm, then 11:55pm.

Apparently there was a snowstorm somewhere and the plane that was supposed to take me to Louisville hadn't even taken off yet from the other airport it was starting from.

"There's got to be a way to meet up with my family before midnight tonight," I thought. The only other flights were going to New York City, San Diego, and Chicago leaving at 10pm. Well, Chicago was kind of between Louisville and Minnesota, so perhaps my Dad could just drive up there and meet me, I thought.

I called to confirm, and Dad was up for it (he was already in Louisville) and driving four hours along the route we already planned to follow to meet me was better than losing at least two hours waiting around in Louisville.

I went to the counter to see if I could switch flights, but the guy said he couldn't figure out how to do it since Chicago was nowhere close to Louisville. Apparently the airlines will only reroute you somewhere within 90 miles or so of the original destination if you're delayed by weather. This did not deter me, however.

I noted the Chicago departure terminal and quickly rushed over there to talk to someone else (it was actually pretty far away and was already 9:30pm by this point). I asked the lady at that counter, and she rudely told me no way, and that only customer service could do anything about my situation. So I rushed over to the customer service desk next (which was also far away). I waited in line an excruciatingly long three minutes before finally talking to a customer service person.

"I'm sorry, Chicago is not a 'sister city' of Louisville so we can't route you there."
"But my family is driving through there anyway and can meet me," I replied.
"Nope, sorry" was her response.

I was still not deterred. It was 9:40pm and I had one last hope. I went back to the Louisville departure gate and there was a different person there this time. I told her the situation and asked if she could put me on the Chicago flight.

"I'm sorry, you'll have to talk to the person at the Chicago gate or Customer Service," she told me.

"I've already talked to both of them and they said they couldn't do it," I responded. She looked surprised and must have figured I was pretty determined. She whipped out a radio and talked to some official-sounding person, then turned back to me.

"Go to the Chicago terminal"
"I can get on the flight?"
"GO-NOW—the flight's boarding," she said urgently.

Success! I ran down to the other terminal and met the same rude lady that hadn't wanted to help me before. I triumphantly gave her my old boarding pass and asked her to print me out a new one. She was extremely skeptical, but everything checked out on her computer and I got on the plane just before it left.

I called Dad to give the OK to drive up to Chicago, then sat back to relish my victory. Matthew and Dad took turns driving across the fascinating state of Indiana at night. My flight landed at 11pm, but my family still had another three hours of driving, so I had a long time to wander around the O'Hare airport. One nice worker even gave me a food voucher around 1a.m. and I had a big second dinner from Starbucks.

By 2a.m. Dad pulled up in the rental van, I hopped in and we started heading north. That's probably the best time of day to drive through downtown Chicago because the streets are completely empty.

By 8am we reached our Aunt Kathy and Uncle Al Toov's home in Austin, Minnesota and took a few hours break to eat breakfast and visit before hitting the road again. Conveniently Hawkeye Point is only a 10-mile detour on the route from Austin to Montevideo, Minnesota (our final destination), and we all felt prepared for a winter ascent. Matthew, me, and Dad had already ascended Hawkeye Point in August 2005 on our way back from California, but we figured we'd better stop by again since we were so close.

We turned south at Worthington, MN and after a few detours due to construction finally saw the huge "Hawkeye Point" highway sign. We pulled up to the summit at 3pm and had it all to ourselves. The last time we had been here in 2005 the high point was just a non-descript patch of grass next to a corn field, but this time there were all kinds of bells and whistles: picnic benches, signs, plaques, monuments, and a dedicated gravel road basically to the top! Thank you to the Highpointers Club for their efforts at Hawkeye Point!

10 Mount Davis

Pennsylvania

3,213ft

Date climbed: September 3, 2005, December 21, 2012

Author: Matthew

Accompanying climber both ascents: Keith Gilbertson

Over the years, driving from home in Kentucky to school in Massachusetts has presented some excellent highpointing opportunities. There are many states along the way, many essentially equidistant driving routes, and our Dad has always been up for driving hours out of the way so we can tag a new hill. We've visited the high points in New Jersey, Maryland, Delaware, and (almost) Massachusetts during the journey to/from school. In the summer of 2005, on the drive back to school following a summer on trail crew in the California Sierra Nevada, we decided to swing by Mount Davis to check out the view from the highest point in Pennsylvania.

We left our grandparents' home in Greensburg that morning and drove sixty miles into the rolling hills and eventually the Laurel Highlands of Pennsylvania. When we were younger we had visited the Laurel Highlands many times, from whitewater rafting the Youghiogheny River, to mountain biking near Ohiopyle, to road-biking the Allegheny Passage bikeway, to skiing at Laurel Mountain. But we had never ventured as far as Mount Davis. After climbing Humphrey's Peak (AZ), Boundary Peak (NV) and Mount Whitney (CA) earlier that summer we were now in the double-digit territory of our highpointing quest list and hungry for more mountains.

When we finally arrived at Mount Davis and stepped out of the car into the cool mountain air we were delighted to see an observation tower peeking up above the trees. First we tagged the big boulder and USGS marker that indicated the true summit and then headed towards the steps to the tower. Our Dad volunteered to guard the van while we climbed up the tower.

From the top you could see a big chunk of southwestern Pennsylvania. Here on Mount Davis we continued a quasi-tradition that we had started back in Sierra over the summer: the shirts-off summit photo. It's difficult to articulate why exactly we feel compelled to remove our shirts on top of a mountain. But I suppose it's just our instinctual way of saying "We conquered this mountain. And it was a piece of cake—we didn't even need our shirts." It was a tradition we would continue sporadically on subsequent high points including Mount Washington (in January) and Mount McKinley (well, just Eric—Matthew was a bit of a sissy).

We snapped a few triumphant photos and congratulated ourselves for yet another successful KY->MA road trip. Earlier that day we had stopped in Garrett, PA in honor of our friend Garrett Marino, the expert meteorologist. Garrett's forecasts would prove to be a vital contribution to the success of our future highpointing adventures.

11 (THE SIDE OF) MOUNT FRISSELL

CONNECTICUT

2,380ft

Dates climbed: July 27, 2006 and Feb 11, 2012

Author: Matthew

Here's a riddle for you: how is it possible for a state's highest point to not be located on top of a mountain? To answer to this important question we traveled to Connecticut to visit Mount Frissell.

It was our big summer on the Appalachian Trail. We had started in Georgia in early June and in order to reach Katahdin by the beginning of school in September we had "yellow-blazed" some southern stretches of the A.T. via motorized means. (We finished hiking the remaining sections by Fall 2008.) By late July we had hiked a thousand miles and reached Connecticut.

The Appalachian Trail provides a nice way to knock off a few state high points: it swings by Brasstown Bald (GA), Clingman's Dome (TN), Mount Rogers (VA), High Point (NJ), Mount Frissell (CT), Mount Greylock (MA), Mount Washington (NH), and Katahdin (ME). So we decided to take advantage of our limited stay in the "Constitution State" to climb the highest point.

Unfortunately, however, Mount Frissell is not actually on the A.T.—it requires a full four-mile roundtrip hike on a side trail ("a blue blazed trail" in A.T. lingo). We groaned at the prospect of adding an extra four miles to our long journey. Sure, we had already hiked a thousand miles and an extra four shouldn't be a big deal. But when you've hiked that far you don't want to add any more miles than you have to. Nevertheless we decided to go for it in the name of high pointing.

On the A.T. we passed by a plaque that claimed that we were currently at the highest point in Connecticut. But we—or should I say SummitPost—knew better. We walked a little farther up the trail and found the side trail that pointed to Mount Frissell.

So here's the answer to our little riddle: Connecticut's highest point is actually on the side of a mountain called Mount Frissell, whose peak is in Massachusetts. The MA/CT border goes right over the side of the mountain. That means we wouldn't even have to climb to the top.

Soon we came upon a little clearing in the woods and in the middle stood a big cairn, triumphantly marking the roof of Connecticut. There wasn't too much of a view but that didn't matter. It was a high point. We took the requisite shirts-off summit photo then returned to the Appalachian Trail and continued hiking north.

12 MOUNT GREYLOCK

MASSACHUSETTS

3,491ft

Dates climbed: July 30, 2006 and February 26, 2011

Author: Matthew

Accompanying climbers: Jacob Gilbertson and Garrett Marino

We had some unfinished business with Mount Greylock. Our first ascent while hiking the Appalachian Trail in 2006 had been successful, but there were a few critical summit souvenirs that we had failed to capture. First: some jumping photos. Sometime in the 28 intervening state high points between #13 Massachusetts and #41 Georgia we had begun the tradition of taking a jumping photo on each summit. We needed one for Mount Greylock. Second: a photo of Eric juggling. Taken with Eric's camera, Eric's official 2006 juggling summit photo had been erased when his camera got wet. So he needed another one.

There were two other important reasons for climbing Mt Greylock. Our younger brother Jacob was in town and Garrett was free. Garrett and Jacob were both hot on the state high point trail and eager to taste the crisp summit air from the roof of the Bay State.

For the four of us the journey to Mt Greylock began that day in Garrett's shiny new Clubman Mini Cooper outside of the Alewife T Station. You might ask: how do you fit four people + four large backpacks + four winter sleeping bags + four pairs of snowshoes into a Mini Cooper? Answer: very carefully.

After driving west on the Mass Pike we passed through the Appalachian Trail town of Adams, MA and wound our way up the mountain towards the trailhead. The parking lot was unplowed but fortunately just minutes after we arrived a nice woman with a plow excavated it out for us.

This was Jacob's and Garrett's first opportunity to use snowshoes but they wielded them like experts. After a short 1.5 miles we ditched the heavy overnight gear at Peck's Brook Shelter and continued on up the Gould Trail. The plan was to spend the night at the shelter. After dodging some snowmobiles and hiking another 1.5 miles we were on top of Massachusetts. A very cool War Memorial tower christens the summit and in the summer you can see five states from the observatory. Unfortunately it was cloudy today so we could only see the town of Adams below us. But that wasn't a big deal; the summit itself was a spectacular sight.

Half of the summit tower was plastered in rime ice, which really brought out the "MASSACHVSETTS" carved into the granite. Replacing the "U" with a "V" must be a Massachusetts thing, we figured, because that's also how it's spelled below MIT's Great Dome. If they replace the U with a V because it's too hard to carve the curve, we wondered, then what about the S?

On the summit we went through our checklist: Genuine summit photo—check. Jumping photo—check. Shirts-off summit photo—check. Summit rock—uh oh, no check. We couldn't head down before finding a rock. Unfortunately though finding a rock proved extremely difficult because everything was covered in snow. We scoured the summit but couldn't find anything better than a miniscule pebble. It was getting desperate. But finally we came upon a little rock wall and found the perfect little stone waiting for us on top. Whew. We breathed a sigh of relief.

With plenty of summit photos along with an official summit rock, our climbing objective was satisfied and it was time to head down. When we arrived back at the shelter we began the important task of collecting wood for a big campfire. I'm always amazed at how it's possible to have a campfire when there are two feet of snow on the ground. I've learned that one effective strategy is to place some big logs on top of the snow, forming a platform on which to build the fire.

Everyone had an important job. Old "one-match" Matthew got the campfire roaring in about ten minutes. Meanwhile "eager-to-eat" Eric worked on dinner. "I-just-lost-my-gloves" Jacob thawed his hands over the fire. And "meteorologist-man" Marino (a.k.a. Garrett), exercising his meteorology black-belt skills, gave us an updated snowfall forecast based on the wind direction and speed. We were an efficient team.

The first dinner course was cheddar + broccoli pasta, followed by couscous + mashed potatoes. Sometimes you might have a little excess water when making couscous but we learned during our A.T. days that you can absorb some of the water by mixing in some powdered mashed potatoes. I don't think any of us actually knows exactly how couscous + powdered mashed potatoes tastes indoors. But we do know that it's one of the most compact meals you can get for backpacking.

We (well, some of us) slept peacefully in our subzero-rated sleeping bags. Some of us had a Nalgene full of boiling water to keep our toes warm during the night. We awoke the next morning to 3 inches of fresh snow on the ground outside the shelter. Eric won the bet because he had guessed 2.00001" while Jacob had guessed only 2".

Hiking back down was like walking on a big soft pillow. The fluffy snow grew deeper as we descended and cushioned every step. Soon we arrived back at the parking lot where Garrett's trusty olive-colored steed awaited us.

It was time to head to Dunkin Donuts for a celebration. It was rumored that it was possible to obtain the elusive powdered-sugar jelly doughnut at Dunkin Donuts locations in western MA. This wonder of modern food engineering was too radical to be found in Cambridge. Garrett was yearning to find out for himself if the legends were true.

We did indeed find the powdered-sugar jelly doughnuts he sought, a fitting end to the noble quest to climb the highest point in Massachusetts.

13 Katahdin

Maine

5,267ft

Dates climbed: March 27, 28, 29, 2006 (Eric), Aug 24 2006 May 23, 2009, Feb 18, 2012

Author: Matthew

The Final Day of the Appalachian Trail (August 24, 2006)

Our 2 a.m. alarms jolted us awake in the shelter at the Birches Campground, five miles and 4000ft below the summit of Baxter Peak.

We shivered as we unzipped our sleeping bags and replaced the 98 degree air for a 40-degree chill. It seemed like it was too cold for August, but we had just woken up and our fuel tanks were empty; the 1/2lb of pasta from the evening had already been spent, and we were ready for some cereal—8 "servings" of it to be precise—but when you're hungry and tired you can divide that number by 4.

Fate would have it that Eric lost his headlamp the previous morning and we were forced to rely on mine alone. It was difficult enough to eat breakfast by one headlamp, but we worried about scrambling over boulders above treeline with no more than starlight and half a headlamp apiece to illuminate our path. But we had to do it. We knew that we couldn't merely walk up to the top in broad daylight and then march straight back down the mountain like many other thru hikers surely do. We wanted to end with a bang. Our plan was to see the sunrise from the very top of Katahdin, no matter how much energy or sleep deprivation it would require.

We found the trailhead at 2:40am and proudly signed into the register as Thor and Sven—our trail names. But we were extremely surprised and dismayed that someone else had already beaten us to the trail . . . an "Adam Stewart" had signed in at 1:30am! We knew that we had to beat this guy to the top. The summit had to be ours alone and we didn't want to share it with anyone else so Eric and I began the climb with a jog.

But the tough terrain and poor lighting combined to give us the most challenging hiking we had encountered all summer. I was in the front and Eric in the back with the headlamp as a sort of a punishment for forgetting his, and eventually we perfected a technique where I would walk on the left side of the trail and Eric walked behind me on the right. He tried to illuminate my path, and then he would have to remember the terrain as it went into the dark zone just before he stepped on it. Often I would have to wait for Eric's light because there were so many big rocks in the trail that we couldn't maintain a direct line of sight between us. The trail wasn't simply rocky—it was "bouldery."

The technical terrain proved too tricky for poor Adam Stewart, whom we passed with relish at 3:10am. Once we reached treeline at about 3:45am the trail picked up the pace and began to climb about a 1000ft/mile rate with many short vertical sections that we had to conquer one person at a time. Above treeline we were surrounded by an uncountable number of stars; there were so many in fact that it was tricky to pick out some of the constellations. We continued our ascent with rising Orion to our right and Polaris to our left.

Gradually the sky grew brighter and soon we could no longer see Sirius, the brightest star of all. We knew we needed to hurry. We could not let the sun beat us to the top. As the terrain started to level out we knew we had reached the 2 mile marker, and we decided to pull out all the stops and launch into an all-out run. We were racing over sharp and often loose rocks at 4:40 in the morning, trying our best to follow the last few white blazes of the Appalachian Trail. After ten minutes we were both totally drenched with sweat but our adrenaline compelled us to keep moving. We refused to miss the sunrise by one minute merely because we were removing our saturated rain jackets. Finally we caught a glimpse in the distance of the distinctive Katahdin summit sign, its silhouette beckoning us to make one last sprint to the finish line.

"If you're tired now," I yelled at Eric, "you're gonna hafta suck it up cause we can rest at the top, I ain't slowin down now!"

"Yeah we didn't get up at 2am to see the sun already up! We're gonna make it!"

We stepped over the last rock and got our first good view to the East. I tagged the summit sign first and Eric followed one second later. The official time was 04:58:07 EST on August 24, 2006! "We made it! How do you like them apples!?" I screamed.

The view was absolutely amazing. Not a single cloud tainted the sky, just humid, cold Maine air. The lights from Millinocket and other distant towns to the East were waning, and we could see limitless lakes stretching northward. To the west there was nothing but mountains and trees all the way to Quebec. We were on the roof of Maine and at the climax of the Appalachian Trail. After hiking countless miles in the Green Tunnel with nothing but trees and the rocks beneath our feet to look at, this moment atop Katahdin was our payback. This made everything worth it.

Now we had to wait for sunrise. "Umm, it should be coming up any minute now" I told Eric. "Yeah," he said, "in the ranger station it said 5:40am, so it should be earlier at the top." Right. The thermometer read 31.4F at that point and the wind gusted less than 20mph, but our MITOC Polypro along with a thin rain jacket and T-shirt was no match for the frigid August air. We used smelly socks for gloves and I had to stick my legs into my empty pack like a cocoon because one pesky pant leg refused to cooperate. We opened up our bags of trail mix and scarfed down the food like animals, for we did not have enough dexterity to grab the food with our hands, nor did we want to dirty our sock mittens with the smell of food.

Eventually these warmth measures proved insufficient, and we had to resort to tactic B for keeping warm: jumping jacks. Eric and I both found a flat spot and alternated between jumping jacks and taking pictures: 30 seconds of intense jumping jacks would provide enough warmth for 2-3 minutes of picture taking. As the sky grew even brighter, it was just like we were in candy land and we could take our fill of pictures. Every direction we turned presented an awesome picture, one that would put most of our previous pictures to shame. We would prance around on the rocks to get the perfect angle, then we would have to recharge our body heat by some hard-core running in place for a change.

Finally the sun officially poked over the horizon at 5:38am (we should have trusted the ranger station), and we got some more classic pictures: the monster summit cairn, Katahdin's shadow to the west, and me balancing on the sign. We actually ended up hanging out at the top until about 7:30am, long enough for poor Adam Stewart to finally stagger up to the top. He missed sunrise by about two hours even though he had an hour head start on us!

With the solitude broken we decided to head down, but it would be pretty wimpy to get back to camp when it was still morning, and when it was still a perfectly good day for hiking. So the verdict was to summit again, but this time somehow incorporate the Knife Edge ridge. We thus looped down the Hamlin Ridge trail, past Chimney Pond, and up the Dudley trail. Now it was still mid-morning by this time and most of the tourists staying in the lean-tos and the bunkhouse were just starting their hikes. It was amusing how we would pass so many people on the way up Pamola Peak. It was certainly a very steep and strenuous trail, but with 1000+ miles under our belts we could charge up without stopping at all to rest while most people rested every five minutes.

Past Pamola Peak we reached the start of the infamous knife edge, a trail with thousand-foot drops on each side and in some places only one foot wide rocks to walk on. Eric had done it the previous winter, so with no ice or snow it seemed like a cake walk. As we hiked on the Knife Edge we passed a lot of people we had met in camp the previous day. They obviously weren't hard core enough to see sunrise that morning from the summit. As we came back full circle back to the summit we met a crowd of about 20 people milling around. It was so much like Mount Washington, though not as bad as having a road to the summit.

I'm so glad we got there at sunrise when we could admire the area's beauty in solitude. The one advantage of having so many people up there was that someone else could take our picture. We gave some good summit poses and then headed back down to camp. It was definitely a fitting end to our Appalachian Trail adventure to summit Katahdin twice, including once for sunrise.

14 Jerimoth Hill

Rhode Island

812ft

Dates climbed: March 10, 2007 and Nov 6 2010 (Matthew)

Author: Matthew

Accompanying climber: Garrett Marino

Eric and I had been planning to visit the summit of the "Smallest State" for quite some time but somehow we had always managed to avoid it. True, Rhode Island's Jerimoth Hill is the closest state high point to MIT and we figured it should be easily doable in a day by a combination of car, bike, or commuter rail. But a trip to this 812 ft hill just lacked the appeal of a hike to the Whites, and we always ended up hiking Mt Washington, Franconia Ridge, or some other high New England peak instead.

But by the winter of 2007, with thirteen state high points under our belt, we were starting to build up some momentum, and it began to seem more reasonable to devote an entire Saturday to the highest point in Rhode Island. In brainstorming the trip we came up with a few different transportation options: 1) bike all the way there and back, 123 miles total, 2) organize a MITOC trip and drive there, or 3) take the commuter rail part of the way, bike to the summit, and take the commuter rail back. Option 1 sounded like the most honorable to us, but the prospect of biking through thirteen hours of cold, slush, and few hours of March darkness didn't sound too appealing. As for Option 2, we didn't expect any other MITOC person to be interested; I mean, sure the hill has meaning to me and Eric, but it probably doesn't strike the same chord with non-highpointers. Another option would have been to rent a car, but at that time Matthew still didn't have his driver's license and Eric didn't drive frequently, so the thought of renting a car never really crossed our minds. Thus we decided to go for Option 3, a combination of biking + commuter rail.

Early one March morning we biked over to South Station and hopped on the first commuter rail. Luckily they allow bikes on the commuter rail during non-peak times. After a relaxing $5 ride to Providence we jumped on the mountain bikes and were under our own power for the remainder of the climb. It was chilly and a little bit icy, but at least we didn't have to worry about there being more snow on the summit. Since air is typically 3-5F cooler per 1000 ft of vertical elevation gain, then we'd expect an essentially imperceptible 2-4F temperature drop as we climbed.

By about 9:45am we began a gradual climb just outside the village of Foster and ten minutes later we were greeted by a brown road sign proclaiming "Jerimoth Hill, State's Highest Point." But not so fast, we thought, we're not exactly on top yet. Earlier that week we had done some Wikipedia and SummitPost research and learned about the checkered history of highpointing on Jerimoth Hill.

Just a few years ago, highpointers had "considered Jerimoth Hill less accessible than Mt McKinley." According to highpointing folklore, the former owner of the summit access driveway, Mr. Richardson, "became known for insulting, threatening or even using violence against visitors who tried to use his driveway" [Wikipedia 2012]. Although Brown University owned the top of the hill, highpointers would have to pass through Mr. Richardson's land to reach the true summit. Legend has it that he became so fed up with highpointers that he installed motion detectors around his property and even fired a few warning shots when highpointers approached.

Fortunately for all of us highpointing nerds, times have changed. Since 2005, the Highpointers Club has worked with the new landowners to make the summit accessible without the risk of being shot at. By 2007 the summit was open on weekends from 8am-3pm. So once Eric and I crested that hill, all we had to do next was walk the nice little 800ft trail to the summit. As we proceeded towards the summit we gave a mental nod to our fellow highpointers for blazing the way and for making our job today so much easier.

At the top we were greeted by a nice giant rock sticking out of the ground, so you could be sure that you were standing on genuine Rhode Island terra firma and not some pile of Connecticut dirt brought in by a dump truck for a construction project. Nearby there were some dilapidated buildings and what looked to be old telescope mounts. Apparently Brown University astronomy students still come up to the top for occasional observations. We were hoping to see some cool telescopes, but I guess with so many visitors it's probably a good thing that they don't store their nice telescopes on the summit.

This was still pretty early in our highpointing career so our summit rituals hadn't fully matured or solidified yet. At that time, a simple photo of both of us with our arms raised was sufficient. We admired the view of the summit trees for a little while longer and decided it was time to head back.

Just to put a little icing on the day's summit cake, we decided to touch our toes in Connecticut before heading back to Providence. It's not that we had never been to Connecticut before, but when it's only a mile away you have to pay it a visit. We biked a mile west and got some photos of us in front of the CT and RI welcome signs to ensure that our state visitation photo archives were complete.

Three years later, in November of 2010, I had a golden opportunity to revisit the summit of the Ocean State. My friend Garrett was headed to Foxwoods in Connecticut for a little blackjack action and invited me to join him.

"I'll come along under one condition," I said to Garrett, "that we've got to stop by Jerimoth Hill along the way."

"Sure thing, Matt," Garrett said.

On the way to Foxwoods we took a little two-mile detour and crested Jerimoth Hill from the west. The familiar 800ft trail led us to the summit and it looked exactly as it had three and a half years earlier. Well, I guess that shouldn't be too surprising because it's basically just a big rock and a bunch of trees at the top. The summit cairn was a little shorter and the trees did look a bit bigger though.

For me, a state high point is a special place, a place that I can visit over and over and it never gets old. Even if Jerimoth Hill doesn't have an awesome view, it's still in the same class as great mountains like Denali or Rainier or Gannett. Another visit to a state high point means more—another summit photo for the webpage, another trip report for the book, another notch in the belt. Another visit to one of America's sacred summits.

15 Ebright Azimuth

Delaware

488ft

Dates climbed: May 25, 2007

Author: Matthew

Accompanying climber: Keith Gilbertson

Ebright Azimuth. The name just has a certain ring to it. There's nothing cliché about the name of the highest point in Delaware—it's not a Mount, Point, Peak, or Hill, nor is it a Butte, Mesa, Dome, Bald, or Mound—it's an azimuth. What it lacks in elevation and difficulty it make up for in catchiness. What exactly is an "azimuth," anyway? On the drive back home from school in summer 2007 we decided to find out.

It was the end of our junior year at MIT and the beginning of what we expected to be a summer of relative anti-adventure. In preparation for fall grad school applications we needed to boost our résumés and get some more work experience, so we were headed for internships. Don't get me wrong, we knew it'd be exciting work—Eric would be working for NASA's Jet Propulsion Lab in Pasadena and I'd be working on robotics at NASA Goddard Space Flight Center in Maryland. But when compared to the previous summer when we had hiked most of the Appalachian Trail, and the summer before that when we had worked on trail crew in the California Sierra Nevada, spending a summer in the office didn't sound quite as appealing.

One nice thing about driving between MIT and Kentucky is that there are a bunch of different but more-or-less equidistant routes that you can take. That means you can swing down into Delaware or Maryland or even southern Pennsylvania without adding much to the nominally thousand-mile journey. This trip we wanted to check off the highest point in Delaware, which is located on the northern end of the state, right on the PA/DE state border. Armed with the SummitPost.org directions we headed out of Cambridge on May 24, 2007 in the trusty green Plymouth Voyager and watched MIT shrink in the rearview mirror.

The other nice aspect about driving between MIT and Kentucky is that you're guaranteed to cross the Appalachian Trail (the "AT"). This means two things: first, you've got a cool place to hike; and second, you've got a free place to camp. Since the Trail goes from Georgia to Maine, any reasonable KY-MA route is going to cross it somewhere. Toward the evening on May 24 we decided that we'd like to camp just inside of New Jersey at the AT crossing near Stroudsburg, PA.

It's also fun to revisit the AT a few years later and try to remember what we were doing or talking about at that moment back in 2006. Near this particular road crossing, I remembered calling Garrett just as we were entering his home state of NJ on July 17, 2006.

"Garrett," I had said, "We're calling to request your permission to enter the great state of New Jersey."

"Granted," Garrett replied. After crossing the Delaware River, Eric and I knelt down upon the hallowed Jersey soil in Garrett's honor to pay homage to him and his native state.

As we pulled off I-80 at the Tammany Trail Access exit, I immediately recognized the spot. We knew there would be good stealth camping opportunities in the woods up to the left. Eric and I grabbed our camping stuff while Dad volunteered to guard the car that night. In the morning, in order to relive a little bit of the AT, we hiked up a few miles to Sunfish Pond and once again touched our toes into the cool water. According to a sign, this lake marked the southernmost extent of glaciers during the Ice Age.

With the AT nearly checked off our list (we had a few remaining sections we finished up in 2008) our sights were now set on the state high points. As we drove farther south towards Delaware we realized that we were officially high point addicts. Mountains that we had done earlier like Mount Washington, Mount Whitney, or Clingmans Dome—those mountains were one thing. Even if they weren't state high points they were still awesome enough to be worthy of a visit. People who just simply enjoy hiking and aren't working on "The List" climb those mountains every day.

But Ebright Azimuth, now that's in a completely different category. Without a trail, a view, or even the requirement of any physical activity it's not one of those places you generally go out of your way to visit. A "mountain" like Ebright Azimuth is in the "highpointing addict" category, and if you go out of your way to climb it that probably means you're working on "The List." Places like Iowa's Hawkeye Point and Illinois's Scales Mound, which we had visited a few years ago, are also in that category. So, after recalling the drive through hours of cornfields in southwestern Minnesota on the way to a little hill in northern Iowa or the miles of backroads in northern Illinois, along with today's drive towards an *azimuth* in suburban northern Delaware we had come to the conclusion that we were officially addicted to highpointing.

After getting a little turned around in the neighborhoods north of Wilmington we finally crested a low and almost imperceptible rise on the DE/PA state line and spotted a radio tower and some buildings that matched the photos we had printed off from SummitPost. We were on the roof of Delaware!

There wasn't much of a view, but that was OK since the view wasn't the reason we had come here. We had come to take a breath of fresh air from the highest point in Delaware. A week later we'd find ourselves atop Maryland's Backbone Mountain—state high point #16.

16 Backbone Mountain

Maryland

3,360ft

Dates climbed: June 2, 2007, Oct 24, 2010 (Matthew)

Author: Matthew

Accompanying climbers: Keith Gilbertson, Amanda Morris, Mrs. Morris

Backbone Mountain is not one of those mountains that you just stumble across. It's also not one of those mountains you find yourself at the top of unless you're a dedicated high pointer. It doesn't even have a real summit. But it is a state high point. And that's why we needed to climb it.

I've actually had the privilege of climbing to the roof of the "Old Line State" twice, Eric has climbed it once. My first time was in summer of 2007. Eric and I were both going to work for NASA centers that summer: me at NASA Goddard in Maryland and Eric at the Jet Propulsion Lab (JPL) in Pasadena, CA. Eric found that it was actually cheaper to fly to CA from DC instead of from KY, so we all packed up the van and headed to Maryland. Along the way we decided to visit the roof of Maryland.

Backbone Mountain is one of the farthest points in Maryland from Washington, DC. It's on the westernmost corner, tucked into the border with West Virginia. It's located in a part of the state that few Marylanders see.

We pulled off Interstate-68 and headed south. We followed the directions we had printed off from Summit Post and arrived at a nondescript little gravel pull-off on the side of the road. I think there's a small sign that read Backbone Mountain.

Our dad valiantly volunteered to stay behind at the van in order to guard the bikes on the bike rack while we climbed to the top. In retrospect I wish we had just locked the dang bikes up so our dad could have made it to the top with us.

After a 20-minute hike we were on top of a long ridge. Backbone Mountain has topography typical of mountains in that area of the country; it's a long smooth ridge that stretches 40 miles from SW to NE from WV to MD. Once we were on the ridge we followed markers to Hoye Crest, a local maximum on the ridge that happens to be in Maryland. We couldn't be sure, but it sure seemed to us that there were higher points on the ridge.

The summit is marked by a really nice plaque and a huge cairn. You can actually see in the pictures how the cairn has grown between 2007 and 2010. We dutifully added a couple more rocks to the top.

I hiked with Amanda and her mom on my second ascent of Backbone Mountain. We were driving back from Seneca Rocks and decided to stop by. In the summit register notebook at the top Amanda sketched an awesome panorama of the valley below. Now Amanda and her mom have climbed their third high point (WV, NH, and MD).

17 Mount Rainier

Washington

14,410ft

Dates climbed: Aug 21, 2007

Author: Matthew

Accompanying climber: Bilal Zia

Day 1

Snow?! In August? Are you kidding me? I couldn't believe what I was seeing. Our spectacular view of the heavily-crevassed Emmons glacier was now suddenly obscured by white out. The cold, 40° rain had abruptly turned into heavy, wet snow as we crossed the 8,500ft contour. We were happy to see that the precipitation was now bouncing off our clothing instead of saturating it, but it was not the time for rejoicing. It was 7pm, with the sunlight fading, and we still had a couple thousand feet to ascend over rocky talus to reach a place that might be campable. We were getting worried. The date was Saturday August 18, 2007.

We had done so much work just to get us to that point, that our determination to reach the summit was unshakeable. I had arrived in Seattle Friday afternoon, and had five hours before Bilal and Eric would show up. In the meantime I walked about ten miles through Tukwila and Seattle procuring white gas, maps, pulleys, and food for the journey ahead. When Bilal and Eric got in, we rented a car and finally left SeaTac airport at 11:30pm. We wouldn't think of staying at a hotel that night. Come on, we were on vacation; we could stay inside any night of the year. So, being the cheapskates that we are, we crashed in a campsite for just long enough not to have to pay. We were on our way to Rainier by 8am Saturday.

Saturday was supposed to be a sort of glacier travel practice day, where we could practice knots, z-pulleys, and self-arrest, but we decided to hike in instead. After being advised by the Paradise ranger to change our route from the Fuhrer Finger to the Emmons Glacier instead, we headed toward the Sunrise park entrance, in the northeast. Our three hour drive quickly took us from the lush forests of Rainier National Park to the dry desert near Yakima. We were getting a taste of the varied climates of Washington.

When we arrived at the White River trailhead we spread all our gear onto the ground and made the critical decisions about what to take and what to leave behind. Our decisions turned out to be mostly good ones, except for the white gas. Our choice to go light and take only about 8oz of fuel later nearly forced us to turn around and abandon the trip. But for now, with me and Eric carrying the tents and Bilal hauling up the rope, we started the five-mile, 4500ft climb to Curtis Camp around 4pm.

The first few miles were easy to follow, but after the Glacier Basin camp, the maintained trail vanished and it was up to us to find a route. We forded the White River and began our climb up a steep scree slope of volcanic pumice. Soon we reached the ridgeline and gained our first good view of the Emmons Glacier below. It was amazing. Until that point, I had thought of glaciers as relatively well behaved pieces of snow. Really big, but pretty much a nice big layer of snow with a few cracks here and there. You know, something that you could probably sled down, but you'd just have to stop every once in a while to get around a crevasse or two. But once I saw the Emmons Glacier my rosy picture of glaciers went out the window. We were looking down at the most intimidating obstacle course we could have ever imagined. Thousands of gaping crevasses spread as far as we could see. These miniature Grand Canyons of snow could swallow a whole house, let alone a person. I think that from the right vantage point you could probably look into the throat of the crevasse and see to the center of the Earth. The glacier was made even uglier by a uniform coating of black rocks and boulders, deposited by millennia of rockfalls and avalanches. Wow. We knew that our route did not meet up with the glacier until several thousand feet higher, but we hoped that we would never have to cross anything like that.

As we continued our ascent our daunting view of the Emmons Glacier was soon obscured by clouds around 7,500ft. A steady, cold rain began to fall, but we were hopeful that we would reach soon the freezing line and the saturating rain would turn into more benign snow. And what a freezing line it was. As we were poured on by the heavier and heavier rain we could actually look a couple hundred feet above us and see snow. We continued our ascent, with me in the front, followed by Eric, and then Bilal, and our shower abruptly changed from rain to snow at 8,000ft. At last.

But now things were getting tense. Bilal was feeling some effects from the altitude, and the thinner and thinner air was holding him back. We were now aiming for a closer camp than we had originally planned, and even that was looking like a stretch. The heavy, wet snow began to blow, and turned into near white out. Our topo wasn't much good when we could only see 100ft in front of us. We relied on Eric's fancy camera and Bilal's GPS to estimate our altitude. But we still had a thousand feet to go.

We couldn't stop now. Our sweat was mixing with the snow and by now our shorts, tennis shoes, and thin rain jackets were saturated. But we had to keep moving. If we stopped to change clothes we'd cool down fast and get our new clothes all wet. So we practiced two of the most critical MITOC Winter School techniques: moisture management and "wet clothes minimization" (i.e., minimize the number of wet layers). We continued along the ridge, buffeted by a strong southwest gale and stinging snowflakes. With the thick clouds we could no longer see the crevassed glacier below us. But we wouldn't have noticed it anyhow. We were on a mission: to reach camp before dark.

And we did. The sharp, 20ft wide ridge finally leveled out a little bit, and we reached an area that looked like it had been camped at before. "Is this the campsite?" I asked. "I don't know, but it's where we're gonna camp" said Eric. We hastily pitched our two summer tents and hoped that they wouldn't be flattened by the strong winds and heavy snow that surely awaited us that night. We cooked a quick gourmet supper of pasta and dehydrated sauce under the vestibule and slathered it with about a half a pound of parmesan cheese. Mmm. The best seasoning they make.

Day 2

We had originally hoped to attempt a summit the next day, but in the backs of our minds we knew this was unreasonable. Indeed, we awoke the next morning to the same wall of white that restricted our view to a couple hundred feet. We would have to wait until the evening for our first good view of our mountain.

We were in pretty good spirits to start the day; we knew that the weather was supposed to clear in the evening, so we would have to push the summit attempt to Monday. But our first meeting with another climbing party soon began to erode our confidence. The six-person group said that they had arrived at camp last night, and had decided that they would go no farther. They had abandoned their bid for the summit based on the latest forecast: storms and clouds all day until Tuesday. They seemed to imply that we should do the same. We thought about it for a while and quickly dismissed the idea of turning back. We hadn't even hiked on glaciers yet! We told them thank you, and then moved on towards Camp Schurman.

Camp Schurman is a precarious little outpost. It's perched on a thin little wedge of rock slicing into the Emmons Glacier. It's basically the last solid ground you can stand on before you step on glaciers and begin the actual climb. As we neared the camp we proceeded down the slope one by one and Eric and Bilal got the first view of Schurman. They immediately chuckled. "What is it?" I asked. I couldn't see around the corner. "You'll see in a second," Bilal answered.

Is was quite a surprise. There was a tiny little ranger shack perched on the narrow, almost knife-edged ridge. It looked like the hull of a submarine had been cut into short sections, and the section nobody else wanted was helicoptered to this spot and declared the ranger's hut. As luxurious as it was, I was satisfied with a tent.

As soon as we got to the camp to check it out, to our surprise we saw a couple of other guys leaving to head up the mountain. "They're crazy," we said. You couldn't see more than 200ft. We took a picture of them as they reached the edge of visibility, so we could have an idea of the route tomorrow morning in case their footprints disappeared.

And then of course . . . it was time for the snowman. How many places in the lower 48 get four inches of snow in August? We didn't have a choice. It was pretty much our civic duty to kids everywhere to erect a snow monument to commemorate this historic event. We also hoped that it would still be there to greet us during our hopefully triumphant return to camp the next day. Time would tell.

After setting up our little "advance base camp" at Camp Schurman (9510ft) we roped up and practiced some crevasse rescue techniques on the nearby glacier. Bilal and I successfully lowered Eric into a little mini crevasse and tried to get him out. As glacier travelers know, we had the most trouble getting him over the "lip." There's no good solution to that problem. Just practice, practice, practice.

Whew. What a long, arduous day. We hiked for one mile, climbed 800ft, and did a little glacier walking. It was now 5pm and time for some dinner, then bed soon after that. I like the mountaineer's schedule.

We knew tomorrow would be a big day. Because the snow gets really soft under the blazing afternoon sun and the snow bridges over the crevasses weaken with the heat, the best time to cross glaciers is in the morning. So we set our alarms for 1 a.m., hoping to leave at 2 a.m. and get back to camp by noon. As we ate dinner we caught a few quick glimpses of Rainier through the clouds, and hoped that this meant the clouds were clearing. Finally, right before we went to bed, two holes in the two cloud layers lined up and we could finally see the frosty top of the mountain. For a brief couple of minutes we stood in awe and snapped picture after picture of the glacier in front of us. Soon the clouds closed up. We hoped that we wouldn't have to rely on our pictures the next day to find the route. We went to bed around 7pm with a feeling of excitement mixed with a little bit of nervous anticipation.

Day 3

Beep beep! Monday August 20th, 2007. Ouch. 1 a.m. came really early. It felt like we just went to bed. But we quickly perked up and the pumping adrenaline soon erased any sleepiness. It was showtime. Our big moment had come. This was it.

My hands were already twitching with excitement as I ripped open the zipper on the rainfly to assess the weather. It revealed a cloudless sky with phenomenal visibility. You could see the distant lights of Seattle to the northwest, almost 60 miles away! Yes! Perfect weather at last! We rapidly scarfed down a quick meal of cereal and powdered milk—the perfect hiker-in-a-hurry, no-fail energy breakfast. Now it was time to rope up. Done. "Everybody doubled back and locked?" Yep. Even with a couple hours of sleep our minds were as clear as day and with a quick check of everyone's knots we were on underway. "Let's do it!" I yelled.

The whistle had blown and the game had started. So far it was Rainier 0 and us 0. Rainier was going to be a tough adversary, but we hoped our attack would fall on a vulnerable day. With Eric as the forward, Bilal at midfield, and me taking up the defense, we began our assault on Mount Rainier.

Even in the moonless, starlit sky we could still see the tracks of our predecessors easily with our headlamps. With Eric as lead tracker, we slowly inched our way like a caterpillar around the crevasses and up the glacier. Thankfully, this part of the Emmons Glacier was much more well behaved that the part we had seen down below. The crevasses were numerous, but not insurmountable, and smooth snow actually made up a majority of the glacier's surface. But crevasses are crevasses. We knew not to stray too close.

Despite the need for great attention and caution when traveling over a glacier, I paused a couple of times to steal a glance up at the brilliant sky. Without the moon, you could clearly see the Milky Way stretching like a cloud across the sky. There were so many faint stars in the sky that would easily be drowned out by the slightest light pollution: The Pleiades, Andromeda Galaxy, and Orion Nebula. It was actually difficult to recognize familiar constellations because there were so many other stars to confuse you. Our distance from city lights helped, and so did the altitude. The starlight had to travel through half as much air to reach us as at sea level.

But soon the spectacular light show began to fade. A strong west wind had begun to pick up the fresh snow and throw it with a stinging speed into our faces. I was quickly brought back to reality by a jerk in the rope caused by my falling behind. Now we had to concentrate. Our awesome visibility was gone and we could only see about a hundred feet. Our headlamps reflected off the snow like the high beams of a car in the fog. And now the tracks that we were following began to disappear as they were buried by the blowing snow.

Communication was getting harder and harder. Actually now the communication was only one-way. The howling wind blew from Eric to Bilal and then to me and thus the sound of everyone's voice was thrown to my ears. At first I couldn't understand why nobody in front could hear me. I heard Eric and Bilal deliberating on the direction of the route, but even when I voiced my opinion at the top of my lungs nobody could hear it. You see, we had to keep tension in the rope, and all three of us had to remain as collinear as possible, so I had to maintain my 50ft distance from Bilal, who had to be 50ft behind Eric. Whenever I spoke the sound was torn from my mouth and pushed uselessly down the mountain. As a result, I was pretty much in my own isolated little world. Sometimes they would be just out of sight, apparently deciding on the route but I could only move when the rope started pulling again. I got a couple nice pictures in the meantime, but I couldn't wait for the wind to die down so we could all start talking again.

From what I later learned, Eric and Bilal were faced with some tough decisions. The tracks had totally disappeared and it was now just a matter of choosing the route that looked best. It was tough work. We came to several dead ends that ended up in sheer ice walls or gaping crevasses, and had to turn back and try another way. We traversed all around the glacier well into the morning and the frustration was building.

A little after sunrise we spotted a couple of other climbing parties way off in the distance on what we figured was the Disappointment-Cleaver (DC) route. Now, the DC route is basically a superhighway to the summit. It's the route that all the rich people pay to have guides hold their hands all the way to the top. No thank you. I'd rather not even hike than pay a guide to lead us like a bunch of elementary students to the top of a mountain. From what we heard the DC route was marked with a bunch of wands, and had a deep trench cut in places by the hundreds of people that are led up each climbing season. You can tell, we didn't have to much respect for the DC route. When we were in the Paradise Ranger Station, Bilal asked the ranger to suggest a good route, as long as it was "anything but DC." It felt like more of a challenge, more thrilling to pick our own way up the glacier and not have to wait in line for other groups to get out of the way. So from our vantage point on the Emmons Glacier we looked at the DC people off in the distance, gave them a nod, and continued on our own way. We refused to let our route ever intersect with theirs.

But route after route always ended up in a dead end. We were still determined to get to the top, but we were concerned that we were seriously off the correct route. Slowly that agonizing feeling began to emerge that we had deviated from the true route early on, when it was still dark. We groaned at the prospect of having to backtrack any more thousand feet down the mountain. We stopped around 9 a.m. to assess our situation. As we munched on some "breakfast" we couldn't help but notice the DC people marching steadily up the mountain. We gradually began to realize that this late in the game our last option might be to actually meet up with the DC route. As hard as it was to accept, we were desperate. We had to get to the top, and we were willing to swallow a little bit of pride to do it.

Even meeting up with the DC route proved much more difficult than we had expected. We backtracked a little bit, trying to find not just the best route, we were looking for *any* route that could bring us over to DC. After five tries or so Eric came upon a path with some promise. But it was going to be tricky. Eric and Bilal were taking a long time in front of me to get down, and I couldn't figure out why. After ten minutes of waiting there, the rope finally tugged again and it was my turn to go. I immediately understood their trepidation. I gazed into a vast ice field full of crevasses and massive house-sized blue ice chunks. We christened it the "Khumbu Icefall place," after the famous Everest obstacle.

Pretty soon we knew that this wasn't going to work either. Although we could see a reasonably feasible route across, we had no sense of scale and couldn't see how far it actually was. We also knew that if we made it across, we still had a couple thousand feet to go up to the top, then we'd have to

53

traverse over this same route later on in the afternoon, when all the snow and ice were much weaker. Dang it. We would have to turn back again.

We made it back to a safe place and considered our options. It was getting "late" in the day (10am) and we knew that our chances for summiting were waning. The clouds were rolling in now and the entire landscape was almost a uniform white. The sky blended in with the glacier and without sunglasses you would probably be blind. In the end we decided to backtrack a little bit and give ourselves one last chance to find the true route. So we reluctantly headed down the mountain— dejected, but still holding out one small sliver of hope that we could summit.

Just out of chance Eric tried a promising-looking path to the left on our way down, and sure enough, there were footprints! And it looked like a decent path continued for quite a distance. All right! We found it! We decided to check it out. Soon we actually found a lone flag sticking up in the snow and knew for sure that we were on the money. The path to the treasures of the top lay in front of us. We were at 11,600ft, with 2,800 still left to go.

But it was not to be. I could only see about two rope lengths from my perspective in the back. We knew that with time we would be able to make it to the top, but we'd get there late in the afternoon and the way down would be sketchy at best with the melting snow and fading visibility. Plus, some of us were feeling the fatigue from the altitude. Bilal didn't think he had enough strength to try again the next day. I wasn't sure I'd hold up much longer. We thought about our options.

We were very concerned about the fuel. We had heard that there would probably be a trickle of water at camp, so we figured we probably wouldn't need the extra fuel to melt snow for water; we could just treat the water we found with iodine, and the only reason for fuel would be for cooking. But alas, the trickle at camp was frozen up by the recent cold temperatures, and the only way we had to get water was to melt snow. So our fuel was running dangerously low, and we were worried that if we stayed to summit another day we might not be able to make enough water for tomorrow. We saw three options:

Option 1: Push for the top and get back to camp late.

Option 2: All turn back and go home.

Option 3: All turn back and return to Camp Schurman. Bilal heads back to the car that night. Eric and I push for the summit tomorrow and return via DC to meet Bilal who's driven two hours to Paradise Ranger Station.

We soon chose Door #3. Everybody seemed happy. On our way down we recorded a few waypoints with the GPS and made a mental note of some of the features for mine and Eric's trip the next day. We hoped that we could just follow our footprints in the morning, but we weren't so sure. It was going to be a challenge, but we figured that with our experience finding the route this day, we would have impeccable route finding in the morning.

Our little snowman was still there to greet us as we arrived back at camp. Its pleasant rocky grin now seemed to be more of a victorious smirk. It was as if the face of Mt Rainier was looking at us, smiling at our defeat today, and ready to dish out more trouble tomorrow. Maybe it was just our imagination.

We took a quick nap for a while as Bilal got ready for the trip back to the trailhead. Four factors had been beating us down the past couple of days and Bilal was starting to feel the effects: altitude sickness, sleep deprivation, dehydration due to lack of fuel to make water, and hunger because we were starting to stretch our food thin. He decided that he'd conquer Rainier some other time, and tomorrow just wasn't the day. We said goodbye to him around 3pm, and wished him safe travels back to the White River Trailhead.

Meanwhile, I was also having some doubts about tomorrow. The altitude and sheer physical stress were catching up to me too. I laid down to rest with an upset stomach and one mean headache. Eric and I planned to wake up at 2am, and then we'd see what kind of shape I was in. If I was better then we'd start the climb.

Rainier 1, us 0.

Day 4

"Matthew, Matthew . . . time to wake up," Eric said.

"Arghhh." I nervously opened the tent door to check out the weather, and sure enough it was perfectly clear. I immediately felt 100% better. "Let's do it!"

We could feel it. This was going to be the day. Yesterday we had tried to find our way up the mountain and lost. Today we knew our enemy. Yesterday morning we had hesitantly tip-toed onto the glacier, nervous about crevasses and what lay ahead of us. Today we were a confident two-man army. We knew what we were up against and what to look out for. Rainier was going down.

Sunrise today found us a thousand feet higher than the previous morning. The incredible undercast sky made for some of the most spectacular scenery we've ever seen. It was satisfying to see the low clouds rise up ridges and drift in between mountains far below us. We felt like we were in a different world up there, like an airplane above the weather. Like a satellite above the atmosphere. Today was definitely the day.

We kept climbing and the adrenaline kept pumping. We were wearing down fast, but it didn't matter. The top was starting to come into sight and we could taste victory. We took one last look behind us at the Emmons Glacier and stepped onto the rim of the crater. We were on the summit!

Wow. The view was absolutely incredible. With the clouds a mile below us, we really felt like we were in an airplane, flying high over southwestern Washington. We had 100 miles of visibility in every direction. Off to the south, we saw two tall peaks rising like islands out of a sea of clouds. The closest was Adams, and the farthest was Oregon's Mt. Hood, both of which we would conquer over the next week. But we weren't thinking of Hood and Adams, we were thinking of our island, our volcano, Mt. Rainier. It was almost like a different kind of Hawaii. Instead of a tropical volcano rising out of the middle of the Pacific, ours was like an icy Olympus Mons towering above the state of Washington. If it wasn't for Mt. Whitney and Mount Elbert, we'd be the highest in the lower 48 states. All we'd need to do is throw a snowball 80 ft in the air to match California's 14,494ft peak.

But the beauty wasn't just on the horizon, it was right in front of us. From the peak we gazed down into the vast crater of Mt. Rainier. You could probably fit a couple football fields—make that a few hockey rinks—in the circular bowl of snow that made up the top. Immediately in front of us there were a few exposed areas of ground with no snow cover, and we saw the reason why: several columns of steam rose timidly out of the rocks and quickly disappeared in the wind. We had found the perfect place for our picnic.

As soon as we ducked a few feet below the peak the brisk 20 degree breeze vanished and we immediately plunged into a 70 degree oasis of warmth. The quick temperature change wasn't from the geothermal heat, however, it was probably because the air was so thin, that the temperature could swing rapidly, depending on the wind. We collapsed with exhaustion on our pads at our little perch below the summit. We were really feeling the effects of altitude now. We had no desire to eat or drink and had to force our body to accept any nourishment. This was now day three of a vicious altitude-induced cycle, and we were happy we wouldn't have to hike another day. All we had to do was get down the mountain. 5,000 ft . . . but it's all downhill—should be easy, right?

As we munched on some granola and sipped some slushwater from our vantage point we could see a few guided teams that had just made it to the top. A couple of super well-dressed, clean-cut clients trundled up to the summit to meet us. It looked like it was probably their first time walking on snow. With their fancy trekking poles, shiny new crampons and plastic boots we weren't surprised that these were the kind of people who would shell out 800 bucks to have someone escort them to the top. I felt sorry for their guides. These kids needed a little bit of MITOC Winter School to show them the difference between ice and snow, not a guiding service. Eric and I thought back to our Winter School experience. Yeah, we were probably like those guys a couple of years ago, but with a few years of Winter School by now we knew our way around snowy mountains.

Pretty soon we had mustered enough energy for the most important picture of all. We quickly raced up to the summit, set up the camera, stripped off all our upper layers, and posed for the requisite shirts-off summit photo. Not too bad compared to Mt. Washington, we thought, the wind-chill here was a balmy 10 degrees. We bolted back down to our packs and spent the next half an hour warming back up to normal.

10:30 am: Time to start heading down. The sun was absolutely baking in our sheltered oasis, and we knew it was time to head down before the snow got too slushy. We took a few last pictures from the top, and marched over the southern rim of the crater, onto the DC route. We had a vertical mile to go to get down to Paradise Ranger Station and meet Bilal, and figured it wouldn't be too tough. Hey, maybe we'd get to do some glissading along the way and shave off some time.

We were immediately glad that we hadn't taken the DC route up. It was just way too easy. With our route, up the Emmons Glacier, there had been a couple of footprints, and one single flag to let us know we were going the right way. In comparison, the DC route was basically a highway. There was a huge trench to follow, with flags all over the place, and even a couple fixed ropes in places that were a little sketchy. The guided teams we had seen on top were cautiously, slowly marching down and eventually let us pass.

By noon the sun was blazing down on us will full fury and we needed a break. It was like we were in a vast white desert. We searched around for any kind of shade or shelter, but all we could see was white. Each little particle of ice was like a separate tiny mirror, and together they reflected all of the sun's rays straight at us. The icy breeze at the top had become an apparent 80 degree oven and we needed to stop for a second to cool down and reenergize. I took my shirt off for a while; maybe skin would reflect the radiation better than a red shirt.

Despite the burning heat, we somehow still couldn't muster any thirst. The altitude was really starting to mess with us, and we knew we had to keep forcing water down to stay hydrated. While we were resting, I found a small trickle of water dripping from a nearby icicle and put a couple Nalgenes under it. 100% pure glacier melt water! People pay for this stuff back in the city. But after waiting five minutes for the trickle to fill a mere quarter of a Nalgene, I soon gave up my entrepreneurial dreams and chugged what I had.

Time to keep moving. "Argh I don't want to get up," I said.

"We've still got 3,000 ft to go," Eric replied, "we can't camp here." We struggled to shoulder on our monster packs and continued the hot slushy slog down the mountain.

Pretty soon we could see a camp off in the distance, and assumed it was Camp Muir, the end of the glacier travel. Awesome. We were really looking forward to some untethered hiking action after spending two days roped up. The rope was really getting on my nerves; in order to maintain constant tension in the rope we were both constantly speeding up or slowing down. Sometimes, while I was on a smooth, flat slope, the rope would suddenly fall slack. The first few times I looked with confusion ahead of me, only to see Eric struggling up a small hill or cautiously proceeding over a crevasse. And of course, once I got to the tricky spot and had to slow down the rope would yank as Eric continued at a steady pace. Pretty soon we learned the key behind rope dynamics: communication. It was still tough, though, and we were anxious that we would finally have the chance to unhitch.

But the mountain still had one last curveball to throw at us. We rounded a corner and were suddenly faced with a 200ft uphill climb.

"Nooooooooooooo! I thought the downhill was over!" I yelled.

"Dang it!" Eric said.

After climbing 5,000 ft that morning, we couldn't handle one last climb. It's one thing to psyche yourself for a big climb and do it. But when you've already patted yourself on the back for reaching the top and you've settled in to a nice downhill rhythm, an unexpected hill can feel like it's taller than Rainier itself. Plus, we were absolutely exhausted from the past few days of hiking. We were being taxed on multiple fronts:

1. The altitude was making our bodies reject food and water, and no matter how much we forced down, we were still basically relying exclusively on our reserves.
2. We had only gotten five hours of sleep last night, for less than 12 total hours for the past three days.

3. We were carrying fifty-pound overnight packs (all our gear had to go up and over the mountain with us).
4. The air was probably 60% the density of sea-level air, so we basically had half the oxygen to work with.

We were running on fumes. And we still had a long way to go. We sat there in the snow, at the base of the climb, contemplating our destiny. Finally, after about half an hour, our mental determination finally overcame our physical exhaustion. We took one slow step, then two, then three. We were going at 1/3 our normal pace. It was only a gradual slope, but it might as well have been vertical. At last, after draining about half our remaining energy it leveled out and we could finally breathe again.

We actually still had farther than we thought before we reached Camp Muir, but we didn't care. It was all downhill from here. We cruised into the camp in style around 1:30pm and now we could finally cramp-off and unhitch for the first time in days.

Now it was payback time. We had climbed five thousand feet up Mount Rainier, and already burned 4000ft of that on the descent. Now it was about to get a lot easier. We whipped out our trekking poles and summoned our balance, then began our glissade down the Muir Snowfield. The slope wasn't really steep enough, but we were still able to get a few nice runs down the snow. We only had one mishap: Matthew slipped (on camera) near the very end and broke his perfect record.

Now it was really time to celebrate. The end of the snow! In the 90 degree heat of Maryland I had been looking forward to snow all summer. Now we were sick of it. We donned our tennis shoes with relish and started prancing down the rocks towards the trailhead.

We knew we were getting close. Pretty soon we saw some little kids walking around, and a few Seattle city slickers asked us how far to the snowline. Now there were actual plants. Genuine 100% real trees and weeds. Wow. It was an oddity that we had forgotten about for the last three days. Now we were snapping pictures of stuff that was green, instead of white. Before long we made it to the trailhead and staggered into the Paradise Ranger Station to meet Bilal.

It was an awesome trip. We were thrilled to make it to the top, but disappointed that Bilal couldn't be there with us. I know he'll conquer it someday. We knew we had caught Rainier on a good day. We had won today, but many days of the year the Mountain would be unbeatable. By waiting out the weather, we had found the perfect window of opportunity and exploited it. We were lucky.

Equipped with better knowledge of the route and the mountain itself, the next time would definitely be much easier. But that would take all the fun out of it. The whole appeal behind mountaineering is being able to step up to a mountain with limited knowledge, not fully knowing what to expect, and to take your own way up, without someone else telling you what to do. You feel a sense of pride, a sense of ownership knowing that you climbed the mountain with your own power and your own skills. You feel that the mountain's more wild. The mountain beckons, and dares you to climb it. And that's why we climbed it. Because it was there.

Rainier 1, us 2.

18 Mount Hood

Oregon

11,239ft

Dates climbed: Aug 24, 2007 and June10, 2012 (Eric)

Author: Eric

We had heard rangers tell us several days earlier that Hood was too hard and dangerous this time of year and "no one is climbing it." Matthew and I found this hard to believe and decided we'd assess the conditions for ourselves and not be scared away before even seeing the mountain.

After finishing Mt Adams on Thursday afternoon we drove across the Columbia River into Oregon and got to the Timberline Lodge trailhead by dark. Bilal couldn't climb with us this time because he had to fly back east on Friday, and half the battle in climbing Hood was figuring out how Matthew and I would get back to Seattle on Sunday with our luggage. The main problem was that I had my laptop and a big suitcase (since I was interning out west all summer). Normally I'd just stash my extra gear at the trailhead, but I couldn't risk my laptop getting stolen, especially since it had sensitive NASA information on it from my internship work.

After several hours of phone calls, brainstorming, and borrowing a wireless connection outside an apartment complex, we came up with about ten plans to resolve the situation. The one that was completely legal and might actually work was this: Bilal would bring the extra gear and laptop to a "Ken's Frozen food and Storage" place at the airport and store it there. Somehow the airport would not be at all suspicious about a Pakistani man dropping off suspicious bags that weren't his at the airport for several days. On Sunday Matthew and I would hitchhike from the trailhead to the nearest town, Hood River, and hopefully catch a bus north to Seattle in time for our flight.

Finally with this plan we could start climbing the mountain. Bilal drove back to Seattle with our extra gear and we started up the trail in the dark. In the rush to get going we had brought a few things like extra clothes that we didn't need on the mountain, so we stashed these in the woods a little ways in.

By about 10 p.m. we had to make a decision to either try to summit the next day or wait til Saturday. The problem with summiting Friday was that we would have to get our usual 3 a.m.-or-so alpine start, which was getting harder and harder after doing that most days in the past week. So we decided to sleep in til sunrise, then establish an advanced camp as close to the mountain as possible for a climb on Saturday.

We set up the tent that night in what looked like a nice spot in the dark, but by morning we realized we were right between two ski runs. Amazingly the resort on Mount Hood is open year round, fed by glacial snow pushed down the mountain by Snowcats every night, so we were woken up by the chair lifts in the morning.

We packed up quickly around 8 a.m. and got outta there before any skiers could run us over. The hike up to the base was actually pretty easy, just some semi-steep scree fields up to about 9,000 feet, where you have to cross a little snow to get to the crater.

We got to the crater around 10 a.m. and were surprised to meet a group of three climbers who had attempted the summit that morning. (And those rangers said no one was climbing Hood). The guys had tried one of the snow gulleys but got scared away because it was too steep, too icy, and a rock fell down near them. They warned us that it was supposed to rain Saturday and we had better be careful.

We considered our options and thought today might be our only chance to summit, so why not go for it. The snow would have softened up a little and the gulley didn't look steep enough to need two tools (maybe 45 or 50 degrees), so we decided to give it a try.

There were some big crevasses on the bottom, so we roped up as a precaution. We considered climbing the Hogsback route (the most popular one), but it had a fifteen foot-wide bergschrund blocking our path, so we went up the steep gulley those guys tried. I think it was called the Pearly Gates route. Anyway, our crampons dug into the snow/ice perfectly, and the climb was not that hard. There was one black shoot of scree and rocks that we stayed away from, and no rocks fell down.

At the top of the snow gulley we reached the crux—a steep section of rotten 3rd class rock/scree held together by a little ice. As I climbed I accidentally dislodged a softball-sized rock, and yelled for Matthew to get out of the way. Fortunately we didn't climb directly below each other (for this reason), and the rock rolled well away from Matthew.

At the top of this pitch I poked my nose over the final boulder and was met with a monster 2000-foot cliff. It was covered in snow and I bet it never saw sunlight. I sat down and belayed Matthew the rest of the way up.

We were definitely on the summit ridge, but it was hard to tell exactly which part on the ridge was the highest. The views were the same everywhere and it appeared we were on about the tallest point, so that's where we took our victory shots.

The sun was getting hotter so we didn't spend too long at the top. I carefully down climbed the sketchy 3rd class section and was relieved to finally get back to good old snow. The worst part about the descent was that it was too dangerous to glissade—the snow was still too firm and icy. We could wait for it to be perfect, but then the rock fall danger would be too great. So we down climbed the whole thing and got off the snow by around 1 p.m.

Now we couldn't just hike back down to the trailhead and be done with it, since we had packed several more days of food to account for possible weather delays, so we set up camp right there in the crater. I bet not too many people have gotten to camp right there, in the crater of one of the most popular mountains in the country, and had it completely to themselves. It was almost like a true wilderness experience, minus the ski lift visible below.

One problem with our camp was that the whole area reeked of rotten eggs from all the sulfur, but we thought it was worth it for such a cool location. And we could actually use the steam vents to melt snow for water because it was so hot!

The next morning when we headed down we saw about three parties trying to summit (one was a group of snowboarders trying to board all the way down), and one solo French ice climber on his way down. We laughed again at the rangers who said no one was climbing now.

As for our plan to get to the airport—it worked perfectly. Sunday morning we got our first hitch at 8:15am on car number 8, and our second one at 8:45am on car number 2. That left us with enough time in town to swim across the Hood River and eat our fill at the grocery store before hopping on the bus to Seattle. That little swim officially counted as our shower for the week.

19 CAMPBELL HILL

OHIO

1,549ft

Date climbed: Nov 23, 2007

Author: Matthew

Accompanying climber: Keith Gilbertson

Can you boys breathe up there? Did you remember to bring your oxygen masks?" our Grandma Wright asked over the phone with a giggle. She was joking, of course. We were calling her from the top of Campbell Hill, the highest point in Ohio. At 1,549 feet it obviously isn't high enough to require oxygen but still the view that you get from the nice little summit park is, well, the best in the whole state!

Have you ever noticed that, on many US road atlases, the highest point in each state is labeled? All the way from Denali to Britton Hill, the cartographers are nice enough to place a little black triangle and label on the state high points just to add a bit of trivia to their maps. On our many visits to Columbus, Ohio for Thanksgiving each year Eric and I noticed that the highest point in the state of Ohio wasn't all that far from Columbus. At sixty miles, it still seemed like a long drive to us, but over the years, as our high-point driving distance threshold diminished, Campbell Hill began to seem within the realm of possibilities.

On Thanksgiving Day 2007 we asked our dad if he would be up for the long drive, and he enthusiastically said yes. The three of us set out on our little adventure at 8am the next morning and headed northwest. Forty-five miles later we passed by Mad River Mountain, one of the few ski slopes in Ohio, and knew we were getting into the high country. Central Ohio had just gotten some snow so we really felt like we were driving into the mountains.

Campbell Hill began to grow in the distance. We turned northeast and were pleasantly surprised to find that the gate to the Ohio Hi-Point Career Center was open. We parked in the lot and after a quick walk soon found ourselves on the roof of the Buckeye State. Campbell Hill is actually contained within the Hi-Point Career Center, but they're nice enough to open the gates from Monday through Friday for Highpointers like us.

We were pleased to see that Ohio is proud of its high point. At the top there's a very nice plaque, signs, bench, and an excellent view. Our little adventure to Campbell Hill began a day-after-Thanksgiving highpointing tradition that next year would see us on top of the highest point in Indiana.

20 Black Mountain

Kentucky

4,139ft

Dates climbed: Jan 5, 2008 and June 5, 2011 (Eric)

Author: Matthew

Accompanying climber: Keith Gilbertson

Looking back on Black Mountain four years later (2012), it surprises me a little that the highest point in Kentucky was #20 in terms of completion order of our high points list. At first I'm surprised that it wasn't #1. After all, Kentucky is our home state and Black Mountain is less than a three hour drive from Berea. But there are a couple of reasons that we didn't climb Black Mountain until the middle of our highpointing quest. First of all, Black Mountain isn't exactly on the way to anywhere. It's way down in the coal country of southeastern Kentucky. And second of all, in 2008 three hours felt like a long drive. We hadn't yet pushed our boundaries like we later would on road trips such as the <u>1340-mile weekend trip to the CO, OK, KS, & NE high points</u>, or the <u>2700-mile trip through MO, AR, LA, MS, AL, FL, GA</u>, or the <u>2700-mile trip through SD, ND, MN, MI, WI, IL</u>, or for that matter the <u>44-hour/2200-mile weekend drive to the NS, PEI, and NB provincial high points</u>, . . . etc. If you're going to drive three hours from Berea, we thought, you might as well go all the way down to the Smoky Mountains.

But the time for Black Mountain finally came during IAP of 2008. (IAP stands for Independent Activities Period, when there are no MIT classes during January). At that point we still had a few hundred miles of the Appalachian Trail (AT) left, in pieces from Tennessee to Virginia. Back in 2006, when we had hiked the bulk of the AT, we had made the strategic (though somewhat painful) decision to skip a few sections so we could complete Maine before school started in September. Back then, we figured that we could finish up the southern pieces (and New Hampshire) during the winter. So, midway through our senior year at MIT, with the possibility that we might end up on the West Coast for grad school, we decided to take advantage of our classless IAP and finish up the AT.

We were missing two AT sections down south: Roan Mountain (TN) to Damascus (VA), and Lickskillet Holler (VA) to Buena Vista (VA). On January 5th, 2008 we loaded up the green Plymouth Voyager at home with our backpacking equipment and began the drive down to the start of the first section: Roan Mountain. Back in 2004 we had finished the Davenport Gap –> Roan Mountain section of the AT during Spring Break of our senior year in high school. I remember starting that hike out in a t-shirt and shorts with temps in the 80s. But by the end of that week we were postholing through two feet of slushy snow! I still vividly remember the moment when our dad picked us up: we were wrapped up in our sleeping bags, huddled and shivering next to a big snow bank, our cotton clothes completely saturated, when finally, to our huge relief, we spotted our dad in the big green van coming around the corner. But that is a story for a different trip report; this story is about Black Mountain.

Conveniently, Black Mountain was on the way to Roan Mountain—or at least we made it be on our way. Along the way we passed through Pineville, KY, home of the famous, "Chained Rock." In Pineville you can look up to the top of a nearby mountain and spot a huge rock that seems to be balanced precariously over the city. Attached to the massive boulder is a long chain that is said to be holding the rock in place. According to a plaque, the giant 101-ft chain was carried up by two mule teams in 1933 and "by tradition, is to protect the city of Pineville, Kentucky." From afar, the chain looks pretty important to the rock's stability but from nearby it doesn't seem that the chain would do much if the rock slipped.

A little later we passed through the village of Lynch, which is the highest town in Kentucky. We were deep in Kentucky coal country but the abandoned houses in the small town suggested Lynch had seen better days. We continued climbing until we reached the KY/VA border, and spotted a sign for Black Mountain. I remember years ago in elementary school we wrote letters to the coal companies pleading for them to leave Black Mountain alone. In the mid 1990s the highest point in KY was slated for mountaintop removal. At that time I didn't have any idea where Black Mountain was located or its significance, but as we looked through the trees at the mountain in the distance it seemed that our efforts had paid off and Black Mountain was still standing.

Even though there was a decent amount of snow on the ground, our dad, a seasoned "Minne-snow-ta driver," was unfazed. He turned the van onto the side road and proceeded over the unplowed gravel. Soon the road steepened up and it was time to trade out the front wheel drive for the hiking boots. We found a little red board buried in the snow and for a moment we were the highest snowboarders in the state. Later we passed by an interesting FAA radar dome; unfortunately there wasn't much info about what it was for, other than the "NO TRESPASSING" signs.

A few hundred feet later we were on the roof of the Bluegrass State! We threw some snowballs, climbed around on the summit tower, and made sure to take in the view. Over the years we had done a lot of hiking in Kentucky and it was a fulfilling to finally climb to the highest point in our home state. After a little more tomfoolery, ballyhoo, and shenanigans we got back in the van and headed for our next little adventure on the Appalachian Trail.

21 MOUNT MITCHELL

NORTH CAROLINA

6,684ft

Date climbed: May 27, 2008

Author: Eric

Bicycling the highest points in North and South Carolina

Our grand plan after finishing up undergrad at MIT was to celebrate by taking the summer off to do an awesome bicycle tour from Prudhoe Bay in northern Alaska down to the continental US. The only problem was that we had never done more than a two-day bicycle trip and weren't sure what to expect. Our solution was to do a shake-down trip—a trip long enough to teach us some lessons about bike touring but not long enough to get us into trouble.

We both had the foresight to only register for final-less spring term classes, conveniently freeing up finals week for our more important business. Our shake-down plan was thus to bike for a week down south, covering ~600 miles and tagging the highest mountains in North Carolina and South Carolina along the way.

Now there are two main gear choices in planning a bike tour: which type of bike do you ride, and how do you transport your gear. We bought some brand new touring bikes from REI for this trip because they have slightly wider tires than a standard road bike for riding over rough roads. For gear transportation the choice was actually made for us. One day in our hometown of Berea, KY as we were hiking across an overgrown field we found two B.O.B. bike trailers laying upside down and collecting rust. Those run for over $300 a piece new and we had just found two of them! It was clear they had been there for a while and must have been abandoned by some other bikers. (Our hometown is actually on one of the official transcontinental bike routes, so we see a lot of long-distance bicycle traffic go through).

Day 1: Leaving KY

By the middle of May we were officially finished with classes. We flew back to Kentucky with our bikes and packed up for the trip. On day one we biked out of our garage in Berea and started heading south on US 25. Our Dad drove ahead for a little while and met us in Livingston, KY, 20 miles south, for a few final pictures. Then we were on our own.

We hit the 80 mile mark in Pineville in southeast Kentucky and took a well-deserved ice cream break. It was pretty stinkin' hot there in southern Kentucky in May. It was still mid-afternoon and we figured we could probably make it into Tennessee before stopping for the day. As we got to the state border we met our first unexpected obstacle: the Cumberland Gap Tunnel. It was officially closed to bikers, and there weren't really any other roads around it. We didn't know what to do and called our Dad to see what he thought. He made some other phone calls and miraculously some official person in a pickup truck drove over and offered to escort us through the tunnel. Perfect!

We threw the bikes in the back, hopped in, and found ourselves safely on the other side in no time. By now it was time to find a place to spend the night. We had brought a tent but we had no intention of paying to camp. Our only acceptable option was to stealth camp. Unfortunately we were still in the town of Cumberland Gap, TN but we found some woods on the outskirts of town that looked secretive enough for our tent. Matthew walked around our proposed site a little more just to make sure and, dang it, he ran into two people on a four-wheeler.

"You can't camp here," they said. "This is private property."

That was actually one of only two times we've ever been caught trying to stealth camp (the other was in Norway), and we got out of there in a hurry.

It was getting close to dark and we knew it would only get more difficult to find a spot. One thing we were sure of, though, was that if we could get far enough out of town we could find a spot nobody would care about. So we actually biked north out of town for about 5 miles, officially crossing into Virginia and crossing the century mark for the day. Finally we found a secret place on the edge of the Cumberland Gap Park and set up camp.

"It had better not be this hard to find a spot every night or I might just consider paying the $10 to camp in a state park," I told Matthew.

"I refuse to pay to camp," Matthew replied. "That's just a basic human right nobody should have to give up."

Day 2: Mount Mitchell

The next morning we stealthily left our spot and continued biking into Tennessee. Our first objective of the trip was Mount Mitchell, the roof of North Carolina and the tallest peak east of the Mississippi at 6,684ft. Eastern Tennessee is pretty hilly, and there were few easy miles that day, aside from the downhills of course. We had been biking with clip-in pedals that kind of wrap around your shoe, and Matthew figured out that the extra efficiency they provide did not outweigh the discomfort they gave him. That's a useful thing to discover before a much longer tour. We finished the day across the border into Hot Springs, NC, and camped just outside town.

As we were planning out our route for the next day we realized that one of the roads our GPS recommended didn't even show up on our paper street atlas. That meant it must be what we refer to as a "Billy Bob" road—a rinky-dink out-of-the-way tertiary road that most people wouldn't have an excuse to drive on. That sounded fun and traffic-free, so we decided to go for it. We continued riding through the hills the next day until early afternoon we made the final turn to the Billy-Bob road. We didn't see any dead-end signs, so at least that was reassuring.

As we biked up the road it started getting steeper and steeper and the intermittent houses on the side were replaced by forest. Then we started seeing more potholes and eventually the road turned completely to dirt. The grade was so steep that we actually had to walk the bikes up for several miles. Luckily we wouldn't have to take this road back, because that's a terrible waste of elevation gain to burn it on a gravel downhill where you can't safely ride fast. We turned a final corner and magically popped out on the Blue Ridge Parkway. It was indeed not a dead-end road!

At this point Mount Mitchell was about 10 miles north on the parkway, but in the opposite direction of our next destination, Sassafras Mountain in South Carolina. The Parkway was notorious for going out of its way to go over the hilliest terrain, so we decided to make this a fast and light summit attempt. We stripped down our bikes of all unnecessary gear and stashed the extra gear in the woods. Then we took off up the road.

There wasn't too much traffic on this weekday afternoon, and we had the road mostly to ourselves. Gradually we wound our way through tunnels and up above 6000ft until we reached the end of the road just below the summit.

We couldn't believe our eyes—the true summit was covered with construction equipment, fences, and "No Trespassing" signs! But it was literally close enough to throw a rock at from the parking lot!

We walked over to a little visitor center building and found an official-looking person to talk to.

"What's going on with the summit?" I asked.

"Oh, we're building a new observation tower," he said matter-of-factly. "You guys can't go up there now, but you can certainly come back in three months when it's finished."

"Oh well, guess we missed out this time," I replied. Matthew and I then walked out and started planning our next move.

"What do you mean 'guess we missed out'!?" Matthew asked once we were out of earshot of the official person. "I didn't bike no 200 miles to come within 200ft of the summit and just turn around."

We both knew we would somehow find our way to the summit that day. I had purposefully played it cool talking to the official guy so he wouldn't get any ideas that we might just sneak up there anyway. If I had gotten angry he probably would keep his eye on us to make sure we biked right back down the road.

By this time of day the construction workers had all left, so if we could just sneak up the mountain from the opposite side nobody would notice—thus nobody would care. It was kind of like stealth camping.

We started biking up the road until we were certain we were out of sight of the visitor center, and then we darted into the woods. We dropped our bikes behind some trees and then started bush-whacking (quietly) back up and around the opposite side of the mountain until we reached the clearing where the construction was going on. There were no fences on this side. We looked around and didn't see anyone.

The summit was a pile of dirt that would be clearly visible from the visitors center so we'd have to act fast. I got my camera out, screwed it into the mini tripod, and then we went for it. I set the camera up on the ground on time delay and we both ran over to the summit. In the 10 seconds before the picture took we managed to tag the summit and pose with hands raised, then just as quickly we disappeared back into the woods. If someone had blinked they would have missed us.

Mission accomplished, we quietly bushwhacked back to the bikes and took off down the hill. I quit looking over my shoulder after about a mile, finally certain that the authorities were in fact not in pursuit.

The bike back to our stashed gear was incredible—we reached up to 40mph several times on the steep hills. By far the most exhilarating part was cruising through completely dark tunnels at 30mph not being able to see even your front wheel contacting the pavement. We got back to our gear just before dark and managed to find a level spot hidden from the road to set up camp.

(The story continues in the # 22 Sassafras Mountain section).

#22 SASSAFRAS MOUNTAIN

SOUTH CAROLINA

4,139ft

Dates climbed: May 28, 2008

Author: Eric

(Story continued from Mount Mitchell section)

Day 3: Sassafras Mountain

The next morning we continued biking south on the Blueridge Parkway to our next objective—Sassafras Mountain. We reached Asheville, NC in the morning just as it started to rain and decided that would be a perfect time to resupply at the local Wal-Mart. We bought three more days of food and a bunch of town food to gorge on for lunch. We tried to drag our feet and stall as much as we could, but the dang rain just would not let up. Real mountaineers battle cold, wind, snow, avalanches, and all manner of obstacles, and we couldn't be sissies and let just rain keep us from a mountain. So we hopped on our bikes and took the plunge.

Once you accept the fact that you will get completely soaked, biking in the pouring rain isn't that bad. Our gear in the trailers was in waterproof bags so we didn't have to worry about that. The only real difficulty in the rain happens when you go really fast. We were pushing 30mph going down some hills and the rain felt like bullets in our faces. At one point we pulled off the road to consult the map and a driver pulled over too and offered to let us warm up and have a meal at his house. We thanked him but said we'd be fine. We were on a mission and wouldn't let anything stop us from reaching our mountain.

We were biking deeper and deeper into the backwoods of North Carolina. Eventually we reached the South Carolina border at the top of a little pass back in the woods. The highpoint was a few miles farther down the pass and then up some more back roads. It would be another out and back trip just like Mitchell, so again we stashed our unnecessary gear in the woods and continued on fast and light.

When I think of South Carolina I usually think of Myrtle Beach instead of mountains, but there's actually some rugged terrain near the North Carolina border. We descended from the pass to the little village of Rocky Bottom, and then started our climb. At one point we actually had to walk our bikes up the road, it was so steep. But luckily it was all paved. We biked up to about 3,400 ft where there was a small parking lot, and then walked our bikes up the final half-mile trail to the summit—the roof of South Carolina!

We didn't spend too long there, since it was still raining. We cruised back down to Rocky Bottom, then back up to our gear stash. A few hours before dark the rain finally let up and we biked about 20 more miles, putting us up to 90 miles for the day. We were having a particularly hard time finding a level stealth spot to camp in such hilly terrain, and knew it would be nearly impossible once it got dark, so we gave in and stayed at a state park campground that night.

Day 4: Into the Smokies

This was the halfway part of the trip and, with no state highpoints left on the list we planned to take the most direct route back to Berea. Our GPS told us this involved riding on the Blue Ridge Parkway to Cherokee, NC, then cutting through the Smoky Mountains and back up US 25. Our previous day on the Parkway told us it would be hilly, but we figured hills were better than the alternative of tractor-trailer traffic and debris-strewn city roads.

The next morning started with a monster climb—we started around 1,000ft elevation and had to gain 4,000ft to reach the Blue Ridge Parkway. That's the best time to do it though, in the morning when you're still fresh from the previous night's rest. We gained the Parkway and were greeted with spectacular views and very little traffic. The road actually wound up to a few 6,000ft peaks that were higher than almost any other state highpoint on the East Coast. The best part of the day was the descent down to Cherokee, NC 70 miles later—where over the course of five miles we lost all 4,000+ft of elevation we had gained that morning.

It was about 4pm when we cruised into Cherokee and we had a decision to make: 1) push on all the way through the Smokies by dark to find a legal campsite in a national forest, 2) camp right where we were, or 3) bike as far as we could into the Smokies and camp on a trail off the road. Well, we certainly weren't going to stop for the day at 4pm after only 70 miles, and we knew it might be tough to find a stealth spot north of the Smokies in the urban sprawls of Gatlinburg and Pigeon Forge, so we decided to see what options the park would offer us.

We started slowly working our way up into the park, up the road to Newfound Gap, elevation ~5,000ft. We were basically on a roller coaster that day, starting at 1,000ft, biking to 6,000ft, back down to 1,000ft, then back up to 5,000 ft. With only a few miles to go before Newfound Gap, I finally hit the wall and my stomach told me I had to inject calories or else. Biking is the only activity I've found that is so binary like that—I can be fine one minute and the next be dead. Even running marathons or hiking 50 miles at once don't make me hit the wall like biking can. Matthew said he could use the break too, so we both stuffed whatever food was most accessible into our mouths and then continued the climb.

We got to Newfound Gap with about 30 minutes of light left and stopped to take some pictures. Our potential plan was to push the bikes up the Appalachian Trail a little ways until we found a good stealth site, but there were so many tourists milling around that we knew it would be too much of a risk to attempt to camp anywhere nearby. So we decided to cruise down the other side of the gap and keep a close eye out for spots.

This was more difficult than we anticipated. The only flat places were near trailheads, and that's where all the people were. It was getting darker and we were getting dangerously close to the edge of the park, where the Gatlinburg sprawl started. Then, with probably 2 miles left of the Park, we spotted a gated gravel service road off to the left leading up the side of a streambed. Perfect! We made sure no cars were coming, turned off our flashing lights, removed our bright orange vests, and sprinted up the road.

That's the trouble with stealth camping while bicycle touring. You want to be as visible as possible while biking so cars can see you, but want to instantly turn invisible when leaving the road for a stealth site. This always involves at least 15 seconds of stripping off clothing while nervously checking for passing cars and simultaneously trying to act like you're just casually taking a break (in case a car actually sees you there). Someday I'll invent an instant bike invisibility switch to cater to fellow bikers that also face this problem.

We made it past the gate and into the woods with no cars noticing, and then started looking for a site. The road dead-ended at a gravel pile after a quarter mile, but we pushed on farther into the woods and found a perfect spot to camp. Even if someone drove up that gravel road they couldn't have seen us.

Day 5: Northward

The next day it was back to civilization as we biked through Gatlinburg, Knoxville, and north toward Kentucky. By the century mark for the day we were just shy of the state line in Jellico, TN. We had been looking for a campsite since mile 90 but there were just too many dang houses around. Finally we gave up and paid to stay at another state park just outside town. This was getting a little ridiculous with two state parks in just a 6-day trip (a 33% failure rate), and we vowed to avoid them if at all possible when we did our big trip through Alaska and Canada.

Day 6: Heading Home

We officially crossed into Kentucky at 8:30am the next morning, the start of the last day of our shakedown trip. We took US 25 north through Corbin, London, Livingston, and Mt Vernon. By that point, with only 20 miles left Matthew was worn out and called our mom to come pick him up. I decided to end under my own power and biked the final miles back home.

The trip was a great success, with 2 state highpoints bagged, 600 miles biked, and quite a few lessons learned about long-distance cycle touring and stealth camping.

23 GRANITE PEAK

MONTANA

12,799ft

Date climbed: Aug 16, 2008

Author: Eric

Accompanying climber: Darren Verploegen

The summer of 2008 was a spectacular adventure of bicycle touring, mountain climbing, and nothing remotely related to MIT problem sets or internships. Matthew and I flew up to the edge of the Arctic Ocean in Prudhoe Bay, Alaska in early July and there started a long bike ride back to the continental US. We braved the famous 500-miles-of-dirt Dalton Highway in northern Alaska, an angry grizzly bear 10 feet from the road in eastern Alaska, July snow in Yukon, and millions of voracious mosquitos in British Columbia. Thirty-seven days and 3,000 miles after starting we had made it to Montana and were looking to end the summer with a bang.

We decided a fitting end to our summer bike ride would be to climb the highest mountains in Montana and Wyoming—Granite and Gannett Peaks. After biking in to Great Falls, MT we met up with our friend Darren and headed down to Granite Peak in his big Suburban. We had originally planned to bike all the way to the peak, but to get it in before school started, it made more sense to load up the bikes in the truck and drive to the trailhead.

We picked up some climbing gear we had mailed to the Roscoe, MT post office and made it to the Mystic Lake trailhead just as a pouring rain started. Instead of hiking in a few miles and getting soaked for the rest of the trip, we decided to ride out the storm in the truck, which was conveniently big enough for all three of us to sleep in that night.

Trip reports of the mountain rated the crux of the climb everything from third class to 5.7, with the general consensus class 4+. Darren didn't want to take any chances, so we packed a good portion of his climbing rack just in case.

We headed up the trail on Friday morning passing Mystic Lake and eventually gaining the aptly-named Froze to Death Plateau by lunch time. This was where we left the trail and trekked across the boulder-laden plateau towards base camp. It was pretty chilly up there and we noticed patches of fresh snow everywhere, probably from the previous night when we had gotten rained on in the valley. We passed two other parties before reaching our base camp at a level spot below Tempest Mountain.

Here we got our first look at Granite Peak, and it looked almost impossible. Granted, we were looking at the rarely-climbed north face and our route was on the opposite face. Matthew looked at the GPS and noted that the summit was only 0.9 line-of-sight miles away and 400 feet above us (we were at about 12,400ft). Sounds easy, but that didn't take into account dropping 500 feet to a saddle and doing some technical climbing.

Before we went to bed that night we had to make the tough decision of which two lucky climbers would get the tent and who would have to bivy outside. Matthew and I only had a 1.5-man tent that we could squeeze two people in and Darren didn't own a tent, so that was our dilemma. We collectively decided to punish Darren first outside for not having a tent, and we would each take turns afterwards for the next mountain.

Next morning we were woken up at the reasonable hour of 5am by another party passing by, and we reluctantly decided to get up. We dropped down a boulder field to the Tempest Saddle, then began the climb up the talus fields. By about 7:30 we reached the snow-bridge saddle, which was the first sketchy part of the climb. There was a narrow snowbridge with a very exposed drop on the south side and a possible cliff on the north. The party in front of us crossed with ice axes, but since we left our ice axes and crampons in the truck but had plenty of climbing gear we decided to belay each other across.

Darren went first and soon realized that there in fact was not a cliff on the north side and the exposed area was only about 5 ft long. He promptly threw off the rope and told me to break down the anchor because we were being way too cautious.

After Matthew and I crossed we began climbing a series of chimneys that we later read in our SummitPost climbing guide were class 4. The climbing was fun because there were always good holds, just a bit of exposure if you looked back.

Eventually we reached the crux part of the climb, which the party ahead of us was pitching out. It didn't look that much harder than what we'd already climbed, but since we had hauled all that climbing gear up we decided we might as well use it. Darren led the way placing in a few cams, Matthew followed on a butterfly knot in the middle of the rope, and I cleaned at the end. There was definitely one move past an overhanging rock that I was glad to have the rope for, so I'd probably agree with the "class 4+" rating.

After this pitch we packed away the rope and passed the other group as they continued to pitch out the climb. We made the top by about 8:30am and had it all to ourselves. Amazingly there was zero wind and not a cloud in the sky. We could even see the Grand Teton about 100 miles south of us.

It turned out the party we passed was actually a surveying party with fancy GPS equipment to find the exact elevation of the summit. Apparently the elevation had only been calculated by sighting the summit from other mountains, and never precisely with a GPS. The guys said they needed to leave the equipment on the summit for two hours, and then send the data to some official agency to have the error removed. I gave them my email so they could tell me whether the summit is still 12,799ft or if the maps need to be revised.

We spent about two hours at the summit and then started descending. Luckily there were rappel rings for most of the way, so we didn't have to do too much down climbing. When we got to the top of the crux move we met a solo climber on his way down. From the look of it he had nothing with him—no food, water, rope, nothing. He looked a little worried about downclimbing that sketchy part and we offered to let him rappel down our rope. Darren made him a harness out of spare webbing and we lent him an ATC, which we pulled back up the rope when he finished.

The rest of the descent was pretty fun rappelling most of the way to the snow bridge. We passed a mountain goat cooling off in the snow and saw another one walking around base camp. After packing up we started hiking down the 12 miles to the trailhead and got to the truck at about 9:30pm. Time for a good sleep at the trailhead before our next mountain—Gannett Peak in Wyoming.

24 GANNETT PEAK

WYOMING

13,804ft

Date climbed: Aug 21, 2008

Author: Eric

Accompanying climber: Darren Verploegen

Matthew Gilbertson and Eric Gilbertson

Day 1

After climbing the high point in Montana our next target was Gannett Peak, the highest mountain in Wyoming. This is probably the most remote mountain in the lower 48 states, requiring a 20-mile one-way hike just to get to the base. That's not easy considering all the glacier gear you have to haul in. We drove all day from Roscoe, MT to Pinedale, WY, taking one "short-cut" along a gravel road that turned into a long-cut after a wrong turn in the dark.

Matthew needed to call some grad school professors in the morning, so we drove as close to the trailhead as we could while still getting phone service and camped there in the woods around midnight. We officially started around noon the next day, after all our errands were done.

The trail was surprisingly flat, starting at 9,000 feet and climbing only to 10,500 or so. We covered about 12 miles the first day and camped at the edge of Island Lake. Now, who could camp at a lake with a name like that and not say they'd swam out to the island? We all three jumped in and swam out to the island, but were surprisingly out of breath from swimming hard at altitude and enduring 33-degree water.

That night I volunteered to bivy outside while Matthew and Darren shared the tent.

Day 2

We hiked a few miles to Titcomb Lake, where the trail ended, and began our climb up to base camp at Bonney Pass. This pass is another reason why Gannett is such a tough mountain to get to: you have to climb up a 12,800ft pass to set up base camp, then drop down to 11,500 onto the glacier before climbing back up to the 13,804ft summit. Summit day of course ends with a final 1,300 ft climb back to base camp.

We climbed up the steep, boulder-laden slopes to reach the top of the pass around 2pm. We thought we were in the middle of remote nowhere, but there were actually 6 tents set up there! Apparently some guided group was getting ready to summit the same day we were. We looked all around for a boulder-free spot to camp, and the only available spot had a person's pack sitting on the corner. We had to camp somewhere, and reasoned that person wasn't planning to camp there because they weren't around and hadn't set up a tent, so we set up ours.

We then proceeded to practice our crevasse rescue techniques with our rope hanging over a boulder. At about 4:30 some climbers started returning from Gannett, and one woman was extremely perturbed that we had set up our tent where we had. She kept ranting about how we should respect her spot, until we asked her if she was planning to camp there tonight. She tried to dodge the question, but it eventually came out that no, she wasn't. At that point she must have realized her argument had no credibility, and we returned to our crevasse-rescuing practice.

Every party we talked to said it took them around 12-13 hours round trip from Bonney Pass, and that three parties had to tie their ropes together for a 300-foot rappel down a steep snow gully. Apparently the snow was too slushy at 1:30pm when they came down.

We weren't sure how in shape these people were, but to be safe we decided to leave well before dawn.

Summit Day: We got up at 3:30am and started our descent to the glacier by 4. There was a full moon and we could have possibly hiked without headlamps if necessary. This was Darren's first time on a glacier, but he was the most experienced at building climbing anchors, so we put him in the rear with me in the middle and Matthew on crevasse-avoidance duty at the front. From watching the other parties return the previous day we had a good idea of our route. We crossed the glacier down to 11,500 ft, then climbed a scree slope (still roped up) to what we called the smiley-face traverse. (This was a narrow, crescent-shaped band of snow).

At this point it was 5am and still 1.5 hours before sunrise, and we started traversing a steep section of glacier towards an obvious snow gulley. At one point Matthew slipped on the steep ice, but quickly self-arrested. When we got to the base of the gulley we checked the GPS and realized we were headed towards the North Face route, which was a vertical ice-climb. We looked around and found a different gulley that looked more promising and headed there.

By this time the sun was nearly up and we could see footprints going up the gulley, basically transforming it into a staircase. We called all the other climbers a bunch of wimps for being scared of this, and proceeded to climb up unroped but with ice-axes ready (it was still pretty steep if you fell).

At the top the snow melted away to talus and we cramped off for some scrambling. The rest of the route was basically 3rd class scrambling over a knife-edge ridge to the summit. To our left the sometimes vertical, sometimes overhanging cliff dropped about 2,000 ft, and to our right was a fairly steep snow slope terminating in a cliff—definitely a no fall zone. We tried to stay on the rocks and had to venture onto the snow occasionally with ice axes in hand. At 7:15am we reached the summit and had it all to ourselves.

Amazingly Darren pulled off a cell phone call to his parents, but there was no such luck for me and Matthew. We signed the register and hung out for an hour before we saw the next party below us reaching the snow gulley. We decided we should get down that gulley before the snow warmed up, and it would be wise to not cross paths with the other people on the knife edge, so we headed down around 8:15am. By 9am we reached the snow gulley and the snow was still pretty firm.

Darren quickly checked out climbing potential of the nearby Gooseneck Pinnacle, but decided not to lead it on our little 8mm climbing rope.

We down climbed the gulley without needing any rappelling and then proceeded to cramp off and boot ski when the snow got less steep. By 10:30am we had reached the glacier below the smiley-face traverse and saw an interesting snow cliff to our right. We had plenty of time so we built and anchor and lowered Darren down about 50ft to the bottom with two ice axes. We all took turns climbing up and snapping cool pictures.

We finally decided to quite fooling around and climbed back up to camp at 12:30pm, making for an 8.5-hour round trip. Subtracting about 2.5 hours of playing around we would have returned in 6 hours, less than half the time of the other parties the day before. That shows how we can't really trust any other peoples' speed predictions.

With so much extra time we hung out at camp for a while before glissading back down Bonney Pass and camping for the night near the Titcomb Lakes. We hiked out the next day with an extra day left over to mail our bikes and catch our flight home out of Jackson Hole.

25 Mount Marcy

New York

5,344ft

Dates climbed: Nov 10, 2008, May 28, 2012 (Eric)

Author: Eric

Accompanying climber: Dana Sulas

Matthew and I were itching to sink our teeth into a fresh snowball after months of summer heat, and it looked like the opportunity would finally come in early November. Veteran's Day weekend was forecast to be rainy all over New England, but could turn to snow in the higher elevations over 4,000ft. That meant some mountains in New Hampshire were fair game, and some in the Adirondacks of New York.

The Adirondacks were a full five-hour drive from Boston, but it was a long holiday weekend, we'd never been there, they were basically guaranteed to have snow, and we could even bag a new state highpoint (Mt Marcy) on the way. That sounded like the perfect combination!

Dana was up for the trip as well, and we all left Boston early Sunday morning for the long drive up to New York. It rained hard most of the way, but we knew every drop of rain we drove through equated to several flakes of snow on Mt Marcy. By midday we reached the Adirondack Loj trailhead, and suited up for a plunge into winter. The rain had luckily let up and we quickly started up the Marcy Dam trail laden with overnight gear. The shortest way to hit Marcy was a 14-mile round trip, but we didn't plan on doing the whole thing that day. We were planning to hike until we found some snow, camp there, and then tag Marcy the next morning before heading home.

We found a good view at Marcy Dam looking up to Avalanche Pass, and noticed all the mountains were shrouded in clouds above about 3,000 ft. We continued hiking a few hours farther and eventually started seeing little sprinkles of white on the ground. By around 3500ft the ground was fully covered in four inches of snow, and we deemed the situation appropriate to set up camp.

Darkness comes early that in the Adirondacks in November, and we were all in our tents and sleeping by 6pm.

It snowed hard most of the night and we woke up to a few fresh inches on our tents. Somehow we had managed to camp in a location with a view of Marcy, which we just noticed as we poked our heads out of the tents. It looked so close!

We quickly suited up for the cold, scarfed down some breakfast and took off, leaving our tents set up to retrieve later. The brief clearing didn't last long as more clouds rolled in and snow started falling again. Nothing could keep us from the summit now, though. We soon broke through the trees to the exposed summit ridge, and were blasted be wind and snow. It looked and felt like the middle of winter here, not early November.

I pushed through several waist-deep snowdrifts before reaching the windswept summit rocks, and finally the roof of New York. A huge plaque was fixed to the rock, commemorating something that I didn't have the patience to read about. I figured it must have said we were on the summit.

We quickly snapped victory shots, struggling to keep our eyes open in the blowing snow. But we had come in search of winter and were not disappointed. Matthew and I walked around the summit for a little while, sampling how the snow tasted and hoping a view might open up.

The views never materialized, so we turned around before the weather had a chance to get any worse. Back in the trees we removed our above-treeline armor and changed back into normal hiking mode again. We found the tents right where we had left them, and noticed no trace of any other people. In fact, we hadn't seen another person since we started hiking the previous morning. I suppose everyone was scared away by the terrible weather, despite it being a holiday weekend.

As we descended from camp we noticed the snowline kept dropping and dropping, even down to Marcy Dam and the Adirondack Loj. We reached the car by mid-afternoon and celebrated our feat with a couple big pizzas back in Lake Placid, before tackling the long drive back to Boston.

26 Hoosier Hill

Indiana

1,257ft

Date climbed: Nov 29, 2008

Author: Matthew

Accompanying climber: Keith Gilbertson

"Did you boys bring your oxygen masks this time?" our Grandma Wright asked over the phone with a giggle. She was alluding to the previous year, when she had asked us the same question atop Campbell Hill, the highest point in Ohio. Now we were on yet another Midwest high point, Indiana's Hoosier Hill (1,257ft). That morning, we had made the fateful decision to leave Grandma's supplemental oxygen at home in favor of a fast and light attempt at the summit, and it had paid off.

The previous year we had begun our mini-tradition of climbing a high point the day after Thanksgiving by driving sixty miles from Columbus, Ohio to Campbell Hill, the highest point in the state. This year we had decided to up the ante by driving 124 miles to Hoosier Hill, located just within the Indiana border two miles from the Ohio line. We were visiting family in Columbus for Thanksgiving and wanted a little post-turkey adventure.

Our dad was enthusiastic about yet another driving expedition, so we set out from Columbus at 8am the day after Thanksgiving and headed west. In terms of our high point list, we were currently just over the "hill," with twenty-five high points summitted so far. We were starting to realize that within the next few years we might actually finish the list. We were beginning to contract "high point fever," and the thrill of the chase turned a four-hour trip to a remote little hill in east-central Indiana into a worthwhile outing.

We turned off of I-70 near Richmond, Indiana and turned north. With nothing but fields of corn stubble extending to the horizon it was hard to imagine that the highest land in Indiana was lurking somewhere off in the distance. We turned on Bethel Road, then Elliott Road, and began to notice an almost imperceptible rise in the woods to our left. It was definitely a local maximum, but it was hard to believe it was also the global maximum for the entire state of Indiana.

A short walk along a gravel road brought us into a clearing and lo and behold we found ourselves on the roof of Indiana. An all-star Eagle Scout had built a very nice wooden sign, brick-encased mailbox summit register, and awesome picnic table on the summit. We thank him for his valiant efforts.

We found a few green, bumpy, grapefruit-sized spherical fruits (later I discovered that they're Osage Oranges) and Eric decided that he needed to juggle them. On the summit, that is. On one foot, of course. Five of them, to be precise. And the one foot needed to be balanced on a two-foot wooden post. Our dad snapped two photos: one of Eric juggling four Osage Oranges, and one photo of the two of us with both of our arms raised. We gathered a small rock from the top and in so doing we marked the beginning of our high point ritual list. From Hoosier Hill onwards we strived to repeat those three summit rituals on every state high point, as long as juggling materials were available and there weren't any steep drops nearby.

We were delighted to see that there was a summit register, which seemed like it was more of a west-coast concept and isn't commonly seen east of the Mississippi. We left our mark in the little journal and flipped through the other pages. We were shocked to see that our friend Darren Verploegen had signed in a week earlier! He had been passing through on I-70 and decided to check off another state high point on his list. We climbed Montana's Granite Peak and Wyoming's Gannett Peak with Darren earlier that summer and he had caught the high point bug.

We ate some Thanksgiving leftovers at the picnic table and admired the view from the highest point in Indiana.

27 Spruce Knob

West Virginia

4,861ft

Date climbed: March 21, 2009

Author: Eric

Accompanying climbers: Amanda Morris, Mrs. Morris, Cookie the dog

By winter 2009 Matthew and I had officially caught the highpointing bug and were looking for another state to check off the list. We only had a weekend, though, it was still winter, and we had done basically all the highpoints within easy driving distance of Boston.

Could we do Borah Peak in Idaho? Nah—better save that for the summer when we could run up it. Kings Peak in Utah? No—it'd probably take closer to a week in winter. Spruce Knob in West Virginia was still on our list, though, and we could even get on a quick direct flight to DC.

We settled on Spruce Knob, and on Friday evening, March 20, flew down to DC. There we met up with Amanda and Mrs. Morris and rested up at their house to prepare for the trip. Saturday morning we drove out with Amanda behind the wheel and Matthew navigating. The mountains on the West Virginia—Virginia border pose quite a challenge for anyone trying to head west. The mountains are basically long ridges angled south to north, and thus very few major roads head due west. As a result what should have been a 2-hour drive if on interstates turned into a 4-hour drive on secondary and tertiary roads. This route even gave Google directions some trouble. At one point Matthew read off this suspicious set of directions we'd printed from online: "Turn left on Jenkins road. Continue 2.5 miles. Make a U turn. Continue 2.5 miles . . ."

We luckily caught this mistake before going the full 2.5 miles and didn't lose much time. After four hours of driving we finally rounded the last turn up the windy Forest Road 104 and reached the Spruce Knob parking lot. From here we hiked an easy 900 feet on mostly level trail before reaching the true summit, marked by an enormous observation tower. Cookie barked in enjoyment at her first state highpoint, and we all admired the view from just above the treetops. The hike had been easy, but that was no problem with me. My legs were still sore from a 20-mile run on I'd done Friday morning (training for the Boston Marathon), and this day was supposed to be a "rest" day for me anyways.

We didn't want to immediately drive all the way back to DC, but there wasn't much more hiking to be had at Spruce Knob. There was, however, a cool rock formation called Seneca Rocks on the way back and we decided to stop there for some more hiking. A short trail led to an observation deck on the edge of a long knife-edge rock ridge. Matthew and I ventured out on the knife-edge ridge as far as we dared, while Amanda, Mrs. Morris, and Cookie played it safe at the lookout point. We watched as rock climbers carefully made their way up the side of the knife edge to the true summit of the rocks. Unfortunately we hadn't brought any ropes, or that would have been pretty fun climbing.

Back at the car I took over the wheel for the drive back, and we made it back to DC before too late. Sunday we had a relaxing day at the Morris's house before flying back to Boston.

28 Mount Mansfield

Vermont

4,395ft

Date climbed: July 4, 2009

Author: Eric

Mount Mansfield by Bike

Mount Mansfield was our last remaining highpoint within easy striking distance of Boston, and it had proven a difficult mountain to get to. It's not as close as the White Mountains, and thus it was more difficult for us to convince someone with a car to go on a trip there. After a failed attempt in February 2009 to convince drivers to come with us, we finally decided to take matters into our own hands—we would just bike to Mansfield. Well, not the whole way (that would be over 460 miles round trip—quite a lot for one weekend), but with a little help from public transportation. On a Friday night we biked over to South Station, put our bikes in boxes, and hopped on a Greyhound to White River Junction, Vermont. It's quite a hassle disassembling your bike to fit it in a bike box, but worth it for another state highpoint. Next time I do a trip like this I'm definitely getting a foldable bike.

We arrived at White River Junction around 10pm, and immediately reassembled our bikes and started riding. We were still 85 miles from Mansfield and needed to find a place to stealth camp for the night. Luckily we knew exactly where the Appalachian Trail crossed the road only 10 miles from the bus stop, and we knew we could camp there without qualms. We were on the trail and sleeping under a tarp by midnight. The next morning we started biking north, taking a short ice-cream break in Montpelier and reaching Smugglers Notch and the trailhead by about 6pm. We ducked into the woods looking for a place to stash our bikes just as it started to rain. Somehow we stumbled upon a huge overhung boulder just out of sight of the road—perfect! We could keep the bikes dry while we hiked and keep ourselves dry at night. We were trying to go ultra light and had just brought a measly tarp instead of a tent, which would have still left us wet in the rain. With all the extra gear stashed we started up the trail, determined to reach the top before sunset.

There were a few different routes to choose from and the Hell Brook looked the shortest, steepest, and most interesting. So up we went. It was probably three or four miles up and we made it to the roof of Vermont—the chin of Mount Mansfield—just before sunset. It was really cold up there for early July! Probably in the mid 40s with rain and wind, so not too much fun. We did our traditional state summit rituals of jumping pictures and me juggling 5 rocks on the summit, and then headed down. It was a little tough navigating above treeline in the fog at night, but we found our way back to the Hell Brook trail eventually, and made it back to our nice dry boulder by 10pm. This happened to be the 4th of July, and we could hear fireworks going off in the valley but it was too cloudy to see anything.

There was no time for fooling around the next morning as we had 85 miles to bike to catch a 7 p.m. bus back to Boston. Luckily it was mostly downhill this time and the sun had finally come out. We made it back in time and our bike boxes were miraculously in the same place we had hidden them on the side of the bus stop. We spent about half an hour disassembling our bikes again and got everything on the bus without a hitch, making it back to Boston late Sunday night for the end of another action-packed weekend.

29 Mount Elbert

Colorado

14,440ft

Date climbed: Aug 29, 2009

Author: Matthew

Roofs of Colorado, Oklahoma, Kansas, and Nebraska in a Weekend

11:25pm 8/28/09 to 4:25pm 8/31/09
6 states: Colorado, New Mexico, Oklahoma, Kansas, Nebraska, Wyoming
4 state high points: Mt Elbert (CO), Black Mesa (OK), Mt Sunflower (KS), Panorama Point (NE)
1342 miles/30 hrs of driving
63 hrs on the ground
ZERO down time

I think Eric and I have discovered the upper limit to the amount of adventure you can pack into a single weekend. We wanted to expand our repertoire of state high points to fill in some gaps out west. Mt Elbert (CO), Black Mesa (OK), Mt Sunflower (KS), Panorama Point (NE) all have the convenience of being relatively close to a major airport—Denver.

Eric: "Hmm . . . I think I sense another adventure coming up"
Matthew: "Wow, is all that even possible in a three-day weekend?"
Eric: "We'll make it possible."
Matthew: "Sounds like a plan to me . . ."

With a quick direct flight into Denver on Friday night, we hit the ground running at 11pm and the clock immediately began ticking. We first wanted to tackle Mt Elbert which, at 14,433ft, is the highest mountain in Colorado and the second highest peak in the lower 48 behind California's Mt Whitney. We signed up for a rental car and cruised west on I-70 until we got tired. With the help of some GPS ninja skills we located some National Forest near the metropolis of Silver Plume around 1am and drove about 90 seconds south before we found a place to camp. I don't think you could find a campsite that fast in Massachusetts.

We packed up the black Dodge Caliber in the morning and zoomed down to Leadville, elevation ~10,000 ft. We followed Summit Post's directions for the Northeast Ridge trailhead of Elbert. The little car handled well on the rough gravel road. The Elbert parking lot was already filled up by 9:30am. Most people who were going to climb that day had already started, in order to avoid the pop-up thunderstorms that populate the high peaks in the afternoons. We quickly got moving from the trailhead at 10,000 ft.

The trail was well behaved, with moderate grades the whole way. The nice thing about trails out west is that they're graded for horses (unlike many trails out east) so they never get too steep. We huffed and puffed in the thinner and thinner air and reached the top in 2 hrs 18 minutes. Wow, that was a lot easier than we thought. I think we've taken longer to hike up Mt Washington than Mt Elbert. There are a lot of similarities between hiking up Mt Washington and Mt Elbert: in both, total ascent is about 4,500ft over 8.5 miles round-trip; treeline is about half-way up the hike; and it's always cold at the top. The only difference is that Mt Elbert has about 50% less oxygen at the top!

We have a few traditions for the top of state high points: we've got to collect some rocks, we need a picture of Eric juggling 5 objects, we need a picture of me jumping, and a picture of both of us with our arms raised. We dutifully carried on these traditions on the summit of Mt Elbert.

After an energizing 45 minute rest at the top we began our descent. For some reason our metabolism was on fire. We hopped down the talus and jumped over the boulders. It seems like it's sometimes easier on your knees to descend quickly rather than slowly because your energy gets dissipated into your muscles like your quads and calves instead of into your joints.

But when we looked to the south at the Southeast Ridge trail we saw the best way to descend: by mountain bike. One hard-core dude had ridden/carried his bike to the summit and was now cruising down in style. Eric and I made mental note that we had to do that some day.

We touched the car at 1:42pm, for a round trip time of 4hrs 12 minutes (including resting at the top). Most of the other cars hadn't been moved since we started. But climbing the highest point in Colorado wasn't the end of our adventure, it was just the beginning.

(Story continued in Oklahoma section)

30 Black Mesa

Oklahoma

4,973ft

Date climbed: Aug 30, 2009

Author: Matthew

(Continued from Colorado section).

After resting to eat lunch for 15 minutes, Eric quickly assumed command of the Caliber and we headed south on US highway 24 towards Buena Vista, where we picked up some groceries. We drove through the spectacular Arkansas River Canyon before we burst out of the mountains and onto the High Plains in Pueblo, CO. Driving into Pueblo felt a little like driving to the ocean; the farther east we got the more the mountains opened up and the Great Plains began to stretch before us to the horizon, as flat as a giant majestic pancake. We were about to experience an entirely different topography.

We turned south on I-25 and began our drive towards the middle of nowhere. We turned off near the giant city of Trinidad, about 15 miles from the NM border. As we drove east a spectacular lightning display illuminated the horizon. It was one lightning flash every three seconds and the sky grew ominously darker. Pink streaks of light streaked across the horizon like a giant spider web. With flat terrain and not a tree in sight we drove in awe at the storms around us. Fortunately they were probably ten miles away, so the most action we experienced was just a little rain.

As we cruised down US-160 towards Kim, CO we were relying dangerously heavily on Google Maps' directions. It pointed us to a shortcut on gravel roads to the Black Mesa area. We took it. It was already well after dark at this point. But the deeper we got onto roads like "County Road 20.6" and "County Road 16.5" the less trust we had in Google's directions. We drove by a few remote ranches and finally reached a sign that said DEAD END. We were already about ten miles deep down these tiny gravel roads so we didn't want to give up. According to the GPS it should not be a dead end, just an intricate maze of roads with no clear exit. We could gamble and keep going south on random roads, or we could drive back to the nearest main road and take it instead, adding 2 hours. We couldn't afford any more setbacks, so we turned around in frustration and headed back towards Branson, the surest way to get us where we needed to go. Google Maps had failed us.

We cruised through the CO/NM border late and needed to find a campsite before we got any more exhausted. We had climbed the highest point in Colorado and somehow also driven for about 11 hours so far this day. I consulted the GPS while Eric drove. We were looking for small side roads that we could pull off on and camp next to without anyone minding. But the few side roads off of NM-456 all ended up being driveways toward people's ranches. By 12:30 am we finally found a suitable campsite under a big tree next to the prickly pear cacti. A few nearby cows mooed in confusion throughout the night.

The morning light revealed the beauty around us. Rugged red and white mesas dotted the open rangeland around us, on top of each mesa were sprinkled small cactus bushes, sunflowers, and cattle. It reminded us of parmesan cheese sprinkled on top of a mound of spaghetti. From the map we noticed one such feature called "Wedding Cake Butte." Maybe that just meant we were hungry.

"I think we're getting closer to the middle of nowhere," I told Eric, because there wasn't another car or a house in sight, just us, the mesas and the endless red gravel road in front of us. We finally made it to Kenton, the westernmost "town" in Oklahoma, with a population of about 50. We asked someone on the street for gas because we were getting low. "Gas, ha! You'll have to go 35 miles east to Boise City for that!" In that case, gas could wait; first we needed to climb Black Mesa.

We followed the signs to the trailhead and started walking around 10am. The trail to the top was about 4.2 miles, not much shorter than Mt Elbert! The path wove through the rangeland, dodging all kinds of cacti and other mesas. Black Mesa itself is wide and flat at the top, so it almost appears that you're back on the plains once you get to the top. We looked around for the official high point on the mesa, but didn't see any variation in the topography greater than 6 inches. The surveyors must have been pretty skilled to find an actual highest point on this mesa; it all looked pretty much the same to us. The USGS quad we had printed out from online indicated a slight rise a little farther to our west, so we kept going.

A gigantic granite obelisk marked the true "summit" of Black Mesa, 4,973 ft. It must have been helicoptered in because there aren't really any roads to the top. Eric climbed on top of the monument for a better vantage point. His view didn't change much. We met some guys on top who had mountain biked much of the way up. Man, we were jealous. After engaging in our requisite high point traditions, we hiked back to the car. We had just climbed to the top of Oklahoma. Kansas and Nebraska were next.

(Continued in Kansas section).

31 Mount Sunflower

Kansas

4,039ft

Date climbed: Aug 30, 2009

Author: Matthew

(Continued from Oklahoma section)

We needed some gas so we headed down into Boise City ('Boise' is pronounced as a single syllable around there). The mesas quickly disappeared and now it was flat land as far as the eye could see. There weren't any crops, just open rangeland for cattle. But it was slim pickings for the poor cattle—there wasn't much growing besides sagebrush and some little bushes. I think I read that around there you need 40 acres per cow.

I said to Eric "I think we're getting tantalizingly close to the middle of nowhere."
Eric: "I think the 'Middle of Nowhere' is one of those places you can get closer and closer to, but can never actually reach."
Me: "Just like the end of a rainbow!"

Indeed, there wasn't much to see besides the endless dotted yellow line stretching as straight as an arrow in front of us and open land to the sides. I've heard that if you were to shrink the Earth down in size that it would be smoother than a poolball. Judging from the terrain in eastern Colorado, I can believe that.

After passing uneventfully though Springfield, Lamar, and finally Cheyenne Wells, five hours later we were sure that we were on the verge of the "Middle of Nowhere." That meant it was time to look for Mount Sunflower. We followed Summit Post's directions for Kansas's highest point and took a small gravel road north. After weaving around on gravel roads through beautiful fields of bright yellow sunflowers we reached the summit around 5:15pm. A master welder had fashioned the great steel monument at the top which read "Mount Sunflower—4039ft—Highest Point in Kansas." The welder had cleverly coiled a thick chain around to form the inside of the sunflower. It turns out that a nearby rancher and his family own the summit and are nice enough to let tourists like us visit.

The view at the top was impressive. Fields stretched to the horizon with the occasional farmhouse and grove of trees surrounding it. Mount Sunflower is located on the westernmost edge of Kansas. Imagine that Kansas is a piece of paper. Now angle that piece of paper down to the east, and slightly up to the west. That's why you get the highest point on the western border.

(Continued in Nebraska section).

32 PANORAMA POINT

NEBRASKA

5,424ft

Date climbed: Aug 30, 2009

Author: Matthew

(Continued from Kansas section).

After the traditional high point festivities, we departed the roof of Kansas around 5:25pm. We had about 11 more hours of driving in order to hit Nebraska's Panorama Point and drive back to Denver before our flight left around 7:15pm the next day. The farther we went this evening then the more buffer time we had the next day.

We turned back into Colorado and rejoined our old friend US-385. We continued north and reached Julesburg, CO, on the NE border, a few hours after the 7:15pm sunset. Then we picked up I-80 west. From the GPS there didn't look to be too much public land in southwestern Nebraska, so we knew we'd have a tough time finding a good place to stealth camp. There weren't really any woods around for us to hide in. So we decided to go for the gold and drive all the way to Panorama Point itself for a good night's sleep.

After running around the car a little bit and eating some chocolate, we were wide awake enough to make the drive to Pine Bluffs, where we turned onto some back roads. We used a combination of directions from Summit Post, Google Maps, and the GPS to get us to "The Point." I guess back in the good old days people just needed a good map. We didn't want to take any chances.

The final pitch up to le sommait massif was a rugged gravel road on which the Caliber, under Eric's control, handled nicely. We reached the roof of the great state of Nebraska around 10:30pm MST and pitched our tent in triumph on the summit. Victory! A few distant lights from farmhouses shone in the darkness around us. A long line of mysterious blinking red lights stretched for miles to our south. We wondered what they could be. We would have to await the light of dawn to fully admire the view from Panorama Point, elevation 5,424ft.

It was a little windy so we drove the car around near the tent, angling it in such a way as to shelter it from the southwest gusts. That's probably the first time we've ever used a car to shelter a tent. It was a surprisingly chilly night for late August, but we slept in comfort knowing that we had just conquered three state high points and driven across the state of Colorado all in one day, touching six states in the process.

We awoke in the morning to the sound of another car door slamming. "What's going on?" I blurted out as I woke up. It turns out that another high pointer had just come and was already leaving the summit. We could only guess what type of mission that person was on.

As I was taking a few pictures, Eric said, "Hmm, that's strange . . . my watch says it's Tuesday September 1st." Me: "Wait a minute . . . ummm . . . my watch says the same thing. Uh oh." For a couple of seconds, we panicked. Our flight left on Monday Aug 31st. I froze in disbelief. Had we really forgotten about a day and missed our flight? Or had we slept through a day like Rip Van Winkle? But wait a minute, I thought to myself, I had just spoken to Amanda yesterday, and she starts class this morning. So it can't be Tuesday already. Then we finally figured it out: when we set our clocks back after we arrived in Denver on Friday, we had set them to 11pm but they had already ticked through midnight by that point, so they were a day ahead. Whew, we breathed a sigh of relief.

It was a peaceful morning on the summit. Low clouds drifted through the endless rolling fields of golden grass. A ~10 mile long line of towering wind turbines spun quietly in the distance. The morning clouds drifted in between them. Cows mooed harmoniously in their nearby pastures.

We were a long ways from Boston. On our adventures I often like take a moment to think to myself how removed I am from the stresses of school. As a farmer out here on the High Plains, your worries are much more connected to nature. You think about tending to livestock, when to plant, when to harvest, and what the weather will bring. You don't encounter the stresses of problem sets, tests, or projects. It's a totally different lifestyle out here, and I'm sure it's even more demanding than being a student. It'd be a tough life being a farmer on the Great Plains.

Alas, for us it was now time to switch back into the "it's time to get back to Boston" mode. We packed up and departed down the lonely gravel road, with each rotation of the tires bringing us closer to MIT once again.

We cruised through Cheyenne, WY and turned south on I-25 into Colorado. At this point, it was just 10:30am and we only had a few more hours of driving to get back to Denver. Our flight didn't leave until 7:15pm. So we decided to pack one more little adventure into the trip by driving through Rocky Mountain National Park. We had driven through the park as a family years ago and wanted to visit once again.

We headed through an awesome canyon on the way to Estes Park, and finally entered into the Park through the Fall River Gate. The gentle Nebraska hills we had woken up to in the morning had been replaced by towering Colorado 14'ers spotted with snow. We wove our way in the car up to 12,000ft. It felt like cheating. All we had to do is step on the gas pedal and we accomplished in 30 minutes of driving what it would have taken 4 hours to hike. We opened our water bottles and heard the high pressure air inside escape. The sunscreen bottle nearly exploded in the lower-pressure air. We went for a quick hike and headed back down.

We took about zero time to acclimate, so Eric got a little altitude sickness. It would be up to me to finish the drive. As we got closer to Denver the traffic heated up. I began to miss driving down the straight, open roads of Eastern Colorado with not another car in sight.

We returned the car and checked in at the airport. We had the vague idea that there was an earlier flight to BOS, but didn't know the time or gate. We hustled nevertheless for some good exercise to see if we could get standby. As it turned out we arrived at the gate about 10 minutes before the previous flight was supposed to leave. The gate agent said: "There are two seats left, would you like them?" "DEFINITELY," we answered. Then she reluctantly opened the door to the jet bridge for us and let us on. Wow, talk about convenient timing! We landed in BOS at a comfortable 10:15pm instead of 12:50am.

We were amazed at how well the trip worked out. We hit every destination and got the bonus of seeing Rocky Mountain National Park without a moment to spare. We had climbed the highest point in four states and had driven 1300 miles across six states all in one long weekend. It wasn't necessarily a relaxing weekend, but it was fulfilling. We set a goal and then we accomplished it. Now it was time to start planning our next adventure.

33 Denali (Mt. McKinley)

Alaska

20,320ft

Date climbed: May 26, 2010

Author: Matthew

Accompanying climbers: Darren Verploegen, Woody Hoburg, Dan Walker

Denali via West Buttress

Schedule:

Day 0:   Sat May 15th: Fly in to ANC, buy & repackage food, stay in Microtel.
Day 1:   7am shuttle to Talkeetna, meet with rangers, fly to Base Camp on glacier.
Day 2:   Move to 7800', camp there
Day 3:   Move to 11,600', camp there
Day 4:   Rest at 11,600'
Day 5:   Cache at 13,500', camp back at 11,600.
Day 6:   Move to 14,200'
Day 7:   Pick up 13,500 cache, sleep at 14,200.
Day 8:   Rest day
Day 9:   Move to 17,200'
Day 10:   Rest day
Day 11:   Wednesday May 26 th: Summit day, sleep at 17,200'
Day 12:   Sleep in until noon, hike down through the night
Day 13:   Hike all morning, arrive at Base Camp at 7:00am, fly out of glacier
Day 14:   Sat May 29 th: Woody, Darren, Dan take shuttle to ANC and fly home. Matthew and Eric have rest day before backpacking in Denali National Park for a week.

Report:

"Let's go see what the top of the country looks like." Darren said. Our elevation was 20,100ft—about 200 below the top.

Through the past eleven days we had ascended 13,000 feet over 13 miles. But the final 2,000ft of climbing had been grueling. Even though we had tiny packs (compared to days ago) each step upward was now a monumental feat. There was one-half the oxygen here as at sea level. Every twenty seconds of hiking you needed to rest for the next thirty to catch your breath and slow down your pulse. Imagine climbing Mount Washington with an extra 200lbs on your back, while breathing through a small coffee straw, while the mountain is made of soft sand. That's the effort level of the final 2,000ft up Denali.

We paused a few seconds to catch our breaths. You couldn't speak a complete sentence without needing to refill your lungs. We had split into two groups; Eric and I had just summitted while Darren, Woody, and Dan were on their final pitch to the top.

Me: "Almost there . . . [gasp] . . . just watch out . . . [gasp] . . . for the Polish people [gasp]"

Dan/Woody/Darren: "Let's do it! [gasp] . . ."

. . .

Day 0-Saturday May 15th:

The five of us had swooped into Anchorage on Saturday May 15th from across the country: Eric/Dan from Boston/Cambridge; me from Maryland; Woody from California; Darren from Virginia. Our goal was to climb Denali (aka Mount McKinley), the highest point in Alaska, the country, and the continent.

Eric and I were seeking the crown jewel for our state high points collection. We could worry later about our remaining 17 state high points (mostly the southern and north-central states). Since Alaska was on the list we had to climb it. We invited Darren, Woody, and Dan to join. I believe all responded an enthusiastic YES within 10 minutes of the invitation email.

We had all managed to push and persuade our advisors/employers to give us the three weeks off that we figured we would need. We had all read trip reports or books that warned that even three weeks might not be enough because of the high potential for bad weather. We heard that sometimes people could even be delayed for days on either end of the trip because the planes needed good weather to land on the glacier.

We thus set up a tight schedule and wanted to get onto the glacier as soon as possible. Eric and I had just handed in our MIT Masters theses on Friday afternoon, and Saturday morning hopped on a plane to Alaska. We descended upon Anchorage first, around 3:30pm on Saturday. Dan/Woody/Darren landed later. We grabbed our bags and put them in the rental car. We each had about 130lbs of non-food gear. We dropped off the bags at Microtel Anchorage (best rates in town) and pulled in to Wal-Mart for some hardcore food shopping. We each took a cart and a deep breath and stepped inside.

We had created a Google spreadsheet for everyone to list their food preferences. Here's the food we bought that we ended up eating:

Dinner: For dinner we picked up pasta, couscous, and some Ramens. Couscous and Ramen are super simple because you just need to add boiling water, and it's a cinch to clean up. We got some good sausage, pepperoni, and brought some meats that we had dehydrated. We also dehydrated some vegetables and pasta sauce. Many thanks to Kate for the dehydrated spices that, along with some Dan Walker cooking, made our dinners particularly awesome.

Lunch: We picked up 20lbs of cheese split up into five gigantic bricks. We also had a cracker mix of Triscuits, Gardettos, Combos, and cheese crackers, along with some Tortillas.

Breakfast: Bunch of oatmeal for some, and cereal/powdered milk for others.

Snacks: Soft fruit bars, cookies, Great Value chocolate chip/fruit/nuts trail mix, Jello (for a real tasty post-dinner dessert)

Eric and I got quite a few looks while we were shopping. I guess not too many people are pushing around two overflowingly-full shopping carts. I think we had about 10 boxes of oatmeal, 10 bags of mini-wheats, 20lbs of pasta, 30 boxes of couscous, 10 huge bags of crackers, 5 x 5lb cheese bricks,

20lbs of sausage, and about 300 Ziploc bags. On three separate occasions people asked us for help because they thought we worked there.

We planned on eating a lot of food in 20 days. On the nutrition facts a box of couscous might say "3 servings" but when you're working as hard as we would be you can divide that number by 3 or 4.

An hour and a half later we traded $950 for 250 lbs of food. I guess for five hungry hikers for 20 days that's not too bad, especially considering that we're in Alaska, where most prices are way higher. Heck, I probably eat for more than $9.50/day in the city. I think a lot of other climbers buy expensive Mountain House free-dried food, which costs about three times as much and produces three times more trash.

When we got back to the Microtel it was time to repackage everything. We began the daunting task of pouring all the food into Ziploc bags. The original food packaging produces a tremendous amount of trash, both in mass and volume. By repackaging food into re-sealable bags you can get rid of all the extra plastic and cardboard. Through years of trial and error and especially from the Appalachian Trail, Eric and I discovered that by far the best bags are the Ziploc one-quart freezer bags. Eric and I cleared the room and began our assembly line.

We poured the food into the bags and lined them up into two huge matrices on our bed. Each column of the matrix was one person's food. Darren, Woody, and Dan landed around 7:30pm and made it to the hotel around 9, and helped us finish up. In the end we had about two big trash bags full of waste packaging. We ended up reducing the amount of trash we carried up the mountain from about 3lbs/person to just a few small, compact ounces of Ziplocs.

We've found that 2lbs of food per person per day is about right. So for twenty days that's 40lbs per person. With Darren's handy hand scale we each picked out about 40lbs of our favorite food bags. It was like a little shopping trip all over again. We ended up with about 50lbs of extra food. I guess that's better than not having enough. Bedtime finally came around 1:30am.

Day 1:

We wanted to get an early start so we had reserved a shuttle to Talkeetna at 7am with Denali Overland Transportation for $160/person. Talkeetna is the town that you fly out of to get onto the glacier. In retrospect it might have been cheaper to rent a big van and park it in Talkeetna during the trip, but we didn't want another thing to worry about.

As soon as we got to Talkeetna after the 2.5hr ride we started weighing our bags. Our air carrier, Talkeetna Air Taxi (TAT), required that each bag be less than 80lbs and have the weight written on it, for better balancing on the plane. Each person is only allowed 125lbs (supposedly a TSA rule, extra weight costs more), so we ended up with 625lbs of gear/food for the five of us. The flight was a staggering $500 per person roundtrip. But TAT had good customer service. They sold us some bamboo wands and let us store our extra stuff during the trip. They have a safe for valuables too.

Next we needed to have a meeting with the rangers. As the park requires, we had registered for the trip more than 60 days in advance with the team name MIT. We each paid the $175 special use fee and sat down. Our ranger discussed the sanitation procedures on the mountain, which consists of using a Clean Mountain Can (CMC). You do your business in a plastic bag lining the small plastic cylindrical can, and when the biodegradable bag fills up you tie it off and throw it into a deep crevasse. (That's much nicer than needing to carry it out!) Our ranger didn't even ask us about our experience. I guess the assumption is that if you're willing to pay that much money you probably know what you're doing. But we later discovered there were plenty of people on the mountain who didn't have a clue.

Once we were done with the half-hour ranger meeting, we noticed a board in the ranger station with climber statistics. So far this year, 235 people had attempted the mountain and only 20 had succeeded. This doesn't look promising, I thought.

TAT informed us that the weather was too bad for flights at the moment. We were getting worried we might not make it onto the glacier that day. But after a quick hour we got a call from TAT that the weather had cleared and flights to the glacier had resumed. We were up. It was showtime.

Four of us would be flying in a single-prop Beaver five-person plane. (I bet Woody knows more of the details of the plane.) Darren drew a short straw and would fly in a different plane. The planes were awesome. They had retractable aluminum skis that allowed them to land on snow. There were a bunch of other bush planes with huge tires all around. These planes were Alaska-tough.

It was one spectacular ride. In a plane that size you really feel like you're flying, unlike in a commercial jet. We flew over some genuine Alaskan bush thick with muskeg. Some lakes still had ice. We flew through a couple of clouds and finally "The Great One" was in sight. Denali. Mountains and glaciers stretched from one end of the horizon to the other but Denali towered a full mile above everything else. It was absolutely massive.

We first followed the Tokositna River, and then flew up the Kanikula Glacier. Soon a high mountain pass came into view; it was called One Shot Gap. "That's our gap," the pilot said. With what seemed like only a hundred feet to spare on each side we shot through the gap and were over the Kahiltna Glacier, which would be our friend for most of the expedition. We turned into a little valley and a small city of tents came into view below. Base Camp. We landed smoothly and the pilot cut the engine. We dragged our monstrous load of luggage out of the way.

Weeks ago I thought, "Man, that seems kind of lame that you need to take a plane onto the glacier—if you can land on snow why not just land on the summit? Where do you draw the line? How high can you land and still say you climbed the mountain?" We found out the location of the 7200ft Base Camp is one of the closest spots to the summit that is free of crevasses and also outside the wilderness boundary. So even if you found a crevasse-free landing zone higher up on the mountain you'd get in trouble for landing there because motorized vehicles are not allowed in the wilderness.

But still, I thought, if your goal is to climb the mountain under your own power wouldn't it be much more honorable to start from a town or a road, rather than getting flown in to a seemingly arbitrary spot on the mountain? Before we left we looked into this option, but that would basically add a month to the trip. Imagine hauling seven weeks of food and 100lbs of gear through trees, bushes, and rocky terrain, then having to pick your own way around moraines and crevasses all the way up the glacier just to get to base camp where most of the 1200 other annual hikers start. Some people do it, and it's admirable, but we didn't have that kind of time to spare. Maybe we'd save a trip like that for next time.

But if starting at 7,200ft still sounds dishonorably high, think about other state high points. For Mt Whitney you start at 8,300ft and climb to 14,494ft; approximately the same is true for Mt Rainier. And for Mt Elbert you start around 10,000ft and climb to around 14,400ft. Plenty of high points even have a road to the top. With that reasoning a net climb of 13,000ft for Denali sounds honorable enough to me. Not to mention the fact that it's glaciers all the way.

We checked in with Lisa, the Base Camp ranger, and she gave us six gallons of white gas fuel that we had paid for back at TAT. Since we would be obtaining 100% of our water by melting snow, we had each brought a stove: three MSR XGK's and two one-piece Coleman stoves (all used white gas). We've found through Winter School that one of the biggest pains of winter camping is huddling around the stoves after dinner and shivering while the snow melts into drinking water. It takes hours each day. So with a stove for every person we could speed the painful process up substantially.

Next, we each picked out a sled from the well-used stack. Normally when towing a sled you want a rigid connection between you and the sled so that if you go downhill the sled doesn't crash into the back of your ankles. People often do this with two skinny PVC pipes. But since we would be roped up the whole time, for downhills we could attach the sleds completely to the rope, by prussiking the front and back. For uphills we'd pull the sleds behind us with a simple rope. The route is pretty much either all uphill or all downhill. Woody had the brilliant idea to bring some elastic cord which absorbed some of the stop and go while walking and eliminated a lot of jerk from the sled.

As soon as we landed we needed full skin protection from the sun. With clear skies above and bright snow all around and below us it was like we had two suns shining upon us. We definitely appreciated our special glacier glasses and last-minute purchase of nose guards. We covered our heads and necks with hats and handkerchiefs. Woody won with a white Arabian explorer-type hat. We slathered on the sunscreen and got to work setting up the tents.

The sun was so intense that the tents acted like greenhouses. Outside it might have been in the 20's (Fahrenheit) in the shade, 50's in the sun, and 70's in the tent. Later on in the day the sun went behind a mountain and thankfully we were in the shade again. We tried to sleep but for those of us with minus 40F down sleeping bags (me) we basically had to lay on top of our bags all night to keep from sweating. Eric and Dan brought thinner bags with thermal liners which allowed them to customize the insulation of their bags. We all brought some kind of vapor barrier liner (VBL) which you would wrap around yourself before getting into the sleeping bag. This waterproof barrier would prevent body moisture from saturating the sleeping bag as you slept and would maintain its warmth. But lower on the glacier most of us were too hot to need the VBLs.

Darkness never really came on the glacier that night but we were all tired enough from two days of travel that we nevertheless slept 12 hours. It had taken us all less than 36 hours to travel from our origins all the way to the glacier, with enough time to purchase/repackage food and meet with the rangers along the way. Things couldn't have gone smoother so far. Now that a big chunk of the logistics had been executed flawlessly, it was time to actually start climbing the mountain.

Day 2:

When we woke up the next morning it was time to put on the armor and prepare for battle. Suiting up for glacier travel with a huge backpack and sled is a lot different that suiting up for a simple climb up Mount Washington. Eric and I were on one rope and Dan + Woody + Darren were on the other, with Darren in the lead. We heard the glaciers were huge in Alaska so Eric and I tied in 40m apart while Dan/Woody/Darren were about 30m apart. We each had enough gear to build an anchor in case the other(s) fell in: a picket, an ice screw, an ascender, beaners, slings, and a belay device.

With my wide-rimmed cowboy-like hat and handkerchief across my face along with all kinds of weapons dangling from my harness I felt like an outlaw in the Wild West. My gear jingled with each step and I could draw an ice screw like a handgun. We donned our packs and hitched our sleds and we were ready for battle. A battle with Mount McKinley. We buried two days worth of food at base camp and marked the cache with a bamboo wand and a flag provided by the Park Service with our name on it. We would use this food if we came back to Base Camp during a storm and had to wait a while for a flight out.

Before we left we got to see the National Park Service helicopter come in for a dramatic operation. First the chopper landed near the ranger tent. Pretty soon it took off with a long rope dangling 100ft below it. One dude with a body harness and fighter-pilot helmet clipped in to the bottom of the rope and was hoisted high in the air. That dude was in for one wild ride I tell you. I hope he's bundled up, I thought, otherwise he'd be a dangling human popsicle in that wind. He and the chopper disappeared down the valley and cruised up the glacier. We had no idea what they were up to. About an hour later they came back and the dude unclipped. Weird, we thought. Later, when we got off the glacier we learned the reason for the dangerous mission.

Now it was time to head out. Eric and I marched in front with Darren/Woody/Dan (I'll call them 'DWD' from now on) covering the rear. We started down the only downhill of the ascent, 'Heartbreak Hill.' It's only heartbreaking on the way back when you have to climb it. Pretty soon we were down on the good old Kahiltna Glacier. Luckily we were early enough in the season and the snow bridges were thick enough that we couldn't see any crevasses in our path. This demonstrated the benefit of hiking on such a popular path: we could see where 200 people before us had walked this season and hadn't punched through into a crevasse, so we felt pretty confident that we would be safe.

The sun blazed overhead and Eric and I stripped down to shorts and a t-shirt and slathered on the sunscreen. It felt like 90 degrees. The bowl of the Kahiltna Glacier acted like a heliostat with us at its focus. By mid-afternoon another tent city came into view: 7800ft camp. This would be our camp for the night. There were already a bunch of snow walls from previous climbers, which were built to shelter the tents from the wind and drifting snow during storms. "What storms?" we thought as we looked at the bluebird sky. But we knew that "the weather can change *in an instant*" around here.

We set up our hardcore MITOC two-person and three-person Trango tents in some vacant spots. It was only 4pm so we still had some time before dinner. Dan rigged up a nifty shade canopy so we could sit without getting toasted. Woody pulled out the snow saw and started cutting snow blocks. The snow in the White Mountains of New Hampshire is never compacted enough for blocks so we were novices at first. In cutting out the blocks, you had to keep in mind the mechanical engineering principle of design for manufacturing, which suggests that we should cut the blocks with the right draft angle so we can extract them. If you angle the cuts the wrong way it might be impossible to extract the block.

Either Dan or Woody cut the angles just right on the first block but then were faced with the dilemma of how to get it out. "This sounds like a job for an ice screw!" Woody suggested. Dan sank two ice screws into the block and extracted the specimen flawlessly. Our campsite neighbors came over to admire it and it became our dinner table. Ah, the simple joys of camping on a glacier. That would be just the beginning of our study of snow block architecture.

That night we met a few of our neighbors. The two guys camping next to us were from Seattle and Park City, UT and brought a life-size, ahem, X-rated blow-up figure whom they named Molly Tucker. From then on we referred to them as the Molly Tuckers dudes. Later, three Japanese climbers silently and swiftly built camp next to us. The three of them cooked and slept in a tent 50% smaller than our two-man tent. Who are those guys, we wondered. A Dutch climber whispered: "those are the famous Giri-Giri Boys from Japan, they're probably doing something crazy." Interesting neighbors indeed.

Day 3:

Next day we woke up a little earlier to beat the heat. The tentative plan was to camp at 9,800ft camp, as recommended in our guidebook (*"Denali's West Buttress: A Climber's Guide to Mount McKinley's Classic Route" by Colby Coombs)*. But we would see how we were doing when we got there.

We suited up for battle. This was starting to feel routine. We pulled out of camp just in front of a 12-person guided group, split into three teams. Approximately 25% of climbers on Denali are part of guided teams, and each client pays about $6000 to the guiding companies, which covers everything except gear once they get to Anchorage. By comparison each of us paid about $1100 once we got to Anchorage for food, transportation, and the permit. Although from what I hear the guided companies had pretty good food.

Eric and I made it to the top of Ski Hill and waited for DWD. We thought it was kind of steep but it turned out to be an ant hill compared to some of the later climbs we would face. The guided group passed us and then we met up with DWD. A little higher up we had a little powwow. We decided to rearrange the groups for increased efficiency: Eric/Matthew/Dan on one rope, Darren/Woody on the other.

We also talked about camp. You climb the mountain slowly in order to acclimate to the thinner air. On other mountains most of us had felt the debilitating headache and nauseousness associated with acute mountain sickness (AMS) before and didn't want to experience that again on Denali. Our book suggested ascending an average of no more than 1000ft a day in order to properly acclimate. But below 10,000ft none of us had really felt symptoms of AMS before so we felt the recommendation to limit our day to only 9800ft was too conservative. I think that recommendation in the book might be fitness-limited and not altitude-limited. So we decided to try and push on to the next camp at 11,600ft. We would spend a rest day there to acclimate.

We all agreed on the plan and split up into two groups. We agreed to radio in periodically with our FRS radios. Pulling all our gear up to 11,600ft camp in one shot was hard work but our first team made it to camp around 5pm. Walking into camp felt like walking into a town in the Wild West. We cowboys strolled in down main street. For a second everyone stopped what they were doing around camp and sized us up, then went back to their business. If there were tumbleweeds they would have drifted across the street. There were probably 75 other people in camp.

Luckily there was an awesome vacant campsite that was perfect for two tents, and complete with an attached cooking area. This was one of the only places in Alaska where it was OK to cook right next to your tent without having to worry about grizzly bears. We chopped out a massive block for a dinner table and pitched the tents. We radioed in and Darren and Woody were on their way up. They arrived by the time we had gotten camp set up.

One of the things to look forward to each evening was the weather forecast. It was given by Lisa, the Base Camp Manager, at 8pm every evening on Channel 1. It was followed by a trivia question. Around 7:58pm every evening the entire camp would go silent and everyone held up their radio. The forecast for the night at 14,000ft was "Up to a foot of snow with lows around 5 above." With weather like that we were glad to be in a solid campsite, with a rest day to look forward to the next day.

Day 4:

We woke up late the next morning to a mere two inches of fresh snow on the tents. I guess that's better than a big blizzard. I don't think any of us felt symptoms of AMS, but we all felt pretty lethargic. Part of us didn't feel like doing a darn thing. But from our fast-paced lives we temporarily left behind I think some of us felt a little torn. From being on the go all the time during the school year and for the past couple of days, part of my mind said "what are you doing just sitting around, you need to be doing something productive!" But we *were* doing something productive: we were acclimating. By resting now we were enabling ourselves to climb higher the next day. Ascending too fast can lead to AMS, which can progress to High Altitude Cerebral Edema (HACE) or High Altitude Pulmonary Edema (HAPE), which are both bad news. So eventually we all felt completely comfortable sitting around doing absolutely nothing.

After a couple hours of sitting around it became time for a little boondoggle. From working on trail crew for the Inyo National Forest several years ago, Eric and I became familiar with the word 'boondoggle.' It's something that you do to feel important, to feel like you're working, but isn't really necessary at all. We decided it was time to "flush the toilet." Around here that action takes on a slightly different meaning than at sea level, since you have to dispose of human waste in deep crevasses. We had identified one such potential crevasse next to camp. There were two bamboo wands stuck into the snow next to it to form an X, the sign for WATCH OUT. We had to check it out to evaluate its suitability for our purposes.

We suited up for business and Eric belayed me out to lip of the crevasse. I didn't want to get too close, but it looked pretty deep. You would not have wanted to fall in. It looked like a good place to empty the CMC. Darren became the designated flusher. He tied off the CMC bag and Eric belayed him out to the edge. With a dramatic flourish he tossed the bag into the abyss and it plunged into the icy bowels of the glacier without a sound. "That was a good four seconds before it hit anything," Darren said. That's how you flush the toilet at 11,600ft.

A little while later it was time for another little boondoggle: crevasse rescue practice. I felt the least experienced with building a Z-pulley so Darren and I tied ourselves together and he jumped into a pit I dug. I was pulled to the ground and had to self arrest. I tried building an anchor but the snow was so soft it pulled out, a scary sight. Dan showed me that if the snow is too soft you don't pound a picket in vertically, instead you bury it horizontally and it holds a lot better.

Toward evening after the skies had cleared and we were back to blazing sunlight we suddenly heard a rumble near the outskirts of town (camp). Everyone around dropped what they were doing and looked up. It was a big avalanche coming down the cliff. Giant snow chunks rumbled down the hillside and pulverized each other into a big cloud of white that made it all the way down to the trail but stayed safely away from camp. That was another advantage of camping in an established site that people used year after year: it was probably out of reach of avalanches.

Ahh, it was nice to have a quiet day on the mountain. We relaxed on our carved benches around the dinner table. We prepared a gourmet meal of pasta with dehydrated sauce, spices (from Kate), sausage, and dehydrated tomatoes. The forecast was good weather for the next few days.

Day 5:

We woke up the next morning refreshed and ready for action. Since the terrain between 11,600ft camp and the next camp (14,200ft) was so rugged and we still had about 120lbs each we decided to make the move in two loads, known as a "double carry." The first climb out of camp was Motorcycle Hill, followed by Squirrel Hill, and then across Windy Corner. We would carry roughly half the gear in our packs up to the well-used cache site at 13,500ft and bury it there, then hike back down to sleep at 11,600ft camp. The next day we would move the rest of our gear all the way to 14,200ft camp, then pick up the cache the following day. That was the plan suggested by the guidebook.

Eric and I took the lead again with DWD behind us. Unfortunately a slower 5-person Polish team had started just moments before us. It's tough to walk off-trail and pass, though, because the surrounding snow is way softer than the trail. In typical Polish fashion (as we later discovered) they refused to step aside to let us pass, so we slowly trudged past them in the soft snow on the side of the trail. It was tough work. By the time we completed the pass Eric and I were totally out of breath and took a while to regain it. But it would have been even more agonizing to hang out behind those guys all the way up Motorcycle Hill.

The top of Motorcycle Hill gave us an awesome view of 11,600ft camp. From above it looked like a small village in a developing country. We could see how campsites had sprung up on either side of the main trail into town and people were working on new campsites on the outskirts. Little alleyways separated the different compounds. Just like a real village, this one had its share of sanitation problems. The rangers instruct everyone to urinate in communal sites to localize impact, so you could see giant yellow stains from half a mile away. Everyone treats or boils their water anyhow just to be safe. It was an interesting lesson in the need for urban planning.

Next was the even steeper Squirrel Hill. As we climbed we got an awesome view of the corniced ridge on the other side of camp. There was so much snow on the ridge that it was hard to tell what was snow and what was bedrock. As we got even higher we realized we were completely above the clouds, called 'undercast' in Mount Washington forecasts. You felt like an airplane immune to the weather below.

Pretty soon we were at the 13,500ft cache site. "Wait, where's Windy Corner?" I asked Eric. "We already passed it," he said. I guess Windy Corner wasn't so windy today, we didn't notice any difference between it and any other mountain pass. We tried to radio in to DWD, but the signal didn't carry far enough. We hung out by a big hole that our Dutch predecessors had already dug and looked for something to keep us occupied while we waited for DWD.

I came up with a brilliant idea for a boondoggle: building a house structure out of bamboo wands. We needed to mark our cache site with some style, we couldn't just stick a little flag in the snow like everyone else. We needed to make ours stand out. First I made a cube and Gorilla-taped the ends together. Then I made a square-based pyramid on the top. Voila. We had the only house-shaped cache marker on the mountain.

We needed another boondoggle. We needed an official flag. I cut a section of yellow trash bag out and taped it to a wand. Then, in red Duck tape, I taped 'MIT' on the flag and made a skull and crossbones beneath it. DWD made it up at that point and we buried a bunch of stuff. Unfortunately Darren had a runaway altitude-induced nosebleed. But we made the most of it, and piled a bunch of the bloody red snow on top of our cache pile. With a bamboo house, MIT skull and crossbones flag, and bloody snow watching over our cache we were confident nobody would dare to lay a finger on it.

We turned around and headed back to camp. Descending was an order of magnitude easier. Gravity was now cooperating with us. It made the air denser and gave us less potential energy as we descended. Good old gravity.

When we got back to camp I had to take care of a little business. While we were waiting at the cache site for DWD, another climber on his way up had approached me and Eric and bashfully requested a special favor. It turns out that his group had accidentally forgotten to dispose of their CMC bag in the crevasse at 11,600ft camp before they had left. They had left the bag in their campsite. If a ranger found their special surprise and discovered the owner they could get a big fine (this actually happened to someone when we were back in Talkeetna). So the guy respectfully asked if we could throw the bag away for them, and we would be duly rewarded. I said no problem. As soon as we got into camp I found their little surprise and pitched it into the toilet crevasse.

When we got back to our campsite we were amazed at the effects of the intense solar radiation. Objects that aren't colored white heat up a lot more on the surface of the glacier. A pair of pot grabbers (a 'spondonnagle' if you're an Aussie) that we had left on the dinner table had melted their way about three inches deep and had frozen into place. A snow shovel that was anchoring our tent had heated up the snow around it and had crept about 6 inches, extruding snow through two holes as it moved.

But more importantly, our sleeping bags had dried completely in our greenhouse tents and were nice and fluffy. I remembered how difficult it had been for me and Eric to dry out our sleeping bags when we hiked across New Hampshire in January a few years back. Basically, every day they got wetter and wetter from body moisture and lost most of their insulation after just a week. We were planning to be on Denali for three weeks. That's why Dan suggested that everyone use a vapor barrier liner. But with intense sunlight we could get away with a little bit of moisture in our sleeping bags and wait for them to dry out during the day. If it got stormy and cloudy things might be different . . .

We finished dinner at a reasonable hour and it was time to get to bed. It was still weird to go to sleep at 11 when the sun was still out, but we were getting used to it. We found that it never really got dark, just twilight. The sun would officially set around 11:30pm in the north-northwest and rise around 4:30am in the north-northeast. The darkest part of the night occurred around 2am, but even then you could see outside just fine without a headlamp. At night the sun would drop just a little below the horizon for five hours. From 11:30pm to 2am was just one long sunset. From 2am to 4:30am was one long sunrise. Over the entire trip we couldn't see any stars, just Venus. When the moon was full it did just the opposite of the sun, rising late and setting early, and stayed just a little above the horizon. It was bizarre. Later on in town I heard someone ask a local, "isn't it hard to get used to all this daylight?" I thought to myself, it depends where you're from, if you're from Alaska it'd be hard to get used to so little summer daylight in the Lower 48!

Day 6:

Today the plan was to move the rest of the gear to 14,200ft camp. We stashed our snowshoes since we would just be using crampons higher up on the mountain. We said goodbye once again to our camp and climbed back up Motorcycle Hill and then Squirrel Hill. Once again Windy Corner was no big deal. We were delighted to see that people had heeded our warnings and nobody had touched the cache. The bamboo house, MIT flag, and bloody snow were still diligently watching over as we walked by. They would need to watch over it another day because the plan was to retrieve the gear the next day. Eric and I strolled into 14,200ft camp first and were stunned by its size. There were probably 50 tents spread all over the place. Even though we had beaten the rush, including our Polish friends, there was no room for us at the inn so we pretty much had to make our campsite from scratch.

We needed to rest first though. At this point we were currently higher than probably 99.999% of the rest of the country. We were 300 feet below the elevation of Mount Rainier, Mount Whitney, and Mount Elbert, the three tallest mountains in the lower 48. The air was pretty darn thin. But we were only at the base of Denali. We still had over a vertical mile of climbing to go.

As we rested I brought out one of the little toys I had hauled up: a solar charger for my camera battery. I bought a waterproof, durable 7W Powerfilm Rollable solar panel online before I left. The nominal output was 12V. Theoretically, even with 10% efficiency it should have enough juice to charge my battery via the battery's car charger with 12V input. I tried for weeks to test the system in Cambridge but it was never sunny enough to produce enough current. I was worried I would need to buy another solar panel. But finally, just before the trip, the sun finally shone upon Cambridge and the charger seemed to charge the battery successfully. I decided to bring the system on the mountain but didn't have too much confidence after only one test.

But it turned out the sun was so intense at 14,200ft high up on the glacier that the system worked beautifully and charged the battery successfully. The whole reason I brought the system was to ensure that Eric and I would always be able to take pictures (I also brought two extra batteries and so did Eric). Now we were in business. Woody also brought his own solar charging system that charged an intermediate battery and had success too.

After a little breather it was time to get started digging camp. There was some talk of a chance of snow so we wanted a bomber campsite to shelter us. Eric and I started sawing away in our own little campsites. With each campsite we got more and more ambitious and demanded a greater level of perfection. This one was going to be awesome, we resolved. We would cut blocks out of the middle of the campsite and pile them up for walls. This way the distance between the top of our tent and the top of our wall—our level of protection against the wind—increased twice as fast than if we had excavated outside camp.

Pretty soon DWD made it up and now we had five construction workers excavating the site. Before long we had two tent spots with roughly 6ft walls along with a sheltered cooking area. Behind our compound we had a plush super secret latrine area where you could use your CMC without anyone seeing you. Privacy was otherwise scarce at 14,200ft camp.

While we were working on camp we experienced a thing I called "Mountain Magic." When hiking the Appalachian Trail you're lucky if you come across what's called "Trail Magic," which is where nice "Trail Angels," often AT alums, park at road crossings and offer food to hungry hikers. Sometimes you'll discover Trail Magic in the form of coolers with drinks and fruit that "Trail Angels" leave in the middle of the woods. While we worked on camp a few nice climbers on their way down the mountain were pulling around sleds offering free food. They said they summitted early and had extra food they wanted to get rid of so they wouldn't have to carry it down.

It was mutual benefit: they were exhausted and still had 7,000ft to descend and wouldn't need the food anymore—it would just slow them down. We didn't necessarily need the extra food, but it was nice to pick out a few items that were different than what we had brought like cookies and different bars. This wasn't a favor that would be repaid immediately. Hopefully we would also summit early and be able to reciprocate the favor to the next round of climbers on their way up . . .

As we finished up camp, a guide from another expedition on their way down asked if we could do them a favor and watch their tent to make sure it didn't blow over. They would be back with another group of clients the next evening. In exchange we could use the tent for cooking. We gladly obliged. It turned out that the tent was absolutely perfect. It was a huge pyramid-shaped tent with a big pole in the middle. The bottom was dug down about five feet and had a nice circular bench for people to sit around. Most importantly, it enabled us to cook without needing sunglasses and headgear to protect us from the sun. Every day so far we had worn our sunglasses and hats pretty much from the moment we crawled out of the tent in the morning until the moment we crawled back in for bed.

It was a debate between couscous and Ramens this evening. Woody, Eric, and Dan selected a Ramen/couscous combination while Darren and I stuck to couscous. While we were eating, a dude knocked on the tent and asked if we were the MIT group. He thanked us profusely for cleaning up his group's little surprise back at 11,600ft camp and gave us a nice bar of premium Toblerone chocolate to show his appreciation. We said thank you and split up the bar as well as we could into five precisely equal portions, but two small chocolate triangles were left over. All five of us concentrated on the two pieces and contemplated how to split them equally between five people. This could be complicated, we thought. It would be difficult for each of us to get exactly 40% of one piece. We could melt the two pieces down, Dan suggested, and cast them into molds in the snow so we all got exactly one-fifth. Wow, that could be cool, we thought. Or we could mash them up and split the mashed chocolate into fifths. Or maybe a neutral person or middleman could cut them into 40%-sized chunks and unbiasedly distribute them.

We focused our brainpower onto the problem. Surely three mechanical engineers, an aeronautical engineer, and a chemical engineer from MIT could develop a workable solution. Woody went outside to meditate for the solution on the latrine. I stared at Dan. Dan stared at Eric. Eric looked at Darren. Darren looked at the chocolate. We were deadlocked. It was a hung jury. Just about that time Woody ran triumphantly back into the tent and declared he had the solution. He threw me the two tiny chocolates and said "Matthew should get both of them because he's the one who did the dirty work and threw the CMC bag in the crevasse." Brilliant! Everyone nodded in agreement. I gave one chunk to Eric because he also initially agreed to do the dirty work for the person. We all sighed with relief that that problem had been solved justly.

Day 7:

The next day our plan was to pick up the cache we had buried at 13,500ft. I think we were all feeling a little bit of AMS and dehydration from the day before. We needed a couple of low-key days to recuperate. As we hiked down we noticed that the trail transected a gigantic crevasse via a thinning snow bridge. We could see a giant crack on each side of the trail and it looked like the snow bridge the trail crossed didn't have too many more days. Indeed, our guidebook showed that later on in the season the route changes and goes around the crevasse. I definitely wouldn't want to be last person on the current route, who prompts the change to a different route!

Our bamboo house, MIT flag, and Darren's bloody snow had watched vigilantly over our cache the past couple days. Now it was time to relieve them of their duties. We exhumed our stuff and put it in our empty packs. Before long we finally had all our gear at 14,200ft camp. We were exhausted from the little two-hour workout and the past couple of epic days.

We lounged around camp the rest of the day reading fine literature. Three of us brought books to kill the time while resting and waiting out bad weather. Without a book in my hands keeping me busy I might have been compelled to walk around and waste my energy. I read *Skunk Works,* while Eric read *Seven Summits,* and Dan brushed up on his *Freakonomics.* Dan's sun canopy made a nice shelter. We lounged about in our down booties beneath overboots. We put on our down jackets for extra warmth and puffiness. There were plenty of cozy spots around camp to dive into a book and immerse ourselves for a few hours in a different world.

Day 8:

I think we all finally felt pretty good today but our schedules and bodies called for another day of rest. We were planning to haul our gear up to the next camp—17,200ft camp—all in one shot, called a "single carry." The route between the two camps contained the trickiest and steepest terrain of the entire route. We could see the infamous fixed ropes on the steep 55-degree slope high above us. The fixed ropes had been placed there by guiding services and/or the Park Service because it was too icy to self arrest. So if you started sliding you'd go all the way to the bottom, or end up in a crevasse. Without the fixed lines we would have needed a whole bunch of ice screws for protection. The fixed lines would be safe because we would just clip one of our ascenders onto the rope and slide it up as we climbed. If we fell the ascender would catch and we wouldn't slide more than a couple feet. But from the bottom it looked incredibly steep. It looked like Alaska's "Golden Staircase" from the movie White Fang.

"I don't want to have to climb that twice," Darren said. We all agreed. It would be miserable to have to do a double-carry up that steep slope. And descending the lines didn't look like a cakewalk either. Plus, beyond the fixed lines was the also-infamous Washburn's Thumb perched on a knife-edge ridge. This was another shorter set of fixed lines with a 3,000ft slope on either side. From what we had heard and read, most people do indeed double-carry this portion. If we double-carried and cached gear high up on the ridge, we thought, we would want to cache five days of food (10lbs/person), along with some stoves, fuel, and shovels (about 10lbs/person), for a total of only about 20lbs/person. I said: "if someone told me, 'you can either climb that whole route twice just because you can't handle the extra 20lbs, or you could suck it up and quit being a dang Nancy and do it all in one shot,' I'd opt to avoid the Nanciness." Everyone else nodded their heads in agreement. So the plan was for one epic day tomorrow with packs of probably 75lbs. We needed a rest day to prepare for it.

We lounged about some more in the morning browsing our fine literature while observing the climbers on their way up. A couple of 12-person guided groups were on their way up the fixed lines. It looked absolutely brutal. From our camp far below the people seemed to be standing still. Either they're sissies or it's really steep, or both, we thought. The weather was so beautiful a huge number of people were on their way up; we counted probably 30 people strung along the route.

With such awesome weather prevailing above us and in the forecast it was a little agonizing to sit around camp and twiddle our thumbs, but the name of the game today was once again patient acclimatization. The reason 14,200ft camp was so massive was that this was the camp where people waited out the weather. Even with just a little wind or snow the trek to 17,200ft camp would be dangerous. We saw a bunch of people headed up in front of us, but it seemed that even more were behind us. By flying in to the glacier on a weekend we had picked a popular starting day. But by avoiding a double-carry farther down the mountain and with plans for a single-carry tomorrow we had set ourselves up to be slightly ahead of the pack. As more people poured in camp grew throughout the day.

It was time for another boondoggle; our minds could only absorb so much text at this altitude. We decided to head over to the "Edge of the World" for a good view and the chance for cell phone service. Our guidebook said some people can get a signal if they stand close enough to the edge. We roped up and headed out towards the edge of camp. Along with about three other groups with the same idea we arrived at a rock outcropping above a who-knows-how-many-thousand foot drop. We prudently placed some pickets, ice axes, and screws in for protection and a few of us whipped out our phones to try to contact that special someone down in the States.

After the crowds had cleared and it became clear that our cell phones wouldn't get service Darren decided that he needed to inspect the edge a little more closely. Woody built a bomber anchor and belayed Darren out to the top of a rock that you wouldn't want to fall off. I don't think he could even see the bottom because we were above the clouds. When Darren was satisfied Woody and Dan determined that they needed to take a look as well.

Our Polish friends showed up and also determined that they needed a good look. But they wanted to spice it up a little bit, to make it a little more thrilling. Instead of building an anchor one burly Polish dude crouched down and got a wide stance. That was their anchor. With the five of them still roped together, three stood right behind the burly dude and one smaller woman walked out to the edge. The burly dude had coiled the rope around his torso because he was too cool for a belay device. He "belayed" the woman out to the threshold of the abyss. We held our breaths because if she fell they were all going downtown. Their system had actually multiplied their individual risks of falling by a factor of five. "Let's get out of here," one of us whispered, "I don't want to see them get killed."

For the past three days I had been itching to make one vital improvement to the aesthetics of our campsite: we really needed an arch. Something like that could really elevate our campsite to a new level. The others concurred. As the others excavated a new kitchen site I took the extra blocks and started building the arch. Toward the top of the arch I started cutting the blocks at a slight angle so they would begin to arch inward. I cut a keystone block and one block for either side. Eric and Darren each placed a block and I dropped in the keystone block. It was kind of amazing to see everything go together like that and reinforce itself, it worked surprisingly well. I granted Woody permission to christen the keystone block as he saw fit. He carved 'MIT' on the keystone to credit our cumulative engineering prowess. We got some compliments from our neighbors.

To make rest day even more exciting we got to see another helicopter landing. While we were on the glacier we had seen the helicopter buzzing overhead nearly every day so far. "I thought that was only for emergencies," I said. The chopper swooped down and in a big cloud of snow touched down near the ranger tent. We got some lessons in helicopter dynamics from Woody. Days later, when we were already off the mountain, we learned the reasons for all the helicopter excitement that week. We heard rumors that a French climber had fallen high up on the mountain and died. The helicopter was retrieving his body. In another bizarre case, a Polish woman had apparently hiked up to 14,200ft camp and decided she didn't want to go up or walk down. She wanted a helicopter to come pick her up. NPS determined that there was nothing physically wrong with her and she could hike out easily. She refused and hung out for three or four days before her relatives back in Poland had persuaded the Park Service to fly her out. I'm sure it was not a cheap ticket off the mountain.

We tuned into the weather from Lisa the Base Camp Manager on Channel 1 at 8pm that evening and it looked to be beautiful for the next three days: no snow, clouds, or wind. The temp was forecast to stay below zero at 17,200ft with minus15F at the summit. That's about as good as it gets for late

May. After the weather came the eagerly-awaited trivia question. "Which animal injures the most hikers each year worldwide?" You're supposed to think "bear" because we're up in Alaska. "Other people," one person answered, "dogs," another replied. "Dogs is the right answer," Lisa said. That was the extent of our communication with the outside world today.

Day 9:

8am: time for action. We wanted to head out of camp 'early' to beat the guided groups. It would be agonizing to be stuck behind a slower group all the way up the fixed lines. We took only the essential gear and cached the rest. We packed five days of food, our most reliable MSR XGK stoves, a gallon of fuel, camping gear, and mustered our strength for what would be our second-to-last epic climb. We pulled out just ahead of our neighboring guided group and with me and Eric in the lead we struck up the mountain. We had had three solid days to gaze upon the fixed lines and contemplate our destiny. We could see 2,000ft of climbing right in front of us, two-thirds of the day's total. We were hungry for some more altitude. We were psyched.

After about half an hour we were above 14,500ft, and higher than any land in the lower 48 states. The only way you get higher than this in the rest of the country is with an airplane. Pretty soon we passed a group of South American climbers. One of them had collapsed and sat down next to the trail. Eric offered to help, saying the Spanish word for help: "ayuda," but the climber and his buddies waved us off. We slowly inched by. Pretty soon six of his eight companions had abandoned him and kept climbing. The two others kept him company. It must have been the altitude. I guess his companions didn't want to be showed up by five Americans each hauling four times as much weight as them.

Now near the beginning of the pack, Eric and I reached the bottom of the fixed lines. It was so steep—supposedly 55 degrees at the steepest part—that snow didn't stick. It was solid blue ice with a few dustings of snow. A giant crevasse would eat you up if you slid the whole way down. A predecessor had dropped a trekking pole a few feet off the trail but it was too dangerous to recover. We couldn't make any mistakes here. First Eric clipped on his ascender, then backed it up with a beaner attached to some independent webbing from his harness. That allowed him to safely transfer his ascender from one section of rope to the other. We remained roped up because it would be too dangerous to unrope with a giant crevasse right below us. And plus if I fell and my protection failed I would hopefully be saved by Eric's equipment.

Pretty soon it was my turn to attach myself to the fixed rope. Ascenders are pretty cool devices that allow rope to slide through them one way but a cam-shaped piece with teeth jams the rope if it tries to go in the other direction. The alternative would be to use a prussik but you would need to re-tie the prussik for each of the ten or so different ropes which would take a while.

It was excruciatingly steep. For 800 vertical feet we climbed up steep, smooth ice without a comfortable place to rest our feet. That section alone gave my feet blisters that persisted for the next week. Our gigantic packs resisted every vertical step. My crampons seemed to just barely stick. I fell twice against the ice and thankfully my ascender caught me immediately. Just getting up from the fall was a monumental feat. Once I had muscled my pack into position I stood in place for a few seconds to catch my breath. Finally, after about ten sections of rope we were at the top of the fixed lines and looked triumphantly down at camp far below. DWD were just starting up the fixed rope in the midst of a traffic jam of other climbers.

We paused for a few seconds to revel in our newfound view. We were currently at 16,200ft, higher than most of the mountains around us. Glaciers stretched out like rivers in every direction. It was down every way we looked, except for one: the West Buttress. We still had a long ways to go. But we were beginning to taste it. Pretty soon Eric and I were at the base of Washburn's Thumb, a gigantic rock outcrop above a steep section, named after the famous cartographer and route pioneer, Bradford Washburn. By now we felt like pros at the fixed lines so we cruised up.

The next part of the route took us over a knife-edge ridge. On the right was a nearly-vertical 2,500ft drop to 14,200ft camp. On the left was a rocky 2-3,000ft slope onto another glacier. Luckily the Park Service had pounded pickets into the snow along the ridge. Most pickets already had webbing and some even had beaners. With 40m of rope between us we could comfortably clip through one or two pickets at a time. In the longer gaps Eric would place one of our own pickets or ice screws. I guess you could call it "sport mountaineering."

Pretty soon we rounded a little hill and staggered exhaustedly into 17,200ft camp, the final camp before the summit. There were only two partially-made campsites remaining when we arrived so we grabbed them in a hurry. Half the work was already done for us, all we needed to do was dig out the campsites a little more and strengthen the walls. I threw down my pack victoriously. "How do you like them apples!" I yelled.

We were exhausted but there was still plenty of work to be done to make the campsite livable and awesome. We spent the next two hours excavating blocks from our little quarry before DWD arrived. At first we saw Darren appear on top of the last hill. I threw my shovel in the air to indicate it was us. Life moved at half-speed at 17,200ft. There was a little nub of a hill to climb to get to our campsite but it morphed into a small mountain. Darren, Woody, and Dan trudged in quietly. We were all too tired to even speak or congratulate each other.

I could cut only about three blocks before I became exhausted. The air was definitely thin but I didn't really perceive myself as being out of breath. It felt like there was something mysterious slowing me down. I could rest for a minute and feel fine, but after five short minutes of activity I needed a break. I felt out of shape. Dan had a nifty device that fit over the fingertip and could measure heart rate and blood oxygen saturation. Like little doctors we eagerly tried it out whenever we got to a new camp. Most everyone's pulse was near 100 bpm with about 88% oxygen saturation. As expected, our oxygen saturation had been decreasing the higher up we went, while our pulse increased to compensate.

Finally we had two nice tent sites and a kitchen carved out complete with stylish benches and tables. In the meantime probably twenty other climbers had slowly trickled in. Every one of them exhibited the half-speed "17,000ft stagger." Most were too exhausted to say anything and quietly got to work on their campsites. About a third single-carried like us. We were pretty darn lucky to be the first ones in camp because all the latecomers had to start from scratch on new campsites and didn't get walls that were even half as tall as ours.

We were all really happy to have our big down jackets at this camp. In the sun it felt warm, like temps were above freezing but in the shade of the snow wall our thermometers read minus 5F. But to me it didn't quite feel as chilly as the minus 5F in New Hampshire that we were used to. Maybe that was because around here, unlike New Hampshire, the sun was always shining and the wind was light. But another factor might have been in play: the thinner air. It seems reasonable that air with half the density would conduct and convect your heat away more slowly than sea-level density air, making it feel less cold. That would be an interesting thermodynamics problem . . .

Another big plus of the lack of darkness was the pleasantness of cooking. In New Hampshire in the winter you're always fighting darkness. Most often on overnight trips in the Whites you get into camp just around dark and have to sit around the stupid stove for hours on end in the darkness melting snow while it gets colder and colder. Here at 17,200ft you could sit for hours and cook in the sunlight. Cooking wasn't faster here, it was just a lot more pleasant. I think that's why we didn't end up needing more than three good stoves the entire trip. In NH we would have used all five stoves.

The forecast predicted good weather for at least the next few days, but we needed a solid rest day to recover and acclimate. It had been a monumental day and we fell asleep rapidly. I had incorrectly assumed it would be our toughest.

Day 10:

I awoke late the next morning to the sound of a jet circling loudly overhead. "What's going on," I wondered. It looked like a Boeing 737 and it seemed really low. "Why's it flying so low and so loudly?" But then I remembered that we were at 17,200ft, about twice as close to the big jet cruising altitude as at sea level. Not to mention there was probably only one-fourth the air between us and the jet. The jet made a giant circle around Denali within a period of 13 minutes. We could see seven huge circular contrails in the sky already.

The other big news item at 17,200ft camp this morning was the number of people attempting the summit. We saw a long line of people headed up the hill outside of camp, on the way up to Denali Pass. The weather looked perfect for it. We hoped it would be just as good for our summit day tomorrow. We saw the line of climbers traversing a steep slope. We wondered why it was taking them so long. We guessed they were probably placing a lot of protection along the way.

Today was another day for reading fine literature. We settled back into our sun-warmed tents and sleeping bags and looked forward to a day of rest to build up our energy for the planned summit day tomorrow. My book, *Skunk Works,* talked about the secret Lockheed stealth projects back in the 60's and 70's. Eric read about the first guys to climb the Seven Summits. I turned the pages and grimaced from the deep crack developing in my thumb from the dryness. We observed that no matter how good a care you took of scrapes, nothing healed at this elevation. I had a few cuts on my hand that hadn't healed at all in the last five days. It's easy to get infections at altitude because wounds never close. I guess our bodies were working so hard they didn't have the resources to devote to healing superficial wounds.

We kept this day low-key and felt good about it. We seemed to be acclimating well and none of us ever had a headache for long. We also maintained our voracious appetites, which can sometimes dwindle at altitude.

We tried to psych ourselves up for the day tomorrow. We heard that some teams take up to 12 hours round-trip to summit. "Why could it take so long," I wondered aloud, "it's only 3,000 vertical feet over 2.5 miles, that's about 30% less distance and elevation than Mount Washington." Altitude was the answer, we figured. But nevertheless we predicted that with light packs we should cruise up the mountain, as we had so far.

We tuned in for the weather for one final confirmation that tomorrow would be the day. "Forecast for the summit . . . ," base camp manager Lisa said " . . . for tomorrow—[howling]" We heard a bunch of howling on the radio. "What?" Woody said. All we could hear on Channel 1 was a bunch of bizarre howling. Then we heard "everyone at base camp is dead . . . [howling]."

It turned out that some idiot somewhere on the mountain was overpowering the weather transmission from Base Camp. "I'm not going to give the weather because people are howling," Lisa said indignantly. A random person on the mountain broadcasted "Hi Lisa, this is the howling person and I'm really sorry, could you please hook us up with the weather?" But then the howling began again. We didn't hear any forecast that night because some jerks wanted us to hear their howling instead. If we had seen the howling people they probably would have gotten tackled by everyone at 17,200ft camp.

"Jerks," Woody said, "tomorrow is the day we need the forecast the most." But we figured that since the forecast from yesterday called for decent weather, with temps around minus 15F at the summit, it probably hadn't changed in the past day. We figured we still had a perfect day of weather to look forward to . . .

Day 11:

Dawn broke on our summit day. The ranger had advised us to start late, around 10am, when it was a little warmer, and there would still be plenty of sunlight on the way down. Over the years plenty of people had gotten frostbite on summit day. We didn't want to join their ranks.

I knocked on DWD's tent. "Rise and shine, it's showtime!" I yelled. We sat around the kitchen and ate our power breakfasts: me with my cereal and powdered milk, DWD with their oatmeal, and Eric with his Pop tarts. We each had our own recipe for success. The rest/acclimation day had paid off yesterday and we were all feeling ready. Months of planning, weeks of physical effort, luck, and the help of our fancy gear had brought us to this spot.

We suited up like soldiers preparing for war. I punched Dan in the shoulder to test his armor. He reciprocated. We were ready. DWD took the lead with me and Eric bringing up the rear. "Ok, move out," Darren said. Like a two-pieced hundred-meter snake we slithered out of camp.

Pretty soon we were reunited with our long-lost Polish friends. They were a bizarre sight to behold. Four of them were tethered about 3ft apart. One small Polish woman walked unroped in a big down jacket without a pack close behind them. She looked like a small lost child. They marched with synchronized footsteps. Darren, in the lead, caught up to the five of them before the first hill. He patiently waited behind them and when it became apparent they wouldn't step aside he began to pass them. The kept marching along. Finally they got the message and let us pass. DWD slowly crept by them and then Eric began to pass. But up ahead Darren got to a steep section and needed to go slower. We all slowed down. Then the Polish people suddenly decided to keep going. They were walking in the middle of mine and Eric's rope but tried to ignore it. We crept along but pretty soon Darren got to a steeper slope and needed to place in a picket for protection. No matter, the Polish people kept marching in the middle of our rope. They got to the steep section and decided to forego the fixed pickets altogether.

Things were getting complicated. I was still standing on flat ground at that point twiddling my thumbs and watching the little fiasco unfold in front of me. The problem with the Polish people walking in our rope is that if they fell they could pull us with them. Luckily the five of us were anchored so we wouldn't fall far. On the other hand, if we fell we could dislodge the Polish people and they would start falling without protection to catch them.

The Polish people clearly had no idea what they were doing, as well as no sense of climbing etiquette. They were a walking contradiction. The purpose of being roped together is so that you can clip through pickets. That way, if one person falls a picket stops them and the whole team from sliding down the mountain into a crevasse. For goodness sake, the Park Service provided the blasted pickets so you could be safe without needing to carry your own. By tying in so close to each other, the team couldn't even use the NPS-provided pickets, and didn't bring any of their own. Since they were roped only three feet apart, if one of them fell they would immediately bring the other three down with them. Now instead of one person needing to self arrest all four would need to self arrest to catch a fall. They had successfully multiplied their chances of falling by a factor of four. We didn't want to have them reducing our own safety.

As I nervously watched ahead while they stepped on and got their crampons tangled up in the rope between Dan and Woody I could see two other teams of about five people starting to catch up to us. They were roped in a similarly senseless manner. My sixth sense told me they were also Polish. "Oh great," I thought, "this is about to get even more interesting." Pretty soon Darren stopped and let the five original Polish people pass. Our rope was so long that I was still standing stationary on flat ground and starting to get cold. At last we all started to move and things became a little more efficient.

Pretty soon the other five-person group caught up to us. They were roped up about ten feet apart—slightly safer—but didn't want to use the pickets either. Of course, they were also Polish. Yet another five-person group appeared behind them roped up in a similarly scary manner. "Yes, we're all Polish," the guy said to me. "Did you come here together?," I asked. "No, we're all different groups," he answered. Darren was placing pickets and clipping in up ahead which explains why we were slower than all the other groups that avoided the pickets. I sat at the back of our 100m snake stationary as Darren wrestled with an obstacle far ahead. I couldn't really see Darren, let alone hear him. I stood there, stationary, and observed the lead Polish dude shuffling about impatiently. He's gonna do it, I thought, he's gonna pass us too.

He cocked his head to the side and asked, "You predict to slip?" with a look of confusion. "No I don't expect to slip," I answered, "but since the pickets are already here we might as well use them, it doesn't take any extra work." "But your rope, it's so long," he commented. "The longer it is," I answered, "the more pickets you can clip through and the safer you are!"

He turned around to his companions, said something in Polish, and they decided it was time to pass us. I mean, I felt bad that we were standing stationary there on the trail and they had to wait for us, but that's just how it is on the mountain. It's not really safe to pass on such a steep slope. He said, "we going to pass, OK?" There was nothing I could do. "Just stay out of our rope," I said, "stay below it. BELOW IT." "OK no problem. Bye." Of course they walked above our rope. Luckily mine and Eric's rope was comfortably clipped through two pickets. If the Polish dudes fell, they would be in trouble, not us.

It was like the Polish dudes had taken to heart just a single sentence from the Denali climbing book: "you need to be roped up to each other to climb Denali." They didn't seem to know *why* they needed to rope up or *how* to do it. The just got the shortest rope they could find and tied themselves to it. Oh, you're supposed to be 30m apart? Why, you can't talk to each other when you're that far apart.

I watched painfully as they slowly trudged past us. Up ahead Eric banged his ice axe against the snow, a universal sign of frustration. We were probably twice as fast as those Polish guys but the five of us clipping into and out of pickets slowed us down significantly. As frustrating as it was though, slowing down a little to clip into some pickets and protect ourselves from falling was pretty important. It was definitely worth it. Through clenched teeth I vowed to pass everyone who had passed us.

After two tough, complicated hours everyone including probably twenty Polish people had reached Denali Pass, at 18,200ft. The route ahead was steep with 2,000ft of climbing but thankfully there wasn't enough exposure to warrant too many more pickets.

It was apparent that we cruised at different paces. We decided to split ourselves up independently: me/Eric would go in front with DWD behind. Each rope team had enough safety gear to bivy on the mountain: a pot, stove, fuel, food, pad(s), shovel, and sleeping bag. Our packs were way bigger that everyone else's we passed that day but at least we had a decent safety margin. That's the Winter School way. That's the safe way. The plan was for me/Eric to summit and come right back down to meet DWD. If any of them were feeling bad they could tie into our rope and we'd take them down while the others summitted. If they were all feeling good we would hike with them back up to the summit.

As we discussed the plan we began to realize it was actually kind of cold. We each put on almost all our upper layers including our heavy down jackets. On my upper body I had two polypro layers, two fleeces, a shell, and my heavy down jacket. It must have been cold because I climbed in all those layers for the rest of the day and didn't overheat. Thank goodness it stayed sunny with light winds.

All the Polish climbers went by. Now it was our turn. After a little while we officially split up, and Eric and I pushed on ahead. Without the need to place protection we were indeed faster than the Polish groups. We began to pass them. I believe they were surprised. We trudged through the soft snow on the side of the trail and gradually made our way to the front of the pack. Of course it wasn't a race, but it was sure nice not to have to wait behind the Polish teams going way slower that we wanted.

As we climbed we moved slower and slower. We were walking in a slow motion movie. Every few steps we had to stop, rest our heads on our ice axes, and catch our breaths. Features that seemed so close for our brain doubled in apparent distance for our body. We wanted desperately to keep climbing but an invisible hand was holding us back, weighing us down. The thinning air and our yearning for the summit made us forget about our hunger. We tried to force some food down but couldn't stomach more than a few bars. We tried to drink some water but even in our insulators our bottles had frozen shut. It must have been way colder than it seemed.

We could see the summit ridge on the other side of the Football Field. Just a little bit higher and we'll be on top. We dragged our bodies to the base of that last hill. From a distance it seemed like an insignificant little nub, just a false summit before the peak. But when we climbed a few feet up it turned into a towering obstacle. This was going to be way harder than we expected. Five steps . . . rest . . . breathe . . . five steps . . . rest . . . breathe. I didn't want to look down because I knew we hadn't climbed much yet. I didn't want to look up because I knew we still had a long ways to go. I just looked at the footprints in front of me. People had made it up successfully yesterday. We would make it today. It was probably a 500ft hill but it seemed much higher.

We were going to make it. By gosh we were going to make it. Even if I broke my leg at that point I still think I would have made it to the top through sheer willpower. Ugh. My mind was now overpowering my body. So far during the past seven hours of ascent I had two little fruit bars and a few swigs of water. I'm not sure what my muscles were running on, I'm pretty sure I had exhausted most of my body's reserves over the past eleven days. Finally we made it to the summit ridge.

The summit was in sight beyond a sharp corniced ridge. The Polish people were just starting at the base of the hill. If we didn't blow our lead the summit would be ours alone for a few moments. It was awfully tempting to just throw caution to the wind and dash to the top without placing protection. But we didn't come all this way to fall off the mountain just below the summit. Eric was better at placing pickets so he went in front. "LET'S DO IT!" I yelled.

We had a few choices which way to go. To our left we had a 500ft crevassed slope down to the Football Field. To our right we had a full five-thousand foot drop to the Ruth glacier. Behind us we had the way we had come. In front we had the summit. I knew which way I was going. The ridge was literally as sharp as a knife—a really dull one I guess. With no flat top, it was safer to favor the 500ft drop over the 5,000ft drop so we walked carefully on the left slope. Fortunately there were a few pickets placed by the Park Service that we could clip through. I guess it was cheaper for them to invest in a few pickets than in a rescue. No helicopter in the world has ever rescued anyone at this altitude.

Ten pickets later we found ourselves on the roof of America. YEEEAHHHH!! I roared at the top of my lungs. I yelled so loud I actually knocked the wind out of myself for five minutes. We were currently the highest people standing on solid ground in all of North America. We saw the Alaska

Range unfold beneath us. There were gigantic mountains with awesome glaciers a full *two miles* below us. We could see the Kahiltna Glacier spreading like a frozen river fifty miles away. It was like we were in an airplane. Except here on Denali the awesomeness extended 360 degrees around us and 180 degrees from horizon to horizon. Like few other places in the world we had a full and complete hemisphere of unobstructed view all around us. Nothing was taller. The closest taller mountain was Kangchengzhongga on the Chinese/Indian border, 5400 miles away.

A few years ago I had never expected I would be standing here. I thought, "I guess if we're going to climb the 50 state high points that includes Denali. But Denali's for real mountain climbers, like Everest. It sounds a little too dangerous to me." But here I was. MITOC's Winter School had turned the tide. Eric had turned the tide.

After a couple minutes of pictures and awe it was time for the most important picture. I wanted to give credit to MITOC, the MIT Outing Club. Through five years of Winter School we had gained our foundations in winter hiking and climbing. We started out as freshmen students but now we were the senior leaders, instructing the next generation. Just for the occasion my girlfriend Amanda had made one shirt for me that said "MITOC RULES" and one for Eric that said "DENALI." My idea was that the two of us would stand together with the t-shirts and get a picture on the summit of "MITOC RULES DENALI."

Problem was, with temps of minus 15F and a little breeze it was awfully chilly for a photo in just a t-shirt. I was already starting to feel sick from the altitude and wanted to get down soon. I had thought ahead and just slipped my t-shirt over the top of my down jacket. Eric decided instead to go for the glory. I asked Eric, "where's your Denali t-shirt, Amanda worked so hard on it?" "I'm wearing it," he said. "Oh jeez." After a few minutes of hemming and hawing, Eric decided to go for it. "Now you better take this picture quick Matthew," Eric warned. Like a bolt of lightning he stripped off all six of his upper layers and I snapped a quick picture of him posing without his shirt. I guess you could say I chickened out.

He extricated the Denali t-shirt and put everything back on. Not often do you wear a t-shirt over a down jacket. We precariously perched my camera on my backpack and clipped it in. We didn't want that camera falling off the mountain. Finally we got our summit picture.

We had stood for 15 minutes on the roof of North America and needed to get down. I was getting a big headache and was going downhill fast. I had had that same feeling on Mt Shasta years before and knew it was only going to get worse. I needed to get the heck out of there while I still could. Our usual tradition is to get a picture of me jumping and Eric juggling on top of the state high points but we didn't have time for those rituals now.

We staggered off the summit. Now we were only halfway through summit day. We passed some Polish friends on their way up. They had ditched their packs at the Football Field. Next we met up with Darren, Woody, and Dan. They were doing awesome and feeling pumped. I wished that I could go back up to the top with them but I was feeling miserable. We planned to radio in periodically and meet each other back at camp. Eric and I moved out and DWD moved up.

The "towering little mountain" that we had struggled up turned back into a nub of a hill on the descent. With gravity helping us we were probably going four times as fast on the way down. We blazed past all of our other Polish friends on their way up. That day, by our count, 25 people summitted: the five of us and twenty Polish climbers. The numbers were similar yesterday and would be about forty tomorrow. That was probably the most successful three-day period on Denali so far this year.

I felt like we were descending a completely different mountain than we had come up. Now we could walk down at a normal pace; someone had just released the "slow motion" button. We cruised to Denali Pass and faced our last major obstacle of the day: the steep side slope. Unfortunately the wind had blown all day and filled in the trail with soft snow, making it much easier to slip, especially since we were the first ones down. Camp was tantalizingly close; we could see it less than a mile away. It was now 8:30pm, we had already been hiking for eleven hours and were exhausted. We were ready for sleep. Once again it was tempting to throw caution to the wind and make a dash for it without placing protection, we could probably go twice as fast. But I had to remind myself that we didn't come this far just to fall off the mountain on our way down.

I had Eric go in front because I knew he would be more liberal in placing protection. We slowly made our way across the steep slope. About halfway we looked back and saw some Polish friends appear behind us. "You've got to be kidding me if you're not going to place protection on this slope," I said aloud. Luckily they kept their distance and didn't compromise our own safety. The slope felt so long because we could no longer just put our minds on cruise control and march down. We had to concentrate the whole time on our footing, the rope, and placing pickets. We had to make sure each footstep was solid.

Near the end, when there was no longer a huge crevasse below the slope and we had determined it safe enough to stop placing protection, my tired foot slipped and I began to slide down. Come on, I thought, not when we're this close. I planted my ice axe weakly and slowed down after 40 feet. I was too tired to hike back up so I made a new trail.

We staggered on and dragged ourselves up the last little Heartbreak Hill to camp. Eric immediately plopped down on his pack and held his head in his hands. I laid down in exhaustion onto the snow. It was cold but I didn't feel it. I was zapped. I was drained emptier now than after the Boston Marathon. We had done it. We were back.

Now we awaited DWD's return. We had tried to radio in but I guess we were out of each other's range. The time was 10:30pm. After twelve hours Eric and I were wiped so we figured DWD would be zombies by the time they showed up. We had each only eaten two bars all day and drank a few sips of water before the bottles had frozen solid, even the ones in insulators deep in our packs. We would have needed a thermos to keep the water liquid all day. We fired up the only stove we had and began the slow process of melting snow. After an hour and a half we had finally thawed our own water bottles and used their contents to create three liters of boiling water. As tempting as it was to drink it ourselves, we decided that since we were feeling OK we would save all the water for the other guys. We had no idea of their condition. We knew they would appreciate hot water. In the meantime we put the hot water bottles in our jackets for mutual warmth retention.

Next we began to melt some snow for cooking dinner. We finally heard a crackling transmission from Woody that they had reached Denali Pass. Now that we could see them in the distance we relaxed a little. If they had been in bad shape I don't know if I would have even been strong enough to offer much help. At midnight I began to turn into a zombie myself. We sat there on the cold benches around the stove. The sun had set and it was probably minus 10F. We were too tired to talk. We just looked. I learned to appreciate just how much heat it takes to bring one liter of minus 10F snow all the way to boiling.

Around 12:30am Darren emerged over Heartbreak Hill. Then Woody. And finally Dan. We were all back. The three of them sat down on the benches. Nobody really said anything. We all stared distantly at the stove. "You guys did it, congratulations!" I pounded Darren and Woody on the backs. They sipped from their hot water bottles and we all ate some couscous. Then the three of them went into their tent and fell asleep. Eric and I stayed awake for the next hour creating some water for ourselves and finally got to sleep around 1:30am.

Day 12:

Our bodies were totally shot so we slept in until 11:30am. We weren't in any hurry to get down. We knew that the biggest obstacles ahead of us were Washburn's Thumb, the long fixed ropes, and not punching through lower down on the glacier. After that we would be at Base Camp and within reach of Woody's finish line: a cheeseburger in Talkeetna.

A huge line of people was headed up the mountain for the summit. Darren counted forty people, including what looked like two twelve-person guided groups. I'm glad we weren't tangled up in all of that. We packed up and headed out. Camp had grown dramatically over the past day; people were probably encouraged to head up by the stellar forecast. DWD went in front with me and Eric bringing up the rear and together we made our way slowly, carefully, down the sharp ridge. Pretty soon our close-roped Polish friends appeared again out of nowhere and blasted by us. They still didn't seem to understand the purpose of the anchors in the snow that we were using.

After Washburn's Thumb it was time for some more fixed rope action. Going down was going to be kind of tricky because ascenders are designed to work while you're going up, not down. We would have to hold the ascenders open while we descended, and if we slipped we would release them and hopefully they would catch the rope. First Dan, then Woody, then Darren, then Eric disappeared over the steep edge. I'm glad we had the ropes to follow because the clouds had rolled in and we could no longer see the bottom. We were descending into a white abyss.

Pretty soon I joined the rest of our group at the bottom of the fixed lines and the clouds broke, giving us a good view of 14,200ft camp. I was amazed. While we were away camp had doubled in size. New campsites had been added all around the edge of town. People were pouring in. This was probably the peak couple of weeks for climbing Denali.

We remembered our cache and realized with disgust that our packs were about to get a lot heavier. "Hey, let's give away some food," Woody said. Dan and Darren excavated the gear and we put all our food that we weren't going to eat into three sleds. Since the weather had been so awesome and enabled us to go fast we had a huge amount of food to spare. Like the ice cream man with his ice cream truck we towed the sleds around camp hollering "FREE FOOD, get your free food here!" People emerged like prairie dogs from their shelters. Most were bashful at first but when we conveyed to them that we really didn't want to carry all this food down they dug in. We were especially thankful when a guide came out to browse our sleds; he had probably been through this dozens of times before and knew what to grab for his future clients. He grabbed about six pounds of cheese, pounds of oatmeal and crackers, and about six bags of pasta from our sleds. We were delighted. He also grabbed a spare gallon of fuel. Our packs were getting lighter and we were making people happy.

Most of the food was gone in twenty minutes. But we still had a few pesky pounds of pasta. Maybe the Korean team would like it . . . They didn't speak much English but once it became apparent that we were giving away the food instead of selling it they opened up. "Pasta?" they asked. "Oh yes, pasta, macaroni, very good," we said. "OOHH, macaroni!" We stacked four pounds into their open arms. "Sank you, Sank you!" they said. They bowed deeply and I bowed and with big smiles all around our sleds were basically empty and we were on our way.

We had tentatively planned on spending the night at 14,200ft camp. But Woody's cheeseburger awaiting him in Talkeetna was becoming increasingly more attractive. Even though it was 7pm we felt pretty good and decided to push down to 11,600ft camp and reevaluate. I held my head high as we moved out of camp. People in camp were waiting with uncertainty for their shot at the summit but we were already victorious and were on our triumphant way down. I thought I could hear trumpets playing in our honor in the distance.

It's not often that you look forward to "flushing the toilet." But for us that meant the chance to stick our nose over a deep crevasse and throw the CMC bag in. We normally steered clear of crevasses and didn't get to look into them. I had a full CMC on my backpack and needed to lighten the load, so I identified a suitable-looking crevasse a little ways off the route and hollered for Eric to stop. He got in self arrest position in case I fell in. I grabbed the CMC bag and marched toward the lip of the chasm. I pitched the bag in and I'm not sure it ever reached the bottom, the crack was so deep. It might still be falling to this day. We continued on our merry way around Windy Corner which was luckily calm today.

Having the sleds took all the fun out of descending. We tied the sleds onto the rope between us and Eric went in front. My job as the back person was to keep tension in the rope, which meant I was holding the sleds back the whole time, trying to prevent them from crashing into the back of Eric's legs. On the steeper slopes like Squirrel Hill and Motorcycle Hill the weight of the sleds on my harness was so uncomfortable I flipped my sled upside down. That way the duffel bag had so much resistance with the snow that Eric had to work a little to drag it down the hill. I felt pretty clever. On leveler terrain I took Darren's suggestion and tied some extra rope to the nose of the sled, which allowed me to steer it much better and things went much smoother.

Meanwhile, DWD cruised behind us with Darren in front, followed by Woody on skis, and Dan in the back. Woody had skied most of the way up the mountain on his skis while the rest of us trudged in snowshoes. Now it was time for Woody to reap the rewards of his labor. We enviously watched as Woody snowplowed down.

By 11pm we strolled into 11,600ft camp. It was pretty quiet in town that evening so I hope our excitement at having successfully summitted didn't wake anyone up. We still had energy so we decided to cook some dinner and keep going. Hopefully we could push all the way to Base Camp that night. It also felt nice to finally take off the dang sunglasses and not need to put on sunscreen now that the sun had set. We figured we might as well hike all night and take advantage of the lack of sun and far more pleasant temps. That was the nice part about being this far north in the summer. We scarfed down some sausage and pasta, compliments of chef Dan, and rolled out sometime after midnight.

Day 13:

Around 1 a.m. we saw a bright orange light appear just behind a mountain far down the Kahiltna Glacier in front of us and soon saw the full moon appear. It was a serene time to hike. There was the perfect amount of light. We walked toward the full moon, which over the course of the next few hours rose just a little ways above the horizon and then headed right back down. We met a couple of oncoming hikers. I wasn't sure how to greet them. It was 2:30am. There's "good morning" and "good evening" but it doesn't seem right to say "good night" when people aren't going to bed. I'm not sure they understood English anyhow.

Pretty soon I was out of water. I had miscalculated and needed a liter to get me to Base Camp. Dan graciously whipped out the stove and fired it up. As we sat there we looked up at Denali. The massive mountain towered two vertical miles above us. It looked like one gigantic wall. We were five miles away so it seemed to flatten out into one monster face. As we sat there we also noticed that there were some new dips in the trail: the snow bridges over the crevasses were thinning. I had heard this was a low-snow year, but I didn't expect the crevasses to open up this early. We knew we had to be careful. Luckily we were hiking at night so the snow bridges should be stronger. A Polish couple on their way up warned that we better get off the glacier before the sun comes up or it could get "dangerous."

A few miles later we learned what they had been referring to. We were walking through an area thick with postholes from people who had sunk in during the heat of the previous day. Eric tried to step around but as soon as he stepped on virgin snow he sank down up to his waist. Luckily his feet weren't dangling in the thin air of a giant unseen crevasse but still I got ready to self arrest. Was there a giant crevasse underneath?, I wondered. If so, why hadn't he punched through the whole way? We guessed that there probably was a crevasse underneath this big minefield and that maybe the snow bridges were melting faster because they were less dense than the glacier snow. In future minefields we learned to step exactly where other people had stepped and to crawl when we had to in order to avoid plunging through. I wouldn't have wanted to be anywhere near that area in the heat of the afternoon. That snow bridge was probably looking at its final couple of days.

We slogged through five other minefields. It was slow going. Each step you took was a thrill. You wondered if your foot would hold or plunge into blackness. Finally we reached the bottom of Heartbreak Hill. Actually, in comparison to the other Heartbreak Hills we experienced on different parts of the trip this one seemed to be a piece of cake. We had known about this hill since Day 1 and could mentally prepare for it. The other hills came out of nowhere when we weren't psyched up for

130

them. Step by step we inched our way up. At 7am the pirate flag marking Base Camp's landing strip came into sight. We strolled in triumphantly and threw our packs down victoriously.

My favorite part of the day came when I undid my harness with relish and threw it violently against the ground. I was finally off the rope. Eric and I had been roped up pretty much every day for thirteen days. Wherever I went I had to make sure I didn't step on the dang rope, and make sure it didn't get tangled on anything. We had to go at exactly the same pace. If I needed to go to the bathroom we both had to stop. And I always had to hold that ice axe in case Eric plunged in. Base Camp was safe enough that we could finally detach that umbilical cord and be free. I had me a big old bowl of granola and powdered milk to celebrate.

"What do we do now?" I asked Eric, "It's 7am and we've been hiking for eighteen hours straight, we need some rest. But the blazing sun is about to come up and people are waking up in Base Camp. It would be tough to sleep here."

"We fly out," he answered. The glacier planes started flying in around 8am. I really hoped we could get some sleep right after we landed in Talkeetna. While we waited for DWD, I said to Eric, "Man, I can definitely see how people could get hurt on that mountain. On summit day if you don't really listen to your body and get down quick you might not be able to walk out. And the temperature wasn't too forgiving even on a good day like we had."

"Yeah," Eric said, "And lower down on the glacier you better hike at night or you're gonna punch through. I don't think many people know that." Pretty soon we saw DWD appear next to the pirate flag at the end of the landing strip. "All right, we did it!" I said.

We organized our trash to show to Lisa and disentangled our sleds. We hoped they would serve the next climbers as well as they had served us. We talked to Lisa and got into the departures queue. It turns out that a twelve-person guided group had gotten there last night and were first on the list for departure with our air carrier, TAT. We noticed at that point that there were actually three "terminals" at the Base Camp landing strip: one each for Hudson Air, Talkeetna Air Taxi, and K2 Aviation. Each terminal had its very own unique-colored sled protruding vertically out of the snow. On the sleds were duct-taped the letters H, T, and K. Wow, it was a real official airport. Woody joked, "Okay everyone, now you can't take any sharp objects onboard the aircraft." We laughed. Our glacier gear consisted almost entirely of sharp, pointy, dangerous weapons.

Unfortunately there weren't any planes coming that could take all five of us at once. One of us could fit on the first airplane, one on the second, and then three on the last, Lisa told us. "Who wants to be first?" Woody asked. Nobody wanted to be first. It was like we all wanted to stay on the glacier a little longer. We were scared to return to the uncertainties of civilization. In order to make this completely, 100% fair it needed to be randomly decided. But where do you obtain a random number on a glacier? This could be difficult. We proposed a variety of solutions. Darren suggested making five small sticks, with one shorter than the others. The person drawing the short stick would be It. Blast it, though, it turned out we couldn't find sticks (or any plant life for that matter) on the glacier. We would have to use bamboo wands.

But Woody was concerned this wouldn't be random enough. "What if we had a five-sided dice?" I asked. Unfortunately we couldn't find one of those either. Eric proposed another solution: "How about I just pick a secret number between 1 and 100, everyone else picks a number and whoever's closest is It?" "But what about you?" one of us asked. "If nobody is closer than 20 than I'm It," Eric answered, "the chances should be one-in-five for everyone." But then Eric backed off: "When people pick random numbers they usually pick prime numbers though, like twenty three or seventeen, so it's hard to get truly random."

Woody was uneasy. "That doesn't sound random enough to me, what else can we do?" Eric offered an improved scheme: "I'll pick a number between one and five and write it in the snow. Everyone else picks a different number and whoever gets it right is It, otherwise I'm It." Most of us nodded our heads that this could work. But Woody was still skeptical: "But like you said, people often pick prime numbers so this still won't be random enough."

We were deadlocked. Nobody wanted to be It. Nobody would back down. We all stood our ground. Pretty soon the first plane landed and started loading up. This was getting urgent. Lisa hollered "Okay, MIT, first person." Woody turned to us. "OK, fine, we can do it your way Eric but I'm still not convinced we're going to achieve true randomness." We all sighed with relief that the deadlock would end. Eric hastily wrote down a number in the snow behind us. Darren guessed the number correctly so he was It. He would take the hit. He loaded the plane and took off. Without argument I volunteered to be the next person. My decision wasn't totally random but I could live with it. At least it meant I would get to change into tennis shoes before Dan, Woody, or Eric.

After one of the most awesome plane rides of my life I was back on the ground. Changing into tennis shoes never felt so good. While we were gone, spring had come to the rest of Alaska. For the first time in two weeks I saw trees and animals again. Dan, Woody, and Eric didn't end up flying out until three hours later. In the meantime I gave the CMCs back to the rangers.

It was Friday and we had finished the climb a full week early. Dan, Woody, and Darren decided they would rather get some work done and give back to their employers a week of vacation that they didn't really have in the first place, so they moved up their flights to fly out of Anchorage tomorrow. Since Eric and I were taking the whole summer off anyhow, we said to each other "How often do you find yourself in Alaska in the summer with a week to kill?" We decided to go backpacking in the northern half of Denali National Park, an area that contained actual wildlife and not as much snow.

After a few showers in the TAT bunkhouse we strolled into downtown Talkeetna for some food. "I bet we could find my cheeseburger in there," Woody said. We walked in to Denali Brewing Company and sat down. The waiter gave us some water. "Wow, you don't even have to melt the snow to get water here!" I observed. We sank our teeth into our best meal in two solid weeks. Dan played around with Woody's phone and suddenly raised his eyebrow in surprise. Woody slowly put down his cheeseburger. "What?" he asked with a full mouth. "Dude, your phone's got a random number generator," Dan said. Woody: "D'oh!"

34 TAUM SAUK MOUNTAIN

MISSOURI

1,772ft

Date climbed: Dec 31, 2010

Author: Matthew

Accompanying climber: Keith Gilbertson

Every state has a highest point. Some are tall. Some aren't. But if you're trying to climb the highest point in every state, they're all equal. So Florida's 345-ft Britton Hill counts just the same as Alaska's 20,320-ft Denali even though, as we discovered, it's not quite as difficult to climb.

With Denali in May 2010 we had attained high point #33. We needed to knock some more off the list. We had a big missing chunk of states in the southeast that were within striking distance of our home in Kentucky. So we decided to visit them over Christmas Break. We decided to go fast and light. Our most important piece of gear was our Silver 3329lb Mazda-Six. 170 horses would be helping us on our journey.

For our initial planning we used Google Maps. Our goal was to climb the highest points in Missouri, Arkansas, Louisiana, Mississippi, Florida, Alabama, and Georgia in less than 5 days. We would start and end in Berea, KY. It seemed the shortest route at first would be MO-AR-LA-AL-FL-GA (~2800 miles). But Mississippi's Woodall Mountain was inconveniently located in the middle of what would have otherwise been a perfect loop, so it seemed like there were multiple possible routes. We tried several route permutations on Google Maps and couldn't get much less than 2800 miles.

Then it was Matlab to the rescue. One of Eric's lab mates had been working on the "Traveling Salesman Problem," which seeks to find the optimal path to visit N nodes. Eric decided to adapt the solution strategy to our problem, and made an 8-by-8 matrix of all the possible path lengths. Using Matlab he found that the fastest route was actually MO-AR-LA-MS-FL-AL-GA (2700 miles). So Missouri was first on our list.

Hi-pt #1: Taum Sauk Mountain—1772ft (Missouri):

Eric and my Dad drove to St Louis and I rendezvoused with them at the Greyhound Station. I had been visiting Amanda's family in Kansas City. After a few traffic jams, wrong turns, and non-existent roads we headed south into the Ozarks.

Taum Sauk turned out to be less of a pushover than we had expected. The higher we drove the thicker the fog became. Even on Mount Washington I haven't seen fog that thick. We inched along and finally made it to the state park at the summit. We set up the tent by the car's headlights, which pierced through the dense fog.

My GPS indicated the summit was only about 500 ft to the west. (We had entered in the GPS coordinates of all the high points from Wikipedia beforehand.) We figured we might as well go for it now since it was so close. But it turned out to be impossible to navigate by headlamp in the dense fog. It was like trying to swim through milk, and expecting goggles to improve your visibility. We turned around and went to sleep in the tent.

It poured and blew all night and we woke up soaked. But visibility had improved. Following the GPS we bushwhacked toward the "summit." Turns out the GPS coordinates were off by about 500ft, so if we had tried to find the summit the previous night we probably wouldn't have seen much. You couldn't actually tell by topography alone the difference between the true high point and just another pile of leaves.

Soon we spotted a big rock in the woods and a trail leading up to it from the other side. It was the summit of Taum Sauk Mountain. We had made it. Our 211-day high-point drought since Denali had ended.

Now it was time for our traditional summit rigamarole. We need to get pictures of me and Eric jumping, a picture of Eric juggling, and some summit rocks. And we needed pictures on at least two cameras so if one camera was lost, documentation of our accomplishment would still survive. The more high points we climbed the longer the checklist. I think on Clingman's Dome (our first high point) back in 1996 we were satisfied with just a single picture. Now we'll probably have to start over on all those early high points so we can collect rocks from them.

Whew. Our first high point had been exhausting. We had hiked over 1000 ft with an elevation gain of 3 ft. We hoped Arkansas would be more merciful.

(Continued in Arkansas report).

35 Signal Hill on Magazine Mountain

Arkansas

2,753ft

Date climbed: Dec 31, 2010

Author: Matthew

Accompanying climber: Keith Gilbertson

(Continued from Missouri Report)

On our way to Magazine Mountain we toured the boondocks of the Ozarks. The area was surprisingly forested and sparsely populated. We hadn't expected such remoteness in Missouri and Arkansas. The roads were so infrequently traveled that once while I was driving we came upon a big tree that had fallen across the highway. I slammed on the brakes and luckily we stopped in time. Thankfully there was enough room in the ditch to drive around the tree. Otherwise we might have had to drag it out of the way with a rope.

We continued on our Matlab-calculated optimal path which took us through Yellville, Flippin, Hasty, and Subiaco. Then we found ourselves at Mount Magazine State Park. A short hike and a little bushwhacking brought us to the summit of Signal Hill, the roof of Arkansas.

Arkansas is proud of its high point. There was a giant sign proclaiming this point to be the highest in the state. A large stone map of Arkansas paved the ground.

Once again it was time for the summit festivities. Ten other tourists sat down and observed curiously as we jumped and juggled. Our Dad said we did this on every high point and everyone relaxed a little. This was our 35th high point. We were now 70% done with all fifty.

Mount Magazine had been another tough one. We could only imagine what was in store for is in Louisiana.

(Continued in Louisiana report).

36 Driskill Mountain

Louisiana

535ft

Date climbed: Jan 1, 2011

Author: Matthew

Accompanying climber: Keith Gilbertson

(Continued from Arkansas report).

From Mount Magazine we drove off into the sunset. We headed south through Little Rock and soon found ourselves in the southern boondocks region of Arkansas. It turned out that it was actually New Years Eve, and we could think of no better way to celebrate than by visiting the roof of Louisiana.

Driskill Mountain turned out to be a little trickier to get to than the previous high points. We had printed off the Summit Post directions that read "The primary route on Driskill Mountain begins at the parking lot of the Mt. Zion Presbyterian Church, however, those desiring more vertical gain and more distance can park further south at the intersection where Jot Em Down Road comes in."

We didn't want to take any chances, so we headed for the church. Luckily the topo maps I had loaded on the GPS actually marked the church, so we made it there without much difficulty. We didn't see any Sheratons in the vicinity so we decided we'd have to camp. We drove up near the cemetery and spotted a nice grove of trees. It was 11pm on New Year's Eve so we didn't expect too many people to be checking up on us tonight. Eric and I slept in the tent while our Dad guarded the car.

We woke up in the morning and noticed a big NO TRESPASSING sign that was apparently referring to the area we had just camped in. "Huh, they must have put that up overnight," I guessed. We took down the tent and you couldn't tell we had been there.

Now for the hard part: the ascent. We prepared for what would be our longest hike yet: 0.8 miles to the summit. We were fortunate that the weather was favorable, because we had been concerned by the Summit Post entry describing when to climb the mountain: "This mountain can be hiked year-round with no ill-effects posed by weather changes. There are slight chances of being deterred by freak ice-storms or hurricanes, but these are well publicized occurrences."

We headed up the dirt road and followed the signs. Then we reached the summit. A diligent Eagle Scout (probably with some help from his dad) had erected a stunning sign and kiosk at the top. After we finished our summit traditions a father and his young son appeared at the top. The dad asked us how early we had started on our high points quest. We told him we climbed our first one when we were ten. "Then there's still hope for my son," he replied. Indeed, we thought, with a strong start on Driskill Mountain that little kid is well on his way to all 50 states.

Three high points down, four to go.

(Continued in Mississippi report).

37 Woodall Mountain

Mississippi

807ft

Date climbed: Jan 2, 2006 (Eric) and Jan 1, 2011

Author: Matthew

Accompanying climber: Keith Gilbertson

(Continued from Louisiana report).

Now it was time for some serious driving. Since we were so far south here in Louisiana it was tempting to cut across southern MS and visit the highest point in Florida. We figured this might be a shortcut. But Matlab and Google know all the shortcuts. The Matlab-optimized path took us next to Mississippi's Woodall Mountain, 422 miles away. So we buckled up and kept driving.

We cut through most of the state of Mississippi that day and passed through Elvis's hometown in Tupelo. Right around sunset we wound up a steep gravel road and found ourselves on the roof of Mississippi. A gigantic boulder with a plaque marked the summit. It was tricky to get the traditional jumping pictures but our dad managed to get a few good ones.

We hadn't exercised properly for a few days now and our legs were starting to ask questions. So we went for a quick run around the summit to pacify them and hopped back in the car. We were headed to Florida.

(Continued in Florida section).

38 Britton Hill

Florida

345ft

Date climbed: Jan 2, 2011

Author: Matthew

Accompanying climber: Keith Gilbertson

(Continued from Mississippi section)

You don't really think of mountains when you think of Florida. You don't even think of hills. It turns out that the highest point in Florida is actually one of the skyscrapers in Miami. But the highest "natural point," Britton Hill, was where we were headed. Britton Hill is one of the farthest points in Florida from the ocean. So we would be some of the very few people who have visited Florida without seeing either the beach, Disney World, or alligators.

First we needed to cross the entire state of Alabama. Our dad took over driving so we could get some rest. As we drove south we tried to come up with a camping strategy. There weren't any state parks along the way. There was no way we'd stoop to staying in a hotel. Perhaps we could camp on Britton Hill? So we kept driving.

We ended up driving the entire length of Alabama from North to South that night and reached the town of Florala, on the Florida/Alabama state line, around 11pm. There was a state park and a campground but we decided to push on towards the summit since we were so close. But when we got there a police car guarded the parking lot. He was probably there just taking a doughnut break, but this meant that it was off-limits to stealth-campers like us. So, defeated, we drove back to the state park and set up our tent.

The dishonor associated with camping in a state park is that you have to pay and you're not all by yourself. But I suppose we got our $12's worth because we each took a shower in the morning.

8:30 a.m. It was game time. It wasn't exactly an alpine start but we still believed we'd summit before dark. We hopped into the Mazda and drove the long mile to the summit. Soon we found ourselves on the lowest state high point in the country. It felt like a monumental achievement.

Like Louisiana, Florida is also very proud of its high point—a very nice little park surrounds the summit. In fact, I think there were more picnic tables, benches, and parking spaces on the summit of Britton Hill than the summit of Denali. We took the requisite jumping and juggling pictures, but had difficulty completing the traditional summit trifecta, which included the collection of a summit rock. I couldn't find any actual rocks so I had to settle for a bag of sand. It is possible that there's not a rock in the whole state.

After paying our final respects to the summit of the "Sunshine State" it was time to aim for the azimuth of Alabama.

(Continued in Alabama section).

39 Cheaha Mountain

Alabama

2,431ft

Date climbed: Dec 29, 2005 (Eric) and Jan 2, 2011

Author: Matthew

Accompanying climber: Keith Gilbertson

(Continued from Florida section).

We drove north through Montgomery and headed towards Cheaha Mountain. With rolling, forested hills mixed with golden farmland it looked like a different Alabama than I had expected. Cheaha Mountain rose prominently in the distance. On the way up we actually had to switch into a lower gear because the roads were so steep. But we encountered the biggest hurdle of the journey when we entered Cheaha Mountain State Park and turned on the road to the summit: the entrance fee. $3 per car. Ouch.

Eric and Dad had been there a few years before but didn't remember the fee. Well, if it's $3 per car, we thought, then we'll just have to leave the car at the bottom. So we finished the climb by foot. A very nice little observation tower was perched at the summit. It was a little tricky to get a jumping summit photo indoors but we managed by jumping off a chair. From the top you could see a significant portion of Alabama and well into Georgia. It was the best view we had experienced so far.

We spent some time capturing the perfect jumping photo. A good jumping photo requires teamwork between the photographer and the jumper. Here's the recipe for a perfect shot:

0) Photographer first kneels on the ground and aims the camera up at the jumper. Kneeling is essential for any quality picture.
1) Photographer presses the camera's trigger down half-way so the camera focuses, then says "ready."
2) Jumper counts "1 . . . 2 . . . 3" and jumps on 3.
3) The photographer looks through the viewfinder/LCD and when the jumper is at his/her apogee the photographer presses the trigger.
4) Meanwhile, when the jumper is at apogee, he/she pulls legs in so it looks like he/she is farther off the ground.
5) In resulting picture jumper looks to be ten feet off the ground.
6) Repeat sequence as necessary.

Step 3 is the hardest to perfect and requires decades of experience. It becomes even more difficult when there are two jumpers. Together with our dad we followed the sequence perfectly and he captured a few textbook jumping shots.

Next we headed for the roof of Georgia to practice our jumping-photo skillz one last time.

(Continued in Georgia section).

40 Brasstown Bald

Georgia

4,784ft

Date climbed: Jan 3, 2011

Author: Matthew

Accompanying climber: Keith Gilbertson

(Continued from Alabama section)

It was nearing the end of our fourth full day. We had budgeted six days for the whole trip but we had been so eager to keep going that we were a day ahead of schedule. We could have pushed through the night and climbed Brasstown Bald in the dark, but instead we chose to save it for the morning when we could actually get a good view. We camped that night near the Appalachian Trail at Neal's Gap, a pivotal road crossing for many A.T. thru hikers. Only half the thru hikers who start out make it past Neal's Gap.

We cooked a traditional thru-hiker's meal of pasta + tomato sauce and prepared for bed. I filled a bottle with some boiling water and threw it in my sleeping bag to heat it up. It was predicted to drop into the low 20's that night so we were going to need all the heat we could get because we had thin summer sleeping bags. After talking to Amanda on the phone for a while I retired to the tent and looked forward to my nice pre-heated sleeping bag. I smiled with anticipation. But to my horror the water bottle had leaked and the sleeping bag was soaked the whole way through. This was not going to be a good night, I guessed.

I soon realized the cause for the leak: the cheap-O water bottle I had used was definitely not intended for the heat. It seemed that the lid was made from a plastic that had a higher thermal expansion coefficient than the rest of the bottle. So when the lid heated up it expanded more than the bottle opening and compromised the seal.

I knew it wasn't going to be a pleasant night. I put all my layers on and placed a trash bag above and below me to keep the water from wicking into my clothes. Thankfully it didn't get as cold as expected that night so we both managed to get some sleep.

The sun rose on the morning of our 40th high point. It was show time. After a short drive we were at the base of the hike to Brasstown Bald. We discovered that winter time is the prime time to climb. There was only one other car in the entire 100-spot parking lot. A quick 0.6 mile paved walkway took us to the summit.

From the observation deck the view was exquisite. To the southwest we could see the tall buildings of Atlanta, 90 miles away. To the north were the Smokies and to the east we could see well into South Carolina. It couldn't have been any clearer. For this, our last high point of the trip, we needed some extra-special jumping pictures. We scoured the deserted complex for the perfect angle. Finally we settled upon a location with good lighting and the observation tower in the background and captured the shots we were looking for.

Brasstown Bald was ours. High Point #40. We breathed in the crisp Georgia air and took a final look at the panorama before us. Then we slowly walked down to the car. Our adventure was nearing its end.

We hopped in the car and began the long drive back to Kentucky. Along the way we stopped by the Smokies, hoping to re-visit our very first high point, Clingman's Dome. But the road was closed because of deep snow.

We headed north towards home base: Berea. The mountains grew smaller and more distant in the rear view mirror. Meanwhile, my thoughts of mountains were slowly being displaced by the anxiety of one colossal hurdle that loomed at the end of the month: the PhD Qualifying Examinations. Ugh . . .

. . . one month later . . .

We ended up passing Quals. Now it's time to finish up the nine remaining high points.

41 Harney Peak

South Dakota

7,244ft

Date climbed: July 30, 2011

Author: Matthew

Accompanying climbers: Keith Gilbertson, Verdi Gilbertson

Sometime in mid 2010 Eric and decided that we were going to finish the state high points by the end of 2011. We're not really sure why we set this deadline, but it was nice to have a goal for the year.

That meant sooner or later we'd have to visit North Dakota. Now North Dakota isn't exactly known for its stunning topography. Before we climbed White Butte we figured that North Dakota was basically just one giant wheat field in between Minnesota and Montana. During this trip we discovered that that's mostly true, but we're also here to report that the highest point in the state is quite a bit more interesting than you might expect.

During many trips to Minnesota over the years, a couple of trips to the South Dakota Badlands, and a bike ride into Montana we had somehow managed to miss the high points in North and South Dakota. With our Dad visiting our Grandpa in Montevideo, Minnesota at the beginning of August we figured it'd be the perfect week to finish off some high points.

We rendezvoused with our Dad and 87-year-old-but-still-vigorous Grandpa in Rapid City, South Dakota around 11:30pm Friday night. It was going to be a tight weekend because we had a flight that left Minneapolis for Pittsburgh on Sunday morning at 7am. That meant we'd have to climb Harney Peak (SD) and White Butte (ND) and drive 900 miles in just 31 hours. But we knew it'd work out somehow.

After a couple hours of sleep we grabbed our free continental breakfast at Super 8 in the morning and were on our way.

Harney Peak (7,244ft)—South Dakota

We swung by Mount Rushmore and reached the Sylvan Lake trailhead by about 9 a.m. (Sylvan Lake is where they filmed part of the second National Treasure movie.) Since we had a tight schedule our Dad and Grandpa had done their part by getting us to the trailhead early. Now it was time for Eric and me to do our part by finishing the hike quickly. Eric and I didn't want to slow our Grandpa down so we asked him if he would guard base camp while we summitted. Grandpa, with his experience in the Vosges Mountains during World War II, was well-qualified and graciously obliged. Meanwhile, our Dad, a seasoned high point veteran, volunteered to stay back and help guard the SUV.

The trail was pretty easy and certainly runnable. If we had brought mountain bikes we would have ridden them until the wilderness boundary, but running shoes were a lot more portable than a mountain bike. We were glad we hadn't started any later because it was already getting hot and we were sweating out most of the water we drank.

After just three miles and 1500ft of climbing we were on the roof of South Dakota. There's a really cool old stone fire tower at the top. In its heyday quite a few people could have lived in it. There's even a small reservoir near the tower that the rangers probably get their water from. It was a little tricky to capture the traditional ritualistic jumping photos inside the fire tower so we decided it would be permissible to get them outside.

Now spending too much time on a high point can be dangerous. If you hang out for too long you might think of pictures that you wish you would have taken on the other high points. Eric and I had already taken our jumping photos, juggling photos, and arms-up summit photos and were looking for something else to photograph. Recently I had discovered some cool free panorama stitching software called Microsoft Composite Image Editor and wanted to get some panoramas on the rest of the high points. Having a 360 degree panorama really gives you a good idea of what the summit looks like. The panorama we eventually created for Harney Peak turned out pretty well.

Our philosophy today was to rush up to the summit, hang out and enjoy the view, then race back to the car and get moving. On the way back the trail turned out to be extremely runable and we made it back to the car in a total time of 1:39:00, including 25 minutes of fooling around on the summit. Our Dad and Grandpa were waiting for us, and reported that there had been no incidents at base camp. Grandpa had been busy working on his Tablet PC, planning the route to North Dakota.

(Report continued in North Dakota section)

42 White Butte

North Dakota

3,506ft

Date climbed: July 30, 2011

Author: Matthew

Accompanying climbers: Keith Gilbertson and Verdi Gilbertson

(Continued from South Dakota section)

We wiped the sweat off our faces and hopped back in Grandpa's Chevy Trailblazer. There had been enough tomfoolery already and there were still a lot of miles between us and Minneapolis so we didn't waste a second and headed north.

One candidate location for the "Middle of Nowhere" might be northwestern South Dakota. After you descend out of the Black Hills the trees disappear and give way to open rangeland. Incidentally, the northwestern corner of South Dakota is also the geographic center of the United States. This is the point where a flat rigid map of the 50 United States would balance. Despite this prestigious distinction there wasn't a whole lot to see in the vicinity so we kept on driving.

After passing through the towns of Belle Fourche, Redig, and Buffalo we triumphantly reached the North Dakota border. A big blue sign welcomed us to the "Legendary" state. We snapped a few requisite photos and started walking back to the car when another SUV pulled up and seven people stepped out. It turned out they were on the quest for all 50 states (but not high points) and North Dakota was near the end of their list. They took some pictures next to the welcome sign, although I'm not entirely sure they actually stepped across the state border.

We were getting closer to the roof of North Dakota. We could feel it. Instead of rolling hills there were actually a few humps off to the northeast and the GPS indicated that one of them was the high point. We were getting into Butte Country.

The previous week we had done our homework on SummitPost and knew where to go. The GPS told us to turn on some little gravel side roads and we obeyed. Soon we pulled up next to the spot I had marked on the GPS as the "trailhead."

"Uh, there's supposed to be some kind of old farmhouse according to SummitPost," Eric said. We drove up to what looked like a farmhouse and I knocked on the door. No answer. We drove a little ways back down the road to a gate with a Private Property sign. It looked like the road that we had planned on taking based on the satellite photos no longer existed.

"I don't know, why don't we try calling the landowners?" I suggested. White Butte is actually on private property so you're supposed to call the landowners before you climb. I tried the phone number given on SummitPost but there was no answer. "Well, that looks like the top right there so why don't we just start walking?"

There weren't too many obstacles between us and what looked like the top so we decided to go for it. We were originally hoping to have three generations of Gilbertsons at the top, but of course someone needed to guard the SUV. Our Grandpa, being fluent in the Upper North Dakotan farmer dialect, decided that he would be the best-qualified among us to deal with any locals who might give us a hard time, and said "Oh ya, I can guard the car." Eric and I were a little uneasy to be without our translator during the climb, but we figured we could manage. Our Dad, meanwhile, agreed to help guard the SUV and serve as the base camp photographer.

We passed through the gate and headed off into the field towards the summit. It would have been nice to be wearing long pants or possibly some boots to protect against rattlesnakes. We had read that "the butte country crawls with rattlesnakes in the summer" so at first we treaded carefully. We were in kind of a hurry though so we soon gave up on watching for snakes and marched up the mountain, hoping that we'd get lucky and not step on any rattlers.

With a few last steps we triumphantly topped out. But wait a minute. This wasn't the top. It turned out there was an obviously-taller butte a half mile away. Argh. This is what we refer to a "false summit." The GPS confirmed that indeed we weren't on White Butte. We had gotten carried away, and climbed the tallest thing we could see. Oh well, we thought, we'd get some extra hiking in today.

We carefully down climbed some crumbly mud/rock/scree slopes and then after a little bit of scrambling we topped out on another grassy hill that was the tallest thing around and thus the highest point in North Dakota.

The landscape around us was surprisingly awesome. We were on top of a large grass-covered white butte that resembled the Badlands of South Dakota. All around us were similar buttes, all rising a few hundred feet above the surrounding fields. Green grass mixed with sagebrush extended beyond the buttes as far as the eye could see. If we had more time we would have liked to explore some of the little canyons below us.

The summit register indicated that several other groups had been there the day before. They had probably found the official trail, we figured, because the route we had taken was completely different than SummitPost had described.

We fooled around just long enough for a 360 degree panorama, the other customary summit photos, and paused to admire the view. But then, alas, it was time to get moving. We didn't realize it at the time, but every minute that we spent on the climb would mean a minute less sleep that night. To spice things up we found a different route down that required some butt-glissading on mud-scree. We figured that we had probably found the hardest possible way down the mountain. But that made it more interesting.

A little farther down the butte we turned a corner and suddenly came face-to-face with a big black bull. Ok, it wasn't exactly face-to-face but it was pretty close. Turned out we had the bull cornered on a little cliff. He didn't look happy. He glared at my nice bright red shirt. I didn't feel like playing matador today so we kicked it into gear and sprinted out of the way.

After squelching through a few fresh cow pies and getting thrashed by some sagebrush we successfully made it back to base camp around 3:30pm. It is widely believed in the Norwegian-Minnesotan community that if you stood on a tall barn in western North Dakota and waved a white sheet you could see it all the way from Montevideo, 450 miles away. "Could you see us at the car?" our Grandpa asked. "Yep, and we could see all the way to Montevideo," Eric answered.

Pittsburgh (elevation 906ft)

The hardest part about climbing the highest point in North Dakota is actually the drive back to Minneapolis. With our Dad at the helm we made it to "The Cities" around 2:30am, and got a few hours of sleep at our Aunt Kay and Uncle Bob's house before our 7am flight to Pittsburgh.

But the highest points in North and South Dakota were only the beginning of our adventures that week. In a few days we'd be back in Minnesota for four more high points . . .

(Continued in Minnesota section).

43 Eagle Mountain

Minnesota

2,301ft

Date climbed: August 5, 2011

Author: Eric

Accompanying climber: Keith Gilbertson

(Continued from North Dakota section)

Most any serious mountain has an accepted climbing season—generally in the spring when crevasses still have thick enough snow bridges to bear weight and the weather is starting to get warm and pleasant. The climbing season for Denali is generally April—June, and for Everest is generally in ~May before the monsoons start. The climbing season for Charles Mound, the highest mountain in Illinois, happens to be only the first full weekends of June, July, August, and September. As serious mountaineers, we chose to climb Charles Mound in season, on the first full weekend in August. But we also had other unfinished state-highpoint business in the area in the form of Minnesota, Michigan, and Wisconsin—so a full mountaineering weekend was in store.

Minnesota—Eagle Mountain 2301 ft

The journey started at 9:30am Friday morning in a rental car in the small town of Montevideo, in western Minnesota. We had climbed Harney Peak, South Dakota and White Butte, North Dakota the previous weekend and had spent the week visiting relatives in Pennsylvania and then Minnesota. After a big breakfast at the best restaurant in town—Valentino's—our dad took the wheel and we started heading up nort (that's how you pronounce it with a Minnesotan accent). According to Google it would be 7.5 hours driving to get to Eagle Mountain, way up in the northeastern tip of the state almost on the Canadian border. It would take a few hours to hike, and then another few hours of driving to get where we needed to be in Wisconsin that night for the whole plan to work out. So there was no time for fooling around.

We cruised up to Duluth no problem, but then got hit with a double whammy of road construction plus weekend traffic from "The Cities" (that's the Twin Cities—Minneapolis and Saint Paul). Luckily it eased up once we got a little farther north on Lake Superior. We drove through Two Harbors, Beaver Bay, and finally to Lutsen where we turned inland on gravel logging roads. We had a few minutes of torrential rain, but luckily it was short-lived and we arrived dry at the trailhead at 4:45pm. Somehow we had managed to beat Google despite the traffic delays.

Matthew and I had heard legends of the voracious mosquitoes in northern Minnesota, and came prepared with full body cover and head nets. But, when we got out of the car we hardly noticed any bugs. Maybe we'd just been expecting a more north-of-the-arctic-circle mosquito level like we'd experienced last summer, but we certainly didn't complain.

We started hiking at 5pm and had the trail all to ourselves. Not surprisingly for Minnesota the trail was flat most of the way, winding around lakes and over swamps on boardwalks. The bugs got a little more voracious near the swamps but the bite rate was only about 3/minute at the worst. At two miles we reached Whale Lake and the view of a hill that most online pictures claimed was Eagle Mountain. We quickly debunked that myth with a careful inspection of our topo map. So if you ever do a Google image search for Eagle Mountain, remember it's actually the local maximum behind the trees to the left of the one in the pictures.

The trail finally started climbing after we rounded Whale Lake, and we reached the summit by 6:15pm. There was no mistaking this one—a huge 2'x2' aluminum sign marked the 2,301ft summit, and even gave the full history of the surveying of the mountain. We got some jumping and juggling pictures, ate a few wild blueberries, and then headed back down. There was a view on the way back and I couldn't see a single sign of civilization. There's true wilderness in northern Minnesota, and I bet you could get pretty far from any other people if you climbed Eagle Mountain in the winter.

We managed to beat the rain back to the car, and immediately started heading back south. Now came the dilemma—we needed to hit Michigan, Wisconsin, then Illinois and get back to Minneapolis by 3pm Sunday to catch our flight. Unfortunately Charles Mound is on private property and the landowners only open it up these certain weekends, but we weren't sure what times of day it was opened (or whether the property was gated). If we assumed it was open 9am-5pm, then we basically had to get there by 5pm Saturday, since there wouldn't be enough time to hit it Sunday morning and make it all the way back to Minneapolis. But Charles Mound was a 16-hour drive from Eagle Mountain (not including hiking time for Michigan and Wisconsin), and it was already 8pm Friday night. That sounded like a good plan to not sleep at all. So we unanimously decided to bet that Charles Mound opened before 9am, and just plan to get there Sunday morning.

With sleep back in the equation, I picked out a nice-looking national forest just outside Ino, Wisconsin, and we drove there that night, finding a good stealth camping spot by midnight.

(Continued in Michigan section)

44 Mount Arvon

Michigan

1,979.238ft

Date climbed: August 6, 2011

Author: Eric

Accompanying climber: Keith Gilbertson

We were up and out of camp by 7am and soon across the border into Michigan. This highpoint, Mt Arvon, would prove a bit more difficult to find. It was guarded by a maze of logging roads outside of L'Anse, but supposedly the best route was marked with blue signs the whole way. However, we found what looked like a more direct route on Google earth satellite photos, and decided to try our luck. At L'Anse we pulled off onto gravel roads, and plunged into the forest. We hit intersections every few minutes, and navigator Matthew would always point us on the right road. After about 20 minutes Matthew worriedly announced,

"Uh oh—there's a stream ahead that intersects our road. I hope there's a bridge . . ."

We rounded the corner and slammed on the brakes. There was a stream all right, and the road went right through it. Any high-clearance vehicle could have made it, but not our poor little rental car. Our gamble had not paid off, and we reluctantly turned around back to L'Anse. We were on a tight schedule and couldn't afford any more delays, so this time we followed the official route. It was indeed well-marked with blue signs and we reached the dead-end marking the trailhead at 11:30am. Actually there was a big barricade over the road, but a 4-wheeler-size path cut through the woods around it. We figured we could probably drive to the summit in a Jeep, but again not in this car. So we got out and started hiking.

It was only about a half mile to the top, and we actually did see a jeep parked half-way up. Apparently the road was even too rough for the jeep. We passed a woman walking down with her dog, and then reached the summit at noon. Michigan is actually pretty proud of this mountain—there were several benches, a picnic table, and a super-sturdy metal summit register attached to a tree. We found a little concrete summit marker next to the tree, and it was mysteriously very wet while the ground everywhere else was dry. Could the dog have peed on it? Or someone emptied a water bottle on it?

I read the summit register and someone had signed in that morning, claiming this was his 39th highpoint and that he had "pied" [sic] on the summit of each one. I suspect he meant "peed" on the summits, and we must have just missed him. We were impressed by him summiting 39 highpoints (that had been us just a few months ago, though this one was now #44 for us), but not by his summit ritual. I mean, almost any mountaineer pees on or near most summits they attain, if only because that's where they naturally take a break anyways. A much better summit ritual in my opinion is to juggle five objects—rocks/snowballs/sticks—on the summit (that's what I do).

After checking out a little man-made view nearby we soon headed back down and set our sights on Timm's Hill, Wisconsin.

(Continued in Wisconsin section)

45 Timms Hill

Wisconsin

1,951ft

Date climbed: Aug 6, 2011

Author: Eric

Accompanying climber: Keith Gilbertson

(Continued from Michigan section)

It was easy navigating back out the logging roads and we were soon heading south on the open highway. We drove through the metropolises of Eagle River, St Germain, and Tomahawk without incident, but when we turned west with only an hour to go before Timm's Hill the weather started deteriorating. The sky turned dark and we were suddenly hammered with torrential rain. This might have been okay for any other mountain, but Timm's Hill was different.

We had read that there was a 60-ft tall metal fire tower on the summit with a ladder on the outside. A cable ran up alongside the ladder and if you had a harness you could clip in for protection in case you fell. We had come fully-prepared with harnesses and slings to climb this tower. However, it didn't sound too safe now to be climbing a slippery ladder 60ft above the ground on the tallest metal object in the whole state during a lightning storm.

We pulled in to the trailhead around 5pm and it was still raining. We could still hit the top of the hill without climbing the tower, so we left the harnesses in the car and started walking up in our rain jackets (well, Matthew went without a shirt). It was only a quarter mile to the top, and as a consolation prize there was actually a second, shorter fire tower that had a staircase and still offered a view above the trees. It even stopped raining just as we got to the top.

We juggled and jumped back at the bottom of the tower, and then got back in the car to dry off. Forty-five highpoints down and one more left on this trip.

(Continued in Illinois section)

46 Charles Mound

Illinois

1,235ft

Date climbed: Aug 7, 2011

Author: Eric

Accompanying climber: Keith Gilbertson

(Continued from Wisconsin section)

From Timm's Hill it was a 5-hour drive to Charles Mound, and we decided we wanted to be there at 8am Sunday morning. Unfortunately there aren't any national forests to camp at in northwestern Illinois, and it looked like it was going to rain all night anyways, so we made the call to stay in a hotel that night. We made it to Dodgeville by 10pm and found a nice Super 8 with a continental breakfast.

The next morning it was raining hard as we pulled out at 7am (good thing we weren't in our tent of questionable waterproofness). We timed the drive perfectly and made it to the town of Scales Mound (at the base of Charles Mound) at 8am on the dot. Now first it's important to know a little history of the Gilbertsons and Charles Mound. Back in the summer of 2005 we had stopped by Charles Mound on our way back home from Minnesota, not knowing about the restrictive climbing season. We got to the turnoff from the main highway onto the owners land, but didn't dare go any farther because of the multiple "No Trespassing" signs. Only after doing careful research back home did we realize that the highpoint was actually open on four specific weekends in the summer, but no other times. We vowed to return some day, and this was the day.

This time, knowing the mountain was officially open, we drove past the "No Trespassing" signs for about half a mile until we came to some old barns in the woods. Here we saw a sign instructing high pointers to park their car and continue on foot. We were at the right spot for sure!

We walked about a quarter mile up the road into the woods and finally came to the official summit sign. At last! And there was even a nice view to all the surrounding corn fields and cattle pastures. We checked out the summit register and there were at least 20 sign-ins from just yesterday, though we were the first that day. It turns out nothing would have prevented us from going up there at midnight the previous night, though the owners house was pretty close by and we were glad not to have offended them at all.

With 46 state highpoints safely in the bag we strolled back down to the car and headed back north. We got to Minneapolis with plenty of time to spare for our flights.

47 Kings Peak

Utah

13,528ft

Date climbed: Aug 13, 2011

Author: Matthew

"Yeah, I've actually only got three state high points left," we overheard a dude on the summit of Kings Peak say proudly to another hiker.

Our ears perked up. Could there really be a fellow hiker here on top of the highest point in Utah who, like us, had also climbed the highest point in forty seven states? We were impressed. We had to hear more about his feat. "Wow, so you're working on the state high points too?" we asked incredulously. "Which three do you have left?"

"Rainier, Gannett, and Granite," he responded. (That's Washington, Wyoming, and Montana, respectively.) But then his story began to erode. "But I don't count the ones on the East Coast," he said, "they're not *worthy*."

Not worthy? Are you kidding me? Now them's fightin' words. I bristled at his egregiously insulting statement. "You don't count the ones on the East Coast? Well there's some pretty nice mountains out east like Mt. Washington and Katahdin," I responded. He had never heard of them.

"The mountains out west here are a lot taller," he countered.

The discussion was heating up. "How many mountains are on your list?" Eric asked.

"Well, I don't count Alaska and Hawaii, so . . ." he trailed off. " . . . so eight are on the list."

"How many have you done?" Eric asked as politely as possible.

"Well, five."

Now Eric and I hadn't intended to publicly insult the guy right there on the summit, but when he says the mountains on the East Coast aren't *worthy* he's got it coming to him. A few minutes later another dude on the summit inquired "so how many state high points have you guys done?"

"Kings Peak makes forty-seven," Eric answered, "so now we've got only three left."

Our pilgrimage to the highest point in Utah began—nervously—in the back of a taxi in Cambridge the previous afternoon. Eric had an advisor meeting which was scheduled to end at 1pm that he couldn't miss, which made catching a 2:45pm flight with bags to check difficult to accomplish via the T. So I was to meet him with all our bags in a taxi at 1pm sharp right in front of his lab. We wanted to make this a quick and stealthy getaway.

Now it's not that Eric's advisor wouldn't permit him to go on the trip, it's just the simple fact that he didn't need to know about it. Eric would make up for lost work the following week, but we might as well just make the trip invisible to his advisor so that no questions were asked that didn't need to be asked.

PHASE 1: getting to the airport

So shortly after 1pm, Eric strolled casually out of his lab meeting as if he was off to the restroom, but then quickly hopped with me into the waiting cab. We were off . . . sort of. Turns out that it was the taxi driver's first day on the job. At first we thought he was taking us on a shortcut to the airport but we ended getting a tour of all the red lights in Boston. We finally made it to Terminal B and hopped onto our plane with just ten minutes to spare. Phase 1 of the journey was over, but there were eight more phases of the trip that we needed to execute flawlessly.

PHASE 2: flying to SLC

We arrived uneventfully at 9:30pm local time and picked up a rental car at the Alamo counter.

PHASE 3: driving to the Kings Peak trailhead

Our route took us from Salt Lake City through southwestern Wyoming and then back into Utah. There's not a whole lot to see in southwestern Wyoming in the dark (or in the light either) so we needed to switch drivers to stay awake.

After passing through the metropolii of Fort Bridger, Urie, Mountainview, and Robertson we turned off onto gravel "Billy Bob Roads" (as we like to call them) and headed south into Utah's Unita Mountains. We wound around for a good forty-five minutes before arriving at the trailhead. We had expected it to be a popular weekend but were still shocked at the number of vehicles at the trailhead. Cars and tents were parked everywhere, probably 100 cars in all. Well, we thought, this means we can camp wherever we want. We finally got to sleep around 12:30am.

PHASE 4: climbing Kings Peak

But "sleep" before a big adventure is always a relative term. We were lying down with our eyes closed but that didn't mean we weren't thinking about the climb. For me it's always tough to get a decent rest before a big adventure. My brain would prefer to focus on the excitement and anticipation of the next day. It also didn't help that the temperature dropped below freezing that night, causing us to shiver a little in our summer sleeping bags.

The 6:30am cell phone alarm jolted us awake for good and it was time to get moving. We had a big day ahead of us. We weren't exactly sure of the mileage that we faced; online sources said anywhere between 25 and 30 miles. We read that most people take three days in all: hike to the base on Day 1, summit on Day 2, and hike out on Day 3. Well we didn't have that much time since it was just a three day weekend. We had other business with the highest point in Idaho the next day so this trip needed to be efficient without any fooling around.

The trail to the base of the mountain is pretty level and well-behaved so we were able to engage our mental cruise control and think about other things besides where to place our feet. We were trying to plan our attack on the remaining high points. We'd do King's Peak today, Borah Peak (Idaho) tomorrow, Mauna Kea (Hawaii) in a few weeks, and finish on Guadaloupe Peak (Texas) sometime in the fall. But King's Peak would turn out to be less of a cakewalk than we had expected.

During the climb Eric and I began to philosophize on the use of the internet in planning our trip. We had bought our tickets online, used Google Maps to plan our route to the base of the mountain, Summitpost for the route descriptions, and Google Earth satellite photos to select possible campsites and record GPS waypoints for the route. It amazed me that everything just worked out. You simply type in your credit card number and get a flight all the way to Utah. You follow the maps and you actually get to the trailhead. You follow the route description and get to the top. The trails all exist. Kings Peak exists (well, we would find that out later). The whole time you're trusting everything you see on the screen, not giving it a second thought. In the days before internet it all would have been much tougher to coordinate.

With our legs on cruise control and our minds free to discuss the nature of reality, at 9:30am we reached the base of the climb—the climb up to Gunsight Pass. So far it had just been a little walk in the woods. At this point the hike turned into a genuine mountain climb.

We (especially me) were expecting at least a little altitude sickness on the climb to the 13,528 ft summit, so we made sure to breathe very deliberately and forcefully, a known tactic to mitigate AMS (Acute Mountain Sickness). We were hoping to summit quickly and get down from altitude fast enough to dodge the signature symptoms of headache and nausea.

The climb started out comfortably, although we couldn't climb too fast without gasping for air. We assumed a slower pace and climbed through Gunsight Pass. Soon the trail leveled out and we were walking through a rugged talus field. From the aerial photos it looked like this part would be flat and easy, but in reality we had to carefully plan every step over the boulders.

Along the climb a group of "ultra light" hikers passed by us on their way to the top. Looked like they were aiming for a speed record. The lead guy was wearing nothing but a thin pair of shorts and a small vest with pockets.

We kept climbing and reached Anderson Pass, the last flat ground before the summit. We took this opportunity to hike across a little snowfield, even though we could have gone around it. There's just something tantalizing about hiking on snow in mid-August. Soon the shorts-only dude passed on his way down. (He ended up finishing in just 4hours, 47minutes, which must surely be a new speed record for Kings Peak.) A few deep breaths and slow steps later we were on the roof of Utah.

Except for some wind turbines 30 miles away in Wyoming there wasn't a single manmade structure in sight. For 360 degrees around it was nothing but mountains and valleys. It was especially cool to see some valleys to the south that were completely undeveloped, with no sign of human involvement. Such undeveloped valleys are rare because that's usually the easiest ground to develop. Luckily, though, we were in the High Uintas Wilderness which meant that no machines or buildings were permitted.

It seemed that some of the surrounding peaks like South Kings Peak and Gilbert Peak were actually a little taller, but we took the internet's word for it that we were on the tallest ground in the state. We completed the traditional high point rituals with a photo of both of us jumping, Eric juggling, and our arms raised on the summit. And then it was time for the most recent ritual addition: the summit panorama.

We hung out for a little while with the rest of the high point crowd and decided it was time to head down. If we weren't on a tight schedule we would have hung out for hours on the top because the view was so spectacular. But we had scheduled an appointment with Idaho's Borah Peak the next day and needed to get moving.

The descent turned out to be far more difficult that we expected. Our time at altitude was starting to take its toll. We had been at sea level 24 hours earlier and now we were above 13,000ft. We needed some more time to make some red blood cells. I was starting to get a headache and didn't feel like eating anything. To make matters worse we had run out of water and were getting dehydrated. A seemingly insignificant little rise suddenly turned into Heartbreak Hill. From past experiences on Denali and Shasta we knew that the only remedy was to get downhill ASAP.

Before long we found a little creek draining a melting snowfield and filled up our Nalgenes. Soon we were back at Gunsight Pass, and finally reached the base of the climb. For us it felt like the hike was pretty much over, although we still had 11 miles to go. Most of the hikers we had passed that day were incredulous that we would be attempting to do Kings Peak in a day. But it didn't seem like such a big deal to us. We had just finished the climb, it was 3pm, and it was all gradual downhill from here. Easy, right? But one dude ominously asked us, "You guys headed back to the trailhead tonight?" "Yep," we answered. "Oh, I'm sorry," was his reply.

The hike out was agonizingly long. Because of the possible need for crampons on the snowfields I had unfortunately chosen to wear hiking boots instead of more comfortable/traditional tennis shoes and I paid for it in the form of some painful blisters. (Later that night when I removed my boots I discovered seven large broken-skin blisters.) To make matters worse we both had a dehydration headache and hadn't been able to eat much the whole day. We slowly staggered on, thankful that Borah Peak the next day would only be seven miles. We took a quick break and both guessed that we only had a half-mile to go. I whipped out the GPS to confirm, but I just about threw the GPS against the ground when I saw that we in fact had 3.5 miles left.

"Ughh," I groaned. "How can we still have 3.5 miles?" The morning ascent had flown by, but the descent was feeling like a completely different trail. Well, at least we had the GPS to tell us the truth. At 5:45pm Mountain Daylight Time we finally made it back to the trusty Chevy Cruze. I threw off the boots, hopped into the driver's seat, and we sped off towards Idaho.

We figured that we could rest in the car just as well as we could rest at the trailhead. We could bask in the glory of having climbed the highest point in Utah while we drove to the highest point in Idaho. We had executed the first four phases of the trip flawlessly, but still had five phases left.

(Continued in Idaho section)

48 Borah Peak

Idaho

12,662ft

Date climbed: Aug 14, 2011

Author: Eric

(Continued from Utah section)

"Come on, don't be a chicken," Matthew yelled up to me. I was standing on the top of a 20ft cliff protruding up from a knife-edge snow ridge. On the right side of the ridge was a 1,500ft drop, and on the left a 2,000ft drop, and the only way forward was to down climb the little cliff and cross the snow. This was the aptly named "Chicken-Out Ridge" section of the standard Borah Peak route, where a slip could have severe consequences and people often decide to just turn around and forsake the summit. I wasn't chickening out, though, just planning my route carefully. I strapped my poles to my pack, turned around, and started down climbing.

Matthew and I had flown out west for another state-highpoint-bagging weekend in our quest to finish all fifty by the end of the year. We flew into Salt Lake City Friday night and polished off #47 Kings Peak, Utah in a twenty seven-mile hike Saturday, finishing early enough to drive into Idaho on Saturday night.

As grad students we make enough of a stipend to fund a plane ticket once in a while, but try to save a penny whenever possible during the trip. On these trips we usually look for a national forest to drive into and just camp for free in the woods. So at 9pm Saturday night when I pulled off on an appealing gravel road in Caribou National Forest in Idaho and saw the sign "Free Area," I was pretty excited.

"No, that says '*Fee* Area', dufus," Matthew pointed out. I must have been pretty tired. It was a campground and thus I instinctively started putting the car in reverse to look for a better spot. "Hold on a minute," Matthew started, "we're both exhausted, it's after dark, we just found a campground in a national forest that's only $6 a night, we won't have to worry about somebody caring that we're sleeping here, and we still want to turn around and keep looking for something cheaper!? I think we can each afford $3 for a good night's sleep, especially since it's going towards a good cause (the forest service)." I agreed, and we pulled in there for the night.

We were both probably as whipped as we'd been on Denali summit day—we hadn't really acclimated to King's Peak (13,528ft), and had been having terrible headaches most of the day. The altitude sickness had sapped our hunger and we had each eaten hardly anything during the twenty seven-mile trek. And we were both pretty dehydrated, despite each having drunk 1.5 gallons of water. Oh yeah, and sleep deprived from only getting a few hours sleep the previous night. But it's amazing what one good night's sleep can do to a mountaineer's body. It was like someone had hit the restart button on a computer and the next morning we were back to 100%.

Matthew took the wheel and we started driving northwest at 7am. The original plan had been to sleep at the Kings Peak trailhead that night and drive the full 7.5-hours to Borah on Sunday, climbing into the night if necessary. But with our bonus 3-hours of driving already done from the previous night, we pulled in it to the Borah trailhead early at 11:30am. There were nine other cars in the lot, and two were actually from Alaska! Everyone must have already started hiking hours ago, and with good reason: the sign at the trailhead warns: "the climb takes 6-7 hours—plan on a 12-hour round trip."

"We'll it ain't gonna take us no twelve-hours," I proclaimed. It was only seven miles, and we had done twenty seven miles yesterday in ten hours. But we still knew it wouldn't be a cakewalk. The trail gained 5,262ft in just 3.5 miles and involved some sketchy scrambling sections. Moreover, I had some unknown knee injury that hurt pretty badly if I ran or put much weight on it. I knew, though, that I could avoid pain by taking small steps, leaning on my poles, and favoring my good leg on the scrambling, so I wasn't too concerned.

We started hiking at noon. The trail was extremely steep, and we soon passed out of the lowland scrub and into the trees, and then out above treeline around 10,000ft. At least five other parties were on their way down, after what must have been alpine starts that morning. I couldn't tell then, but apparently some of the groups had actually chickened out on the namesake ridge and hadn't actually reached the summit. Nobody announced that to me, though, of course.

After about an hour and a half we reached the fun part. The trail kind of fizzled out at the base of some ledges and the only way forward was scrambling up. Matthew started ahead, climbing up the 3rd class rock, and then traversing to reach a small cairn at the top of a scree field. From there it was more scrambling up along the ridge, avoiding the occasional snow patch and trying to ignore the thousand foot drop below us if we were to fall. That section would have definitely required ice ax + crampons a month earlier, when we had originally planned on summiting Borah. It was no coincidence we had chosen this weekend, though, when the snow level would be at its lowest and we had the best chance of a fast and light summit bid.

Eventually the path of least resistance led us back to the top of the ridge and the infamous chicken-out section. It turns out the down climb is a lot easier than it looks from a distance (either class 3 or 4 depending on your guidebook source), and has awesome hand and footholds the whole way. We got down no problem and the knife-edge snow ridge at the bottom had enough footprints that we crossed without needing crampons.

From here the final push to the summit looked impossibly steep, though it turned out to be mostly class 2 level. We passed two local Idahoans descending who said they were the last ones on the summit. They said they'd passed quite a few people on their way up, but didn't see anyone else reach the summit after them. Must have chickened out, they supposed.

At 2:45 we officially reached the roof of Idaho, and had it all to ourselves! State highpoint number 48! There were all sorts of memorabilia up there: a big American flag, several summit registers, and even a pair of old elk antlers. We admired the view for quite a while, and did our usual fooling around pictures of juggling and jumping. Down on the east side of the mountain we spotted some awesome alpine lakes that brought back memories of the Sierra Nevada. There would be quite a lot to keep a mountaineer busy in the mountains around Borah Peak, and I wouldn't mind too much if MIT would move to Mackay, Idaho (at the base of Borah). It could even keep the same acronym.

The clouds started building up and getting darker and that was our cue to get down. We had each drunk about 3 liters of water on the way up but still felt dehydrated, so we filled up from a melting snow patch on the descent.

The chicken out cliff was easier going back up, but the rest of the scrambling a bit sketchier going down. Some sections had scree sprinkled on rocks (what some mountaineers call "kitty litter"), but we managed to avoid that most of the time.

Shortly after we got back into the trees we saw two more hikers starting their way up. The clouds were building and I could have sworn I had felt a drop of rain. "That could have been us if Kings Peak had taken any longer," I said after they had passed. It was already 5:30pm, and they would certainly be descending in the dark—I just hope they didn't have to go over "Chicken Out Ridge," in the dark and rain.

We reached the car at 6pm. No speed record (I had definitely slowed us down by being careful with my knee) but still better than the supposed twelve-hour time the "average" hiker takes. We were five-hours away from Salt Lake City and needed to make a 2:30pm flight the next day, so we figured we had enough time to check out one more destination—a bonus point you might say. Craters of the Moon National Monument was only an hour away, so we headed there and got in one last evening hike in the ancient lava fields. We left early the next morning and made it to our flight with plenty of time to spare, arriving back in Boston late Monday night.

49 MAUNA KEA

HAWAII

13,796ft

Date climbed: Sept 2, 2011

Author: Eric

Accompanying climber: Jake Osterberg

"This guy has to pick us up," Matthew yelled, sticking out his thumb as a silver jeep approached. We were 12,000ft up on Mauna Kea, the tallest mountain in Hawaii, and Jake was getting hammered by altitude sickness. We had hiked to within 700 vertical feet of the summit, but had to turn around and get down ASAP before Jake got worse. It would take hours to hike back to our car at the 9,000ft trailhead, so we were walking down the summit road hoping someone might pick us up. It was slim pickings for cars driving by on that Thursday morning, and the only other car we'd seen had passed us by, but we were feeling good about this Jeep.

The journey had started Wednesday morning with fifteen hours of traveling from Boston to Hilo, Hawaii, where we all converged at 7:40pm. Matthew and I were hoping to tag our 49th US state highpoint, and Jake was shooting for number three. I guess you'd say this wouldn't be a typical Hawaiian vacation—we would be on the island for just a long weekend, with no plans to visit any tourist beaches, stay in any hotels, or eat in any restaurants. In fact, we were actually hoping to see some snow if we got lucky.

Using Google Maps street view we had carefully planned out multiple stealth camping locations for our first night out, and after picking up the rental car and picking up a few gallons of water at the Hilo Wal-Mart, we sped off into the night. Luckily for us the Big Island of Hawaii is actually pretty sparsely populated, with the only major towns on the coast. We were driving into the heart of the island, toward Mauna Kea, with Jake behind the wheel and Matthew navigating toward campsite #1 marked on the GPS. Unfortunately Google Maps was not as good at notifying us of road construction activity or fog. The first four potential spots were either blocked by construction vehicles or we missed them in the limited visibility. We eventually punched out of the fog and the road construction, but that was also exactly the altitude where the trees stopped (and, consequently, where our pre-planned campsites stopped).

We turned around back down the road to try to find a spot we had missed in the fog, but this one turned out to be no good—construction vehicles were parked in it. It was getting pretty late by now (about 4am east coast time for us), and there was even talk of paying to stay in an official campground or worse—a hotel.

We decided to try looking around above the treeline just in case, and soon stumbled across a gravel access road for the power lines. It got us off the main road, and we could even park the car behind a large boulder out of view from passing cars—perfect! We threw down the tents and finally took a well-earned sleep.

The sun woke us up at 5:30am local time, and we quickly packed up and got moving. Within half an hour we had driven to the Mauna Kea visitor's center at 9,000ft, and got out to assess the road conditions up ahead. Now the original plan for our Hawaii trip was to rent mountain bikes in Hilo and bike the whole 40 miles and ~14,000 ft of elevation gain from sea level to the summit. But I had recently injured my knee and, since the doctor told me to rest it for 6 weeks, I figured such a biking trip would certainly injure it even worse. There was an access road to the summit for the astronomers at the Keck Observatory, but driving up for us was not an option because first, that would be lame, and second, the road supposedly required a 4WD vehicle and we had chosen the cheapskate 2WD rental car.

There was, however, a ~7 mile trail to the summit, and I figured as long as it wasn't too steep and we took a slow pace my knee should be okay. We started walking at 7:15am and were soon stopped by a person driving down (probably from the observatory).

"Did you guys sign in? Do you even have a map?" he asked in a way that suggested he didn't think we were prepared.

—Yes we have a good map, but didn't see a sign-in place because the visitor's center isn't open.

"Well that trail is tough, and there's no water, so be careful," he warned as he drove away. He must have had to bail out some unprepared hikers in the past, we figured. I'm sure if he had known our credentials he wouldn't have been so concerned.

We kept hiking and the trail was indeed steep, but not unmanageable. We started out in scrub land with occasional grass and bushes, but soon rose above the vegetation line into a landscape more similar to the moon or Mars than anywhere else in the US. It was amazing that just last night near Hilo we were driving through rainforests, but now we were hiking through a desert. I guess the clouds always come from the same direction, and dump all their moisture on one side of the mountain with nothing left for the other.

We took a rest break at 11,000ft and noticed how the altitude was starting to make us breathe harder. Matthew and I were quite familiar with the effects of altitude, and we all tried to force down as much food as possible, knowing we'd soon lose our appetites when we got higher up the mountain.

We were all still feeling good enough to keep going, so we pressed on up the mountain. At 12,000 ft we saw the access road to our side and a couple cars driving up. Amazingly, the road was actually paved here. Now I've heard that they pave the last 2 miles of road so vehicles don't stir up dust that might interfere with the telescopes. I think an untold motive is that they *don't* pave the bottom few miles so they can deter most of the tourists from driving up to the summit.

By the time we hit 13,000ft Jake had hit a glass ceiling and could go no higher. He had the classic signs of AMS (Acute Mountain Sickness)—pounding headache, fatigue, lack of hunger, and generally feeling terrible. Somehow Matthew and I were doing okay, but we knew Jake would only get worse unless we got him down immediately. We thought about hiking down, but the fastest way for Jake to get better would be to get him in a car already driving down. So we cut over to the road and started walking down.

Luckily the silver Jeep stopped and a nice couple from Texas offered us a ride. It looked pretty cramped so Matthew and I offered to hike down and meet Jake at the bottom, but they insisted there was room so we all squeezed in. We soon arrived back at the visitor's center and said goodbye to the couple after thanking them again. Jake was feeling a little better, but still not 100%. Luckily we still had another 9,000ft of increasingly oxygenated air to drive down through, so we got in the car and pushed on all the way to Hilo at sea level.

None of us had even considered leaving Hawaii without that summit, and we were already planning how we could make it work. We all decided Jake would recover the fastest with a good night's sleep in a hotel and good meal at a restaurant that night. Then we could trade in the car for a Jeep and drive up to our high point at 13,000ft and continue the hike to the summit (thus still climbing it honorably). Hopefully by resting at sea level and following the climb-high-sleep-low mantra of mountaineers we would all be better prepared the next day.

With our own new silver Jeep at hand Friday morning, we confidently drove back up to the visitor's center and onto the rough gravel road. We soon reached the 13,000ft mark and pulled off to the side to park. We could see the summit, but it still wouldn't feel right to drive up. Since the trail merged with the road soon anyways, we decided to just hike up the road. We were all feeling good and within an hour we reached the road's end at the Keck observatory. After another tenth a mile of trail hiking we reached the top and the roof of Hawaii! State highpoint number 49!

It felt like we were on Mars—the summit was on the rim of a huge caldera and all the rock was red and volcanic-looking. There wasn't a single sign of vegetation up there, only a few huge telescopes and a bunch of red rocks. Across the island we could see Mauna Loa, another volcano only 100ft shorter. Down on the coast Hilo was still covered in clouds, while the other side of the island looked like a desert under clear skies, and to the south side of the island there was smoke rising from some active lava flows.

Unfortunately we couldn't find snow anywhere. It was pretty chilly up top in the low-40s and windy, and had probably dropped below freezing that night. We've seen pictures of people skiing from the summit, but maybe that's only in the winter. We took a bunch of pictures on the top and stayed until we were too cold to last any longer without moving. With no regrets we walked back to the Jeep and drove back to Hilo, going from freezing-cold in the 40s F to the sweltering heat of 90F in less than an hour.

We had a few days to check out some other sites on the Big Island and I'd definitely recommend these destinations. On Friday and Saturday we went hiking in Hawaii Volcanoes National Park and got to see the glow of lava from a caldera (we weren't lucky enough to see any flowing lava, unfortunately).

On Saturday we drove to Ka Lae, the southernmost point in the United States. The best part about this point is the cliff jumping. We jumped off a forty foot overhanging cliff into the ocean many times and it's quite a thrill. The water is super clear and you can see all sorts of tropical fish (but watch out for a big tiger shark that lives there and the marlin that sometimes swim around). To get back to the top of the cliff we swam into a cave on the side of the cliff, and timed our swim with the incoming surf to push us to the top where we could scramble up through a rock tunnel to the surface. We also drove our Jeep out to Green Sands Beach to go camping, and down into the rainforests of Waipio Valley. There's awesome body surfing waves on the black sands beach of Waipio Valley as well.

50 Guadalupe Peak

Texas

8,749ft

Date climbed: Feb 25, 2012

Author: Eric

Accompanying climbers: Amanda Morris and Jake Osterberg

Every US state has a highest point—from Britton Hill (345ft) in Florida to Mt. McKinley (20,320ft) in Alaska—and Matthew and I set out to climb every last one of them. Our quest started in 1996 with Clingman's Dome, the highest mountain in Tennessee, and by February 2012 we had finished off 49 states. The lone remaining state was Texas.

We invited Jake and Amanda to join us in finishing off Guadalupe Peak, the highest mountain in Texas, and we all swooped into El Paso on Friday night, February 24th. We'd come from all over the globe—me and Matthew from Massachusetts, Amanda from Maryland, and Jake all the way from Africa. Saturday would be summit day, with Sunday as a backup just in case. Though, short of armed soldiers guarding the mountain, I don't think anything would have prevented Matthew and me from summiting Guadalupe Peak. Of all 49 other states we were only thwarted by one on our first attempt (Illinois), and that was because we'd tried to climb that highpoint on a day when the private property landowners had closed access.

Amanda had found a cheap deal on a hotel for our first night, so we all got a good night's rest in El Paso Friday night. Somehow Amanda had also used her cheapskate ninja skills to get a car rental for only $8 a day—just $2 per person! We piled in the Toyota Corolla at 7am Saturday morning and started heading east.

The terrain in West Texas is pretty flat, and with no trees, that means you can see a long ways. Guadalupe Peak was officially 100 miles away, but we could already see it 40 miles outside of El Paso. The peak has a huge 2,000ft cliff on the southern side called "El Capitan," and a long ridge extending north to the true summit and beyond. Early settlers used El Capitan as a landmark to tell they were on the correct route, and I can understand based on how prominent the mountain is compared to the flat landscape.

We pulled into the Pine Springs Visitor Center at 9:30am and went inside to quickly ask the rangers about trail conditions. One of my friends had climbed Guadalupe Peak over Christmas break and said there was over a foot of snow on the ground! The rangers assured us most of that had melted, except for a few patches left in the shade. It would be extremely windy, though, they warned. The previous day it was supposedly gusting to 70mph on the summit. Now that's just a gentle breeze by Mt Washington standards, but we still brought some eye protection and balaclavas just in case. The rangers were pretty impressed to hear this was our last state highpoint, and wanted to make sure we signed the log book at the summit.

We layered up with sunscreen, threw some food and water in our backpacks, and headed up the summit trail. In July it would have likely been pushing 100F already, but luckily in February it was a mere 50F at the trailhead. Amanda was already prepared for wind, wearing her ski goggles from the start. I bet she was the only person in the state of Texas wearing ski goggles that morning.

Unlike New England trails this one was well-graded, with all kinds of switchbacks. We soon caught up to and passed a church group hiking up the trail, and then passed a few Boy Scouts hiking down (they must have camped out that night). The trail started out on the south side of the mountain, but soon hooked over to the northeast side. Suddenly the barren desert turned into a lush forest of pine trees, with patches of snow sprinkled around in the shade. Somehow the north facing side of the mountain must provide enough shelter from the wind, and maybe allow more moisture for all those trees to grow. It didn't seem like we were in West Texas anymore—maybe more like Colorado.

The snow was a bit icy on the trail, but no problem as long as we were careful. The trail soon weaved back to the desert on the southern side of the mountain, and we passed a few more people coming down.

"You're almost there; 5 more minutes," they told us. This was Matthew's cue. He'd promised to carry Amanda the last tenth a mile to the summit and this was close enough. I took Matthew's backpack, Matthew replaced the pack with Amanda on his back, and we all continued up the trail. At 12:15pm we rounded the final turn and reached the summit! State highpoint number 50! It was too easy—there weren't even any armed soldiers guarding the top. There *was* a huge aluminum pyramid marking the summit, and that would have been the optimal place to stand during a lighting storm if you wanted to get struck.

I whipped out an American flag I'd bought just for this occasion and we got all sorts of patriotic pictures. My favorite is the one of me and Matthew both holding the flag while at the top of a big jump. Jake got all kinds of amazing pictures with his fancy DSLR camera, and we hung out at the top for several hours taking pictures, juggling (just me), signing the log book, and eating lunch.

"What do we do now that all the states are done?" I remember thinking. For the past 16 years we'd been working toward this goal but hadn't really thought what we would do next if we ever climbed all 50 highpoints. It was kind of like a void had opened up that I needed to fill with some new project. Luckily highpointing is a limitless endeavor—you can always make a new highpointing project to work on. I think the next logical step after completing the 50 states is to work on country highpoints. With ~195 country highpoints to climb, I don't think we'll have to be too concerned about filling another void any time soon.

Jake suggested there'd be good picture potential if we could drive out below Guadalupe Peak to catch the setting sun on the mountain, and that meant we probably had to get back to the trailhead before sunset. So we reluctantly packed back up and started heading down the trail.

We got back to the trailhead with plenty of time to spare and indeed took some awesome sunset pictures of Guadalupe Peak and El Capitan. I think we exactly reproduced the picture on one of the postcards sold at the visitor's center.

You might recall how most national parks have a "junior ranger" program where little kids can do scavenger hunt type tasks and earn a junior ranger patch and certificate. Well, at Guadalupe National Park even adults can get in on the action, and earn a "Senior Ranger" patch. Who wouldn't want a patch that said "Guadalupe National Park Senior Ranger" on it? Me, Matthew and Amanda couldn't resist, so the rest of that evening we spent diligently reading park brochures and answering questions about the park. We camped out at the Pine Springs campground that night, and early the next morning turned in all our paperwork, took the official park oath, and became official senior rangers (with the patches to prove it!).

We had a full extra day to kill in Texas, so we drove a little farther east and checked out the Carlsbad Caverns National Park. That cave is pretty spectacular and I'd highly recommend it if you're in the area and have already climbed Guadalupe Peak.

We spent our last night in El Paso after celebrating our success at a nice Mexican restaurant, before flying back home Monday morning.

You can check out all of our state highpoints at
http://web.mit.edu/matthewg/Public/high_points/,
and follow our progress on the country highpoints here
http://web.mit.edu/egilbert/Public/CountryHighPoints/

You can also Google *gilbertson mit*

EXTRA CREDIT

51 Point Reno

District of Columbia

409ft

Date climbed: April 30, 2011

Author: Matthew

Accompanying climbers: Keith Gilbertson, Amanda Morris, and Mrs. Morris

Just like Puerto Rico, the District of Columbia isn't a state. But it still has a highest point. Just in case it ever does become a state Eric and I decided to play it safe and visit the summit of our nation's capital: Fort Reno.

We flew into DC on a Friday night for an action-packed weekend. Our grandpa, Verdi Gilbertson, a World War II veteran, had been invited by the Honor Flight Program to visit the World War II Memorial. His name had been on the organization's waiting list for a couple of years and in early 2011 he was finally awarded a complimentary spot on an Honor Flight. He flew with 149 other WWII veterans and my Uncle Greg on a chartered flight from Sioux Falls, South Dakota to Baltimore to visit the memorials. Meanwhile our Dad drove 10 hours from Kentucky to meet them. Our plan was to rendezvous with them on Friday.

To add to the excitement, it was Amanda's birthday that weekend. What better way to celebrate than by visiting the highest point in DC?

After a nice time with our grandpa and uncle we bid them farewell on Saturday afternoon and headed towards the high point. We had done our Wikipedia research and found that Fort Reno is the highest natural point in DC. (The Washington Monument, at 555ft, doesn't count in our books since it's man-made.) We didn't expect too many glaciers, icefalls, crevasses, bergschrunds, or other obstacles, but I had input the coordinates on the GPS just to be safe.

We arrived at the parking lot without incident and began our ascent. As we walked the signature summit towers that I recognized from Google Images finally came into view. It was nice to see everything working out so smoothly: I had copied the GPS coordinates correctly, we had driven to the right place, and according to the signs it seemed that Wikipedia was indeed correct, and that we had reached the highest point in DC.

But as we approached the summit an uneasy feeling developed in my stomach. We abruptly—came upon a locked gate that separated us from the summit towers. In my research I thought I had recalled that you could go up in the towers. Maybe they're open during the week? No, some locals said they're never open.

Our dad snapped the customary jumping photos and we grabbed a few summit gravel pebbles but something was amiss. There was no sign that said we were standing on the highest point. As we headed down I began to worry. Had we timed it incorrectly? Was the gate only open on weekdays? Would we have to come back some other time to climb up in the tower to make it 100% official? Had we come to the wrong Fort Reno?

It appeared that there was some higher ground a hundred feet away so Eric ran over to take a look. We were searching for any kind of sign or USGS marker but couldn't find anything. It was apparent that the summit structure was a large underground reservoir, obviously man-made.

There's gotta be a marker somewhere around here, we thought. We walked through the soccer field and spotted a small nub a few hundred feet away. Could that be it? we wondered.

Eric scouted ahead and soon signaled a triumphant thumbs-up. I sprinted to join him. Dad, Amanda, and her mom followed.

Lo and behold there was a small brass marker cemented in the ground that read "National Park Service—In cooperation with the DC Association of Land Surveyors and the Highpointers Club—POINT RENO—Elevation 409ft—Highest Natural Point." We breathed a big sigh of relief that we had finally found it. I suppose that with a little more research we would have known what to look for.

Anyhow, this meant it was time to redo the summit photos that we had tentatively captured earlier. After triumphantly holding a summit rock I decided to up the ante. I triumphantly held a summit Amanda instead. But just holding her wasn't enough, I had to be in the air. I didn't jump too high but Eric and Dad captured a couple of good shots nevertheless.

After a big sigh of relief my watch alarm brought us back to reality: the parking meter time was up and we needed to return to the car. I believe Fort Reno is actually the only high point for which you need to feed a parking meter. But for just 45 cents I think the experience was worth it.

52 Cerro de Punta

Puerto Rico

4,393ft

Date climbed: March 20, 2011

Author: Matthew

Accompanying climbers: Amanda Morris, Mrs. Morris

Day 1

Even though Puerto Rico isn't a state, it is still part of the US and still has a highest point. Officially Puerto Rico is a commonwealth of the United States, but there has been growing discussion about the possibility of statehood. Just to be safe, me, Amanda, and her mom decided to climb Cerro de Punta — the roof of La Isla del Encanto (the Island of Enchantment) — in case Puerto Rico does become the 51st state.

The journey to Cerro de Punta began in Boston for me + Amanda, and in DC for her mom. We decided that Puerto Rico would be the perfect spring break location: it's warm, accessible, has a highest point, and we hadn't visited before. For $300 and 4hrs of flying you can actually get from Boston to San Juan more easily than the west coast. Plus, it has the feel of a different country but provides the comforts of the rest of the US: drinkable water, same currency, some English, and few people trying to rip you off. So we headed first to San Juan, the capital.

We discovered that the best way to get around Puerto Rico was by car, even though the driving is sometimes a little trickier than in the rest of the US. Often lanes vanish and merge without warning. Giant wheel-swallowing craters in the road lurk around every corner. And the mountain roads are so curvy and narrow that you need to honk before every curve so oncoming traffic can slow down.

After obtaining the camping permits at the Jardin Botanico in San Juan we drove west. Our plan was to camp the first night in Bosque Estatal de Rio Abajo (Rio Abajo State Forest), a rainforest area in the north-central region. We had decided upon the park after many hours of research and phone calls.

It's extremely difficult to find camping and parks information for Puerto Rico. There are many nice state forests and parks on the island, but there are very few official websites and details are slim. The best parks/camping guides we found were travel websites like letsgo.com and fodors.com, along with Wikipedia. We also used Google Earth to look at other peoples' pictures and view aerial photos.

To add to the difficulty there's also a huge amount of bureaucracy involved in obtaining a camping permit. You can't just show up to the park and pay for a campsite. You need to reserve a site more than a week in advance (even if it's the low season), pay in advance, and check-in for the campsites in San Juan, 50 miles away. Through hours of phone calls Amanda's mom had luckily identified two key people who enabled us to navigate through the system: Carmen and Darien. Throughout the parks system (DRNA) they were universally known just by first name.

When we arrived at the park we were supposed to get another permit at the guard house before it closed at 3:30pm, but arrived 4 minutes late and the ranger had already left. No problem, we thought, and continued driving towards the campground.

It felt like we had entered a different world. Palm trees and bamboo were everywhere. We had started out that morning in cold, brown Boston and were now in a sunny green rainforest in Puerto Rico. As it turned out we were the only campers in the park that evening so I'm not sure why all of the hassle with the permit was necessary.

To be ultralight we had brought one small two-person tent for Amanda + her mom, along with a tarp and mosquito net-shelter for me. The idea was that we could all hang out under the tarp if it rained. After hiking to an awesome little cave back in the jungle we were lulled to sleep by the sounds of hundreds of chirping Coqui tree frogs.

DAY 2:

We continued on our way towards Cerro de Punta the next day. First we stopped by the Arecibo Radio Telescope, the world's largest telescope. It's a massive 1000ft-diameter spherical aluminum reflector built over a sinkhole in the mountains. Next we headed south to Cabo Rojo, the southwestern most point in Puerto Rico, for some swimming at the beach. We camped that night at Lago Luchetti.

DAY 3:

Next day we explored another interesting state forest, Bosque Estatal de Guánica. It was rumored that the park was home to many tropical birds. By "many" I think they must have actually meant "6."

After Guánica it was time to put on our game faces and head to the high point. We turned north at Ponce and started the drive into the mountains. As we climbed the vegetation changed from cactus and dry little bushes to lush jungle with palm trees.

The roads became much more challenging. We turned east onto Highway 143, part of "La Ruta Panoramica," a highway that transects the island from west to east along the spine of La Cordillera Central. It reminds me of the Blue Ridge Parkway, except that the road is only about 1.5 lanes wide and you need to honk before all the blind turns to alert oncoming drivers. I've never seen a road that curvy in the rest of the US. Amanda's mom did an expert job at the helm.

Navigating in Puerto Rico is also a little tricky. Amanda had purchased a good highway map at Barnes and Noble's that we used to plan the trip. Unfortunately, though, not all the roads showed up on the map and some small windy roads appeared just as large as major highways, even though, as we found out, they were much slower. To supplement the highway map we had printed Google directions, which showed us the "fastest" route. However we soon discovered that it was much more relaxing to take the major highways rather than the curvy little roads suggested by Google, even though they might be a few minutes slower. I also brought my hiking GPS (a Garmin eTrex Vista HCx) on which I had loaded the topographic maps along with the roads. I think that my hiking GPS was more effective than a car GPS would have been because you can easily scroll across the map and you know which roads are hilly because you can read the topo contours.

Thus, using a combination of Google directions, a highway map, and a hiking GPS, and with Amanda's mom at the wheel we navigated our way through the interior Puerto Rican highlands. Soon we arrived at La Hacienda Gripiñas, a beautiful mountain lodge at the northern foot of Cerro de Punta, just outside of Jayuya.

The conventional route up Cerro de Punta is a 0.7mi hike along the steep service road that begins southeast of the mountain on La Ruta Panoramica. But that sounded too easy. I had read that there's also secret route that starts near Hacienda Gripiñas and climbs from the north. Google Maps' aerial photos confirmed that the roads on the north side ended within a mile of the summit, so I figured that even if you couldn't find the secret trail you could still bushwhack to the top.

But when we arrived at Hacienda Gripiñas it became apparent that the jungle would be far too slow to bushwhack through. We would need to find the trail. I asked the secretary at the check-in desk if he knew about the route. He said it existed but "you would need to hire a guide" to show you the route. Ha. To me "need to" is a relative term. The "need" to hire a guide made it sound even more intriguing.

But alas, it was not meant to be. There were only a few hours of daylight remaining and we would have 2000ft of climbing. Our consensus was to wait until tomorrow and drive 20 miles to the conventional route which starts southeast of the summit. It paid off because that afternoon we went for a little hike through a fruit plantation and found plenty of bananas and oranges that had been "knocked to the ground by the storm." It was like we were walking through the fruit aisle in the grocery store.

DAY 4: Summit Day

We got back on Highway 143 and headed towards Cerro de Punta. The clouds became denser as we climbed and we had little confidence that we would get a good view. Luckily I had marked on my GPS the parking lot for the summit trail, because there was no road sign. I had read on SummitPost that there's several radio towers on the summit, which is accessible by a steep service road. SummitPost had advised to leave the car in the parking lot and hike the road because it's so steep. As we began hiking three 4-wheel drive vehicles drove past us and headed up the road. But it turned out we had made the right decision because soon the vehicles encountered a very steep and slippery section and could proceed no farther. They had to back down about 0.25 mi of some of the steepest road in the country, which has a 15% average grade (3800ft-4250ft in 0.6mi).

We climbed upwards through the jungle and the radio towers emerged through the fog. With one final climb up some stairs to the top of a large mound we found ourselves on the summit of the Island of Enchantment. We could only see about 100ft through the thick clouds, but the view wasn't our objective. We basked in the glory of being the highest people on the island. From my research the closest higher mountain was La Grande Soufrière (4,869ft), the highest point on the French Island of Guadeloupe, 353 miles away.

We took the requisite jumping photos, but since Eric wasn't present there weren't any juggling pictures to be taken. Pretty soon the family who had been trying to drive up the mountain appeared, and it was time for us to relinquish the summit to them. We gathered a few of the requisite summit rocks and walked down to the car.

We spent the next 5 days seeing more of Puerto Rico, and here's our itinerary:

DAY 5: hiking in El Yunque National Forest, the only rainforest in National Park System.

DAY 6: Ferry to the Island of Culebra, snorkeling

DAY 7: Beaches on Culebra and snorkeling

DAY 8: Ferry back to Fajardo, explore Old San Juan

DAY 9: Fly back to BOS

Lessons learned:

1) You need a good GPS, map, and driver to drive in the mountains. We took the wrong road only about four times but Amanda and her mom didn't know because I acted like it was just part of the route.
2) There's plenty of good camping in Puerto Rico. You'll have the most success in getting permits if you call and talk to the key people such as Carmen or Darien.
3) Knowing Spanish really helps. I'd estimate that only 10% of people in the mountains speak English. Most people in the cities speak some English.

And that's how you climb the highest point in Puerto Rico.

NEXT PROJECT:
COUNTRY
HIGHPOINTS

*Included is one country highpoint report
from each continent
(except Antarctica)*

Africa: Jbel Toubkal

Morocco

13,671ft

Date climbed: Oct 12, 2012

Author: Matthew

A WARM WELCOME TO AFRICA

Honk honk honk! I had just entered into a two-lane roundabout and had mistakenly merged into the inner lane. The drivers were just simply vocalizing a little of their frustration with my driving techniques. I needed to take the next exit but cars were inches away, all around me, blocking my escape. It was bumper to bumper gridlock, with cars coming from seven different directions and wanting to go to seven different directions. The red brake lights from the car in front of me illuminated and I slammed on my brakes, narrowly averting disaster. The sun had just set and the lights from the beat-up old Peugeot in front of me glowed fiercely like two angry eyes.

I was in fight or flight mode, with my pulse and blood pressure sky-high, my eyes darting back and forth from one obstacle to another, muscles tensed and ready to react to the flowing, evolving chaos around me. Then brake lights of the car in front of me turned off and a gap opened up. OK, this is it, I thought, there's my gap to freedom, just a few milliseconds before that gap closes, just gotta take my foot off the brake and . . . sputter-sputter-sputter . . . lights off. "@#$%&!" I forgot that I was driving a manual!

It was just a pleasant drive through the friendly rush hour traffic of Marrakech.

§§§§§

A FEW DAYS EARLIER . . .

My goal for the trip was to climb up Jbel Toubkal (13,671 ft)—the highest point in Morocco—and I would have four days to do it. I had just come from the IROS robotics conference in Vilamoura, on the southern coast of Portugal, where I had presented a paper on my research. I've gotta admit, the prospect of a trip to Portugal and Morocco is very effective motivation to conduct good research.

A few days before the conference, Amanda and I had flown out to the Azores to climb the highest point in Portugal. Tropical Storm Nadine happened to be tearing through the islands at the time so the weather was not favorable for doing much of anything besides hanging out in the car. I ended up summiting by myself anyhow, in spite of the torrential rain, ferocious wind, and blinding fog.

Amanda did not come back from the trip empty-handed, however. She actually came back from the trip with a shiny ring on her finger because I proposed to her when I got back down to the trailhead. So, given the success of the previous week, I figured that just about anything could happen in Morocco and I'd still be ahead in the game of life.

I had flown out of Lisbon in the morning on a tiny little plane operated by Portugalia Airlines. I was sitting in seat 6B, which was actually a window seat because the seats were in a 1-1 configuration. The flight was especially scenic, because the pilots didn't bother closing the flight deck door during flight, and you could look out the cockpit window as we pierced through the clouds. You had to keep an eye on the pilot's altimeter, however, because there wasn't a flight attendant to tell you when you had reached the 10,000 ft electronics-off altitude.

Even though the closest big airport to Toubkal is Marrakech, I chose to fly into Casablanca instead because, given the flight schedules, it turned out to be faster and cheaper. My plan was to rent a car in Casablanca and drive to the Toubkal trailhead. I'd climb the mountain first and then, if there was extra time that week, I'd drive south and see how far I could get into the Sahara Desert. I mean, what's a few extra hours of driving in Morocco, anyhow? It can't be too much different than the US, can it?

MON VOITURE

After passing through the customs booth at the Casablanca Airport, I made a beeline for the car rental counters. People started to approach me from a few directions, offering taxis and car rentals in English. I was a little stunned at first, but I just smiled, told them "no, thank you," and continued on my way.

A nice gentleman helped me locate the Budget car rental counter and I presented to the agent a printout of my reservation. "Bonjour," the agent said. "Hello," I responded. I soon found out that many Moroccans fluently speak both French and Arabic and many also speak some English, especially in the touristy areas. "Welcome to Morocco," he said. Before long he gave some keys. A man who spoke no English escorted me to the car, and I strained to recall some of my French. "Aujourd'hui, il fait froid en les Atlas?" I asked. [Is it cold in the Atlas Mountains today?] I gave myself a big mental pat on the back for remembering all of that. I couldn't understand a word of his response, other than "Oui," but I just smiled and nodded.

We approached a small black Hyundai i10 and stopped. "Mon voiture?" I asked. "Oui," he answered. "Très bon, très bon," I said. I signed a few papers and started to load my stuff up in the car. I asked about how to get to Marrakech, and with a combination of a few English words and a lot of hand gestures he communicated the route.

I looked in between the driver's and passenger's seats and sure enough it was a stick-shift. But I was expecting that. Ever since early July, when I had known that I would be attending this conference, I had set my sights on Morocco and had started preparing. On Kayak.com's car rental site I quickly realized that basically all rental cars in Morocco were manuals. My Dad's Moroccan student Mustapha also gave me the advance warning that I'd need to know how to drive a "five speed."

To get some practice, Eric and I had decided to rent a manual in Boston and take it on a road trip up to Maine one weekend in September. After some thorough searching, it appears that, in the greater Boston area, there is exactly one manual-transmission car available for rent. It is an orange, circa 2000, Ford Focus from a Haitian-run company called Americar Auto Rental, located in the industrial area of Somerville. I won't discuss the details here, but it suffices to say that we got some pretty good manual training from the rush hour traffic of downtown Cambridge to the logging roads in rural Maine.

With this bit of experience in the psychological arsenal, along with some more practice driving a manual in the Azores a week earlier, I was actually, cautiously, looking forward to driving in Morocco. I hopped in the car and began to arm it with a few of my gadgets. I mounted to the windshield a Garmin car GPS that was packed with Moroccan road maps, pulled out a regular GPS loaded

197

with satellite photos of Marrakech and Casablanca, and unfolded a printed National Geographic highway map onto the passenger's seat. And most importantly, I unpacked some special music CDs to enhance the drive.

Man, it's hot in here, I thought, where's that A/C button? It was probably in the mid 90F's outside and I wiped the sweat off my forehead. As I scanned the dashboard, the rental car dude, as if he had read my mind, knocked on the window. I rolled it down and he said "no A/C" Ugh, I groaned to myself. This is not going to be pleasant. When I was reserving the car online I had noticed that there wasn't the little snowflake symbol that signified A/C. But I figured it must have just been a mistake. I mean, come on, this is Africa, is there a car on the continent that wouldn't have A/C?

Well if there is one African car without A/C, I certainly found it. And it might also be one of the few cars without a working 12V cigarette lighter. That was bad news because it meant that I couldn't charge up the GPS or my camera battery. Well that's pretty unfortunate, I thought, but at least I'll be able to mention that later on in the trip report.

DRIVING TO MARRAKECH

I waved goodbye to the rental car dude and slowly began to back the car out. I'm not gonna stall, not gonna stall, not gonna stall, I said to myself. But, sure enough, the car stalled. I had originally intended to convey to the rental car people the concept that I knew what I was doing. But I think that their confidence was waning. I managed to get the car started again and pulled out of the lot, with a big wave to the rental dude, and I was on my way.

Somehow I made a wrong turn early on, shortly after merging onto the big expressway, which added about ten miles. But soon I was back on track and my confidence began to build. It's nice because the Casablanca airport is right next to a straight, smooth, major expressway with a speed limit of 120 kph (75 mph). There are quite a few tolls, but minimal traffic. Plus, it's fun to accelerate from 0 to 75 mph in a manual. The buildings of Casablanca faded in the rearview mirror and I was on the open road, blasting through the desert. I popped in Born to be Wild, rolled down the windows and maxed out the volume on the speakers.

One hundred forty exhilarating miles later the road signs for Marrakech began to appear. All the road signs in Morocco are in Arabic and French so I could basically figure out what was going on. But I knew that as I neared the heart of Marrakech things would get trickier and I would be relying on the GPS. Unfortunately, however, by now the GPS batteries were almost drained after a few hours of uncharged operation. This not good, I thought to myself, I'm going to need that thing to get through this city.

Slowly the speed limit decreased, the roundabouts increased in frequency, and Marrakech came into view. I needed some food for the next four days so I pulled into a big shopping center-looking plaza near the edge of town just as the sun began to set. I soon came to realize that Marrakech is a very modern, well-developed city and you can buy just about anything you need. It was nothing like the dusty desert outpost I had imagined. I picked up an extra USB/12V car adapter at an electronics store that would hopefully solve the GPS power problem. And I stumbled across a super-awesome store called Marjane that is basically the Moroccan equivalent of a Wal-Mart Supercenter. They've got food, clothing, and electronics just like the Wal-Mart in Berea, Kentucky. But the shopper demographic is a bit different, to say the least.

The food shoppers were all women dressed in traditional, colorful headscarves. Everyone was pushing to get the worker to weigh their vegetables and print out the price tag sticker. I noticed that I was one of the only guys buying bananas and apples at Marjane today. I picked up almost all the items on my list, from fruit to cereal to sandwich supplies, and a red hat and a ceramic cereal bowl to boot. Wow, that was much easier than I expected, I thought to myself. Morocco is my kind of country.

PLUNGE INTO PANDEMONIUM

But that feeling didn't last long. The sun had set, traffic had picked up, and with only a few days of practice driving a manual under my belt, I wasn't exactly looking forward to stop and go driving in bumper-to-bumper traffic. And did I mention that there were hills too? I started the car, turned on some music, took a deep breath, and plunged into the chaos.

It was scary at first, especially at the roundabouts. But soon I began to realize that my car had an invisible force-field around it. It must have, because there's no other way that my car could have escaped that pandemonium without a scratch. Another possible explanation could be as follows: Moroccan drivers can tolerate much closer proximity to other cars than American drivers can, but they avoid accidents because they go slow and everyone just takes their turn.

At one particularly crazy roundabout, I felt that there was absolutely no possible way of escaping Marrakech without getting hit. I seem to recall that "Stairway to Heaven" on my CD was playing at the time. I wonder how police deal with accidents around here, I thought to myself. Would the police speak English? Would they blame the tourist for the collision? Or can I find someone else on the street who can drive my car for me?

Somehow, as the faithful GPS pumped out its last few of joules of energy, I reached the edge of town and turned into the mountains. Success! I had made it through Marrakech! With my hands still shaking, I played around with the connector cable and finally got it charging again. It said I had an hour to the trailhead. Just a little longer, I thought, and it'll just be me and the mountain, and all the variables will be known.

For the next few miles I came to realize that the dangers of driving in Morocco are not restricted to the cities; the country roads have their own dangers at night. I found myself dodging one motorbike after another. Unfortunately, the roads have no shoulders, the motorbikes have no lights, and the roads have no illumination, so it's nearly impossible to see motorbikes taking up half your lane, especially when the oncoming cars forget to dim their high beams. But, compared with stop-and-go city traffic, this danger was tolerable, I just slowed down.

MOHAMMAD #1

The road climbed through Bou Ouglas, Tahnaout, and Asni and the traffic fizzled out. Pretty soon the road steepened up, narrowed, and started to wind up through the hills. Now this was my kind of driving, I thought. I was racing around corners, shifting, and slowing down through the villages. I almost didn't want the road to end but pretty soon I found myself in the village of Imlil. My GPS said the road kept going, and I had read that the trail actually started in a village named Armd, but I couldn't find the correct turn off. (Aside: "Armd"? "Jbel"? You've gotta like those unpronounceable place names.)

I cruised back and forth through town a few times in search of the turnoff and soon a small crowd began to gather nearby. An old, bearded, white-robed man with a cane approached my window. He only had a few teeth but I heard him ask "You go to Toubkal?"

"Yes, I want to climb Toubkal," I answered. "Is this the road to Armd?"
"No, the road ends here, you park here. Then walk to Armd."

I paused to think about it. There were a couple of other cars parked in the little lot, one with an Italian license plate. Surely they're tourists like me who are also climbing Toubkal. If they parked here it must be the right spot. But my GPS said the road kept going, which bugged me. I couldn't see any more road, and in the darkness the mountains looked pretty steep around me, so I figured that the dude must be right and this is the end of the line.

"Can I park here for one day?" I asked.
"Yes, one day is 20 dirhams," he answered.
Hmm, that's only about two dollars, I calculated, so that's a pretty good deal. "OK, I'd like to park here for one day."
"Great," he answered, "my name is Mohammad."

Awesome, I thought, his name will be hard to forget. "I'm Matthew." (Editor's note: he shall henceforth be referred to as "Mohammad #1" in this story.)

I backed into the parking spot, pulled the handbrake, and turned off the car. Whew, I let out a big sigh of relief. Now the rest of the trip would be under my own power, and I won't have to worry about stalling the car or hitting anything.

I was famished, so I opened up the trunk and started scarfing down some food. Mr. Mohammad #1 came over and started watching my every move. It was a bit creepy at first, but I came to the conclusion that he was simply curious. This brand new rental car, this flashy American gear, this strange looking food, this strangely-garbed foreigner. As I ate my power dinner of cereal and powdered milk, I offered him the box of cereal. He gladly took it, and began to scarf along with me.

"Where you stay tonight?" he asked.
"Oh, I'll hike for a few hours, then camp," I said. "I have a tent, see." And I showed him my brand new ultralight tent.
"Camp? No, it is dark, you should stay here. There is a nice hotel in town."
"No, I have a torch, I can hike." And I flicked on my headlamp.
"OK, OK. But it is very far to Toubkal tonight and very cold." True, I was still wearing shorts and a t-shirt even though I could see my breath.

"I have a jacket and warm clothes." I produced my fleece and polypro and he nodded in satisfaction. "And I will run up the mountain. I like to run."

"Do you have a map? The path is too difficult to find at night."

"Yes I have a GPS." And I showed him the GPS, loaded with the satellite photos.

And with that, Mohammad #1 came to the conclusion that he was dealing with a crazy person who could not be reasoned with, and stopped imploring me to stay in town tonight. We stood there, together, munching on some Moroccan granola, and I began to get the feeling that Mohammad #1 was a trustworthy fellow. He told me that I could either pay now or after I returned. I said I would only be one night, and he said I could pay him tomorrow when I returned.

Attracted by all the excitement, a few other locals came over and started milling around. One dude approached me, and in perfect English, told me he was a guide. He said he was born nearby and was Berber. I told him my plans to climb up tonight and he smiled. I was ready to defend my plans, as I had to Mohammad #1, but he just nodded his head and told me how to get to the start of the trail. He and a couple of other guides were curious about my GPS and they gathered around as I showed them some of the satellite photos.

As Mohammad #1 continued munching on the granola he watched me intently while I packed up my bags. As trustworthy as he seemed, I didn't want him to see the laptop that I was leaving in the car. I diverted his attention while I slipped the laptop under the seat. "Wow, look at all those stars," I said. Many more here than in Boston.""Yes, many stars," he said. I sensed that he probably didn't even know what I was talking about. He had probably never spent much time in a big city. I mean, stars are stars, how can it be different when you're in the mountains or in the city?

I grabbed my pack, closed the doors and locked it up. I was ready to roll. "How will I find you tomorrow, Mohammad?"

"Just ask in town and I will come," he answered. I guessed that he probably wasn't the only person in town named Mohammad, but it's a small enough town that people would probably be able to guess which Mohammad I was talking about. I waved goodbye and started up the path. Little did I know that I had forgotten to roll up the passenger-side window.

MOHAMMAD #2

I quickly came to the conclusion that I had been duped. The "trail" was actually just a plain old road. It was rough and steep, but the car could have made it up without any problem. It was nothing compared with some of the rough roads Eric and I had driven in Ontario or Labrador. I marched up the road, frustrated that I had taken Mohammad's word and hadn't trusted the GPS. Was he trying to trick me, so that he could get my parking money? Or was he genuinely worried that I couldn't handle the Moroccan gravel? Either way, though, I wasn't going to turn back so I just kept on climbing.

It felt slow to walk and, energized by the cereal + powdered milk, I decided to start running. Soon I removed my shirt to cool off. I hadn't seen a sign for Toubkal in over half an hour so I was starting to get skeptical that this was the correct route. I passed right in front of a motel and saw a guy standing outside. I'll refer to him as Mohammad #2. "Hello," I said, "is this the trail to Toubkal?"

"Yes, but it is too difficult. You can't do it tonight. My hotel is very nice and you should stay here tonight."

I noticed a few other westerners milling around inside but I would not be distracted. I really wanted to say "look, Mohammad #2, I sincerely appreciate your hospitality, but I won't be staying in your hotel tonight. I've already discussed this with Mohammad #1 back in town. Can you tell me if I'm on the right trail?" But I held my tongue and told him "no, thank you, I'll keep hiking and camp in my tent tonight." Then I resumed running. He began yelling in French but I just kept going and didn't look back. I guess it isn't a spectacle he sees every day: a shirtless foreigner running up this dusty trail, by himself, at 9pm, with just a tiny backpack. I'd read that most people are guided and take 2-3 days round-trip. Not to mention, mules usually carry their gear, as I would later discover.

CLOSE ENCOUNTERS

A little higher up, soaked in sweat, I needed to shed some more layers to keep from sweating so I took off my shorts. I hadn't seen a single car all night, so I figured there'd be absolutely no chance that anyone would see me. Even if someone did, they'd still think I was wearing some tight shorts. But lo and behold, I soon heard a car rumbling around a curve in front of me, and I ducked behind a boulder. Morocco's a pretty liberal Muslim country, right? Nobody would mind, would they? The driver had spotted me, and pulled up slowly alongside me.

"Ça va?" the driver asked. [What's up?]
"Ça va bien, merci," I answered. [I'm fine, thanks.] The car paused for a moment. Then it slowly rolled away. I can only imagine what the driver must have been thinking. I kept running and soon I could see the lights of Armd twinkling upon the hill. I ran though another little village and for a brief moment I could see some more westerners hanging out inside a hotel, presumably waiting until the morning to start their hike. Someone started to yell something in French to me, but I just kept running. There was plenty of mountain left to climb, and no time for chatting.

Finally the road fizzled out and I met a heavily-graffiti'ed sign reading (in Arabic & French): "You are entering into the protected zone of Toubkal National Park." All right, I thought, now I'm making some progress. It was a pleasant night for a run and with the cereal + powdered milk still burning in my belly I picked up the pace. The sky was clear and cool and I could see the Milky Way stretching over me from one horizon to the other.

Suddenly I spotted a pair of orange eyes staring back at me from about 50 feet away. I froze for a moment. But I couldn't think of any animal that I'd need to be afraid of in Morocco, so I just kept running. It was probably a little cat or something. Higher up, I saw more and more eyes every few minutes. They never made a sound, just stared back in silence, unaware that, due to the glare of their eyes, their stealthy gaze wasn't actually that stealthy. I crossed an irrigation channel and spotted a few large toads hopping around. Of course I had to pick one up. I discovered that Moroccan toads are basically the same as Kentucky toads: their body shape is almost exactly the same; they also try to pee on you if you pick them up, and the only difference is their coloring.

By about 10pm my energy started to fade and it was time to activate campsite-finding-mode. But it wasn't exactly the best place to set up at tent. In the dim light I could tell that there was a steep hill to my left and basically a cliff on my right. I saw a couple of lights in the distance, and wondered if they could be the Toubkal Refuge. I had read that there was a really nice stone hut along the way where most people stay before their climb. But my GPS indicated that it couldn't be the refuge, it was still four miles away.

As I approached, I realized that it was actually a little mini-village. Hmm . . . maybe I can just camp here, I thought. As I turned around, trying to locate the trail, a tall shadow emerged from the darkness and I gasped in surprise.

"Is this the trail to Toubkal?" I asked. "No, this is the marabout," a man said. He pointed to the left. "That is the trail to Toubkal." "OK, merci," I said. I didn't know exactly what a marabout was, but is seemed to be some sort of mini-mosque or tomb. Also known as: a place where you can't camp.

FROM FIVE-STAR TO INFINITY-STAR

I kept climbing and soon began to consider just sleeping right on the trail since it was the only flat spot and I was exhausted. But I ruled that out because, and I could tell from the droppings on the trail, there was a lot of mule traffic and they'd probably be walking through pretty early to carry peoples' packs up the mountain. I climbed a little higher and found a pseudo-flat spot that could possibly fit the tent. I was just about to unpack when I recalled Eric's Zeroth Law of backpacking: wherever you set up your tent, there's always a much better campsite just a few hundred feet away, which you'll discover in the morning. It was a law that we'd observed and validated very frequently on the Appalachian Trail.

So, to beat old Eric at his game, I dropped my pack and hiked a little further. Sure enough, after another hundred feet I spotted a little building and a beautiful flat spot right next to it. I didn't know what the building was for, but the big steel door seemed to be locked, so I figured nobody would bother me. Exhausted, I set up the tent and prepared my bed. It was already in the lower 40F's and, with my 45F degree bag I knew it'd be a long, sleepless night. I had packed ultralight on this trip to avoid needing to check any luggage.

In an effort to conserve every last calorie of heat, I pulled out one of the tricks I had discovered on the AT. I emptied my backpack and stuffed my lower third into the pack. My theory was that it would provide an extra tiny bit of insulation for my legs. Unfortunately, it did not. Just after I turned off my headlamp, I heard the creaky steel door swing open and someone started walking around. I was too tired to panic. "Hello," I said from inside the tent, "can I sleep here? I'm very, very tired."

"Oh yes, no problem," a man answered. "Sleep well." "Thank you, sir!" And with that, I collapsed onto my makeshift pillow of shoes and granola bars. It had been a long day, starting at 5:30am at the 5-star Tivoli Marina Resort Hotel in Vilamoura, Portugal, and ending here at midnight on a cold dusty ledge perched high in a canyon in Morocco's rugged Atlas Mountains, in the earth's ultimate hotel—the Infinity Star Hotel.

CLIMBING TOUBKAL

Seven sleepless hours later, I rose to the beep of my alarm. With adrenaline pumping, I was ready to do battle with the mountain. From my GPS I could see that I was only three miles line-of-sight from the summit, but given the ruggedness of the trail, I knew that could take a while. I quickly packed up my stuff and started running. On the way up I passed a few big white tents and saw some local Moroccan fellows preparing breakfast. They looked to be guides; their clients were probably still asleep.

One guide was on his way down, leading a donkey heavily laden with clients' backpacks. I snapped a quick photo. "Hey, no photos!" he yelled at me. "I just got a picture of the mountain, not you," I told him. He must have been superstitious about being photographed. I kept running, and stashed my overnight gear behind a boulder. It was below freezing, but I had stripped down to shorts and a t-shirt to keep from sweating while I ran. I got quite a few stares from guides on their way down—I guess there aren't many people who solo the mountain clad so lightly.

By 8am I had reached the Toubkal Refuge, a spectacular three-storied stone fortress perched near the top of the valley. I had seen photos online, but was still astounded at the enormity of the entire complex. It looked like an ancient stone temple built to serve the climbers of Toubkal. The refuge is situated at about 10,500ft, at the point where the trail steepens up and the real climbing actually begins. A few clients and guides were milling around, getting ready, but it looked like most of the climbers had already started up the mountain. I took a quick sip of water, scarfed down some food, and kept running. By now, the summit was within reach, and I knew I would make it back down to the car with plenty of time to spare. The reason I was running was that I still hoped I'd have enough time this week for my road trip foray into Western Sahara.

SAHARAN SNOW

The trail steepened up and I began to slow down. Headache. Shortness of breath. No desire to eat. Yep, I thought to myself, there's the altitude sickness. But it wasn't too bad yet, I knew I just had to get up and down quickly and then I'd be fine. I passed about thirty people and finally emerged into the glorious sunlight. By now I was walking on snow, and judging by the frozen puddles it must have dropped well into the mid 20F's overnight, but in the dry, thin, low thermal-inertia desert air the sun warmed me rapidly.

I traversed a few small snowfields. No big deal compared with the Sierras of California, I thought, but wait a minute, this is Africa! Can there really be snow in North Africa? I ate some just to be sure, and came to the crunchy conclusion that, indeed, this was genuine, good old-fashioned snow.

The Atlas Mountains and northern Morocco began to unfold beneath me. To the north was a thin sea of clouds blanketing Marrakech and distant Casablanca, and in every other direction, rugged mountains extended to the horizon. I spotted a few bushes in an oasis far below, but this was desert and basically the only other living things on the mountain were me, some goats, and my fellow hikers.

A few steps later, at an elevation of 13,671ft, I was on the roof of Morocco. Well, I wasn't actually on the roof of Morocco, just the highest "natural point." The actual highest point in Morocco was located on the top of the large twelve foot tall pyramidal steel structure straddling the summit. And of course I had to climb it. Luckily it was built Moroccan-tough and had clearly held the body weight of many climbers over the years.

Sure, I could climb it, but the trickier part would be getting a photo of myself on the top. I was currently the only person on the summit so I would have to use the 10-second delay on my camera. But it didn't look like ten seconds was going to give me enough time for me to get from the camera's trigger to the top of the steel summit jungle gym structure. To find the optimal climbing technique, I climbed the structure a few times until I felt that I could do it pretty fluently. Then I pressed the camera trigger, sprinted, climbed up, looked at the camera, and smiled. Darn it! It had already captured. I repeated the little skit five more times until I finally got a photo of myself on the top.

FORGING THE FELLOWSHIP

Pretty soon other people began to arrive until it became a veritable party on the summit: Germans, Spaniards, and then three fellows about my age—the only other young people I had seen on the mountain. People began waiting in line to pose for photos on the summit.

"Nice view today, huh?" I asked the three guys, guessing that they probably understood English. "Yeah," one fellow responded. I was impressed because he wearing shorts and a t-shirt. I got the sense that these boys were tough. "But it's a circus up here! Those people are taking forever—let's get a photo and get outta here."

I took a photo for them and they reciprocated the favor. "Where are you guys from?" I asked.

"Poland, what about you?
"US."
"Cool, I haven't seen any other Americans up here."

We struck up a conversation and I found out that their names were Witek (pronounced 'Vitek'), Andrzej (pronounced 'Andrey'), and Anton (pronounced, well, like 'Anton'). Witek and Andrzej had flown to Fès, on the north coast of Morocco, a few weeks ago and had hitchhiked around the country, rendezvousing with Anton in Marrakech a few days ago. Then they had hitchhiked to the Toubkal trailhead. Anton had to fly back to Poland in a few days but Witek and Andrzej were off the leash. They would go where the wind took them for as long as they liked. I told them my story and how I had gotten from Vilamoura to Toubkal over the past 30 hours. "Yeah, and after this I'm planning to drive south into southern Morocco and maybe see if I can climb the highest point in Western Sahara. It's a long drive though."

Then it hit me. To get to the Western Sahara high point I still had another 24 hours of driving, according to Google Maps—way too much to accomplish by myself in the next four days, especially considering the fact that I needed to be back in Casablanca in three days for my flight back to the States. But these three fellows had no agenda. Like me, they were searching for adventure too. And having a ride would allow them to cover a lot more ground. Meanwhile, my little Hyundai had three empty seats. And travel is way more fun when you've got a friend to share it with . . .

"Would you guys like to join me?" I asked. Witek looked to Andrzej, Andrzej looked to Anton, and they began deliberating in Polish. They thought about it for a few minutes. It was a big decision, one that would shape the course of our adventure for the next three days. The four of us stood at a crossroads. After a few minutes, Andrzej said "Ok, we'd like to join you!" with a big smile. And so our mutual adventure began on top of the highest point in Morocco.

Andrzej's knee was causing him problems, so Witek and I ran ahead to dismantle their tents, which they had pitched at the refuge below, while Anton stayed behind to help Andrzej down. As I talked with Witek on the way down, I got the feeling that the decision to combine forces had been a good one. I could tell that the four of us would get along well together.

As we hopped over boulders, passing about fifty other people, I learned that Witek worked as a window cleaner for tall buildings in Poland. He was fearless of heights. Andrzej worked as an independent investor. The two had saved up for this trip for a long time and would return to Poland when either the money ran out or they stopped having fun. Meanwhile, Anton worked as a firefighter and had managed to carve out a week of vacation for this trip.

Down at the refuge, we dismantled the tents and were joined by Anton and Andrzej a little while later. We enjoyed a hearty meal at the refuge and discussed the plans. They were on board for the plan to drive to Western Sahara, and offered to help drive. Without a license, Witek would only be able to provide moral support, but Anton and Andrzej had grown up driving manual-transmission cars, so I was looking forward to some relaxation in the backseat while they navigated the urban obstacle courses ahead of us. We still had a long hike to the trailhead so we quickly packed up and bid farewell to the refuge.

SMELLY SOCKS FOR SILK

A few small trailside shops had opened up, selling apples and souvenirs from the High Atlas. The apples were too hard to pass up, so we stopped and Andrzej bartered for a bunch of them. He managed to get them for half the original price, an impressive feat. But that was only a prelude—he had his sights set on one of the hand-woven rugs.

"This is very pretty, I want to get this one for my mother," he said to the gentleman who owned the shop, whom we'll refer to as Mohammad #3.
"300 dirhams," Mohammad #3 said.
"300?!" Andrzej replied, "100, I'm just a poor student."
"250."
"I only have 150 in my wallet. Please sir."
"200."
"Ok, how about two for 300? My friend Witek wants to get one for his mother too. I'll give you my last 150 and so will Witek."

Mohammad #3 thought about it. "No, 400 dirhams for two," he said.

"Please sir." Andrzej clasped his hands together and kneeled down as if in deep prayer. "Look into my eyes," he said softly, removing his sunglasses, "would these be the eyes of dishonest man? Please sir, this is for my poor mother, and for Witek's poor mother."

"OK, 300 for two," Mohammad #3 said with a big smile.

Andrzej gave Mohammad #3 a big bear hug and we all shook Mohammad #3's hand. It had been a valiant effort for Mohammad #3, but this time Andrzej had been victorious. Andrzej opened his wallet and, perhaps not completely inadvertently, as he pulled out his "last 150," he revealed five or so hundred-dirham bills that had been hiding. "Oops, I didn't see those!" he said. And the five of us—Mohammad #3 included—erupted with laughter.

We continued on, munching our apples triumphantly. Farther down Anton decided to try his own luck with bargaining. We waited outside a shop while he marched into battle. "Man, what's taking him so long?" Witek said impatiently after a few minutes. "Anton!"

Anton emerged with a huge smile on his face. "I traded them two of my dirty wool socks for this!" It was a beautiful silk handkerchief. "It's for my girlfriend." As we looked at the colorful piece of fabric we marveled at how two foul socks could fetch something so beautiful. "I guess socks are hard to come by around here," I said.

DASH TO THE CAR

As we resumed our descent Andrzej groaned in agony. "It's my knee, guys; I'm going to have to take this slowly. I hurt this many years ago and it comes back sometimes on big hikes." Witek and I took turns carrying Andrzej's pack in order to ease his pain. His knee was already wrapped up in athletic tape and unfortunately there wasn't much more that we could do for him, short of carrying him down.

Then I had an idea. "How about I run down, get the car, and then drive up to meet you guys?" I suggested. The mile or two of road walking I had done the previous night, I had concluded, would have been completely drivable after all. I was a little upset with Mohammad #1 for telling me that my car couldn't get any higher, and getting me to park in Imlil instead of Armd.

"Ok, that sounds good," Andrzej said. He was definitely looking forward to sparing his knee any unnecessary miles. And with that, I took off and kicked it into gear.

A few miles later I was down to the road, finally able to see what I had run by in the dark last night. The road was perched high up on the side of a canyon, with an awesome one-lane no-guardrail bridge leading to a village perched high up on the other hillside. It was like a bridge out of Lord of the Rings, minus the lushness of Middle Earth.

I consulted the GPS and decided to take a little shortcut in order to shave off a few miles. What started out as a trail quickly deteriorated into nothing and I found myself bushwhacking down an ever-steepening hillside. Soon the bushes stopped and I was faced with almost twenty foot cliff. Darn it! I bushwhacked a little farther to the side and the steepness eased slightly. The GPS, meanwhile, proclaimed that I was just a tenth-mile line-of-sight from the car, tantalizingly close. So I took a deep breath and carefully downclimbed the final twenty feet, holding onto bushes. A few villagers had noticed me and stared in bewilderment as I emerged from the bushes. But I kept running and triumphantly crossed the finish line to my car.

Just then Mohammad #1 appeared out of nowhere. "Hey Mohammad!" I said, "I made it up to the top!" He smiled but then directed my attention to a rug covering my car's passenger window. He removed the rug, and to my horror there was no glass. I immediately froze in shock and questions raced through my mind. Someone had broken into my car? Geez, they probably took everything, my laptop, food, extra gear. I wonder how much the rental company is going to charge for this. I wonder if they did anything else to the car? Mohammad #1, sensing my escalating blood pressure, rushed to reassure, "no, it's not broken! You forgot!"

And indeed, I noticed then that the window was simply rolled down, and I had just forgotten to roll it up. I opened all the doors and confirmed that everything was still intact, including my laptop. Whew, I breathed a big sigh of relief, and gave Mohammad a hearty handshake. As I reached for 20 dirhams to pay Mohammad, he gently suggested that he might deserve a little more, and pointed to the window. I nodded, and gave him 40. Hopefully he'll maintain the same level vigilance in the future watching other foreigners' cars, I thought to myself.

THE FELLOWSHIP OF THE HYUNDAI

I fired up the car and began to pull out of Mohammad's little dirt lot. "Wait, have some dinner!" I heard someone shout, "We have many nice places to stay! You need a good sleep tonight and we have many nice rooms!" I put on a big smile. "Sorry, but I've gotta go, I need to pick up my friends."

I waved farewell to Mohammad #1 and turned onto the rough road that wound up the mountain. The road turned out to be equivalent in roughness to a typical Maine logging road. But there were two important differences. First, I was driving a manual transmission car, for the fifth day in my life. And second, there were some obstacles. Little kids, descending the road on their way home from school, noticed a foreigner at the wheel of the car and decided it'd be fun to scare the driver. They took turns jumping into the road in front of me. I'd slam on the brakes, try to start, stall the car, yell in frustration, and repeat. Finally an adult shooed them out of the way and I waved in thanks.

At last, a few hundred feet higher, Anton and Witek appeared from around a corner, with Andrzej hobbling behind them. He looked exhausted. "Y'all want a ride?" I yelled. I parked the car and we started packing it up. "It'll be kind of tight," I said, "you'll all still up for this little road trip?" "Definitely!" they answered. "We'll make it fit." Andrzej collapsed into the front seat, relieved that he wouldn't have to walk another meter. Miraculously we managed to cram four smelly dudes and all their gear into the miniscule Hyundai i10.

"Can I drive?" Anton asked me.
"Absolutely," I answered, "I was hoping you'd ask that."

He threw it into reverse an expertly turned the car around. I breathed a big sigh of relief that there was now a more competent person at the helm of our little ship. He drives manual-transmission fire trucks around Warsaw, I thought, so no wonder it's a piece of cake for him to drive this little car!

"Let's go boys, we're outta here," Anton said, shifting into first gear. We had successfully climbed Toubkal, but the Moroccan adventure had just begun.

Asia: Jabal ad Dukhan

Bahrain

440ft

Date climbed: Jan 19, 2010

Author: Matthew

It's not too often that you find yourself in Bahrain. I therefore felt that I needed to take full advantage of my 11 layover in this Persian Gulf Kingdom on my way back from India.

I was to arrive at 11:00pm local time in the capital Manama, and my flight left for London at 10:00am the next morning, giving me 11 hrs on the ground. I could either try to sleep at the airport or go for the gold and climb the highest point instead. It was a clear choice. Bahrain is an island country only about 20 miles long, so I didn't think the high point would be too tough to get to.

As soon as I got off the plane I exchanged dollars for dinars and approached a taxi driver. They all wore traditional white Arab headdresses. "I'd like to go to Jabal ad Dukhan," I said, and pointed to the high point on my map.

Taxi dude: "Why do you want to go there," he asked with a thick accent, "there's nothing there."
Me: "I want to climb the highest mountain in Bahrain"
Taxi dude: "It's dark, you can't climb it and you can't see anything. There are no hotels there."
Me: "I've got a light, see" and I turned on my headlamp.

He and the other drivers couldn't fathom why a young foreigner would show up in the middle of the night and want to climb a dusty hill in the middle of nowhere. Mostly everyone else at the airport was a well-dressed businessman twice my age. Eventually we agreed on a price of 30 dinars and it was a deal. We sped off into the night.

Driving through Manama felt like driving through Las Vegas or LA; sleek tall buildings with fancy lights, palm trees everywhere, and the only cars on the road were BMW's, Mercedes, and Porsches. After 20km we reached the boondocks of Manama and soon after I could see some hills through the darkness. "That's Jabal ad Dukhan," the driver said. I told him to wait here and I'd be back in half an hour. I knew he wouldn't go anywhere because I hadn't paid him yet. I jumped out the door and bolted towards the tallest of the hills. I didn't even need a headlamp because the lights from the city reflected brightly on the white rocks and sand.

I climbed up a steep little 300ft hill and found myself on the roof of Bahrain. No sweat. The city glowed peacefully in the distance. The temp was a nice 20C with a little breeze. I started to snap a few victory pictures but then noticed something peculiar a half mile down below. I could still see the taxi but a big jeep had pulled up next to it and three people got out. They looked to be questioning the taxi driver.

Uh, oh I thought, I'm guessing that they're not too happy with me being here. I remember the taxi driver saying something about a "defense area" nearby and come to think of it the lights on the other side of the road look to be those of an airbase. I knew I would probably get questioned when I was down but since they couldn't see me up here I might as well get a few pictures (without the flash) and enjoy the scenery for a minute or two. I took a quick glance at the beauty and grabbed a few rocks as souvenirs then headed down to face the music.

But then I started thinking about my pictures. Man, it would be quite a shame if they made me delete all my pictures, or worse, if they confiscated my camera. I had some pictures from the Taj Mahal that hadn't been backed up yet. Plus, I needed proof that I had made it to the top of Bahrain.

So I stopped for a second and made a critical move: I removed the small XD memory card with all my pictures and put it in my pocket. The camera has a built-in memory with a 10-picture capacity, so I took two dummy pictures of me on the top, so if they looked they could see that the pictures were benign and didn't threaten Bahrain's security.

I hopped over a few oil pipelines then made it back to the taxi. For the last two hundred feet I walked coolly. Out of my peripheral vision I saw a tough-looking guy dressed in camo approaching me from the side. I could probably outrun him but didn't want to try. He looked like a Bahraini military guy. I kept a calm beeline to the taxi but he reached me first and demanded "PASSPORT." Uh oh, this isn't good. I handed my passport over, and he said "Wait here." He walked with my passport over to a small guardhouse nearby and radioed something on the walkie-talkie.

I sat in the taxi and nervously awaited my fate. When I asked the driver he said "No problem, no problem. Only a few minute." That wasn't very reassuring.

After 20 minutes the guard appeared again and jumped in the front seat of the taxi. He ordered something in Arabic to the driver and we silently drove to another nearby guard station. "What's going on," I asked. "No problem, no problem," the taxi driver replied. Two other military guards dressed in camo opened the spiky steel gate. And closed it behind us. He told me to come into the office and bring my stuff.

I walked in and sat down. The door slammed shut behind me. The five guards looked down at me. I gulped. The room was silent. A crow cawed ominously in the distance.

"I have an 11 hr layover in Bahrain and I wanted to climb the highest mountain," I said with as much innocence as I could muster. "I wanted to get a souvenir to bring home to my family," and I showed them the rocks I had collected. I offered them the rocks back. They declined. I tried to think of more to say but that pretty much summarized all of it. I could detect a slight smile on some of their faces. One guard demanded to see all my stuff. I hastily dumped out the contents of my backpack on the floor. Six sets of eyes pored over the gear critically.

"Clothes, sleeping bag, medicine, toothbrush, water," I began. They couldn't see anything wrong with me having that stuff. But eventually my list started to come to the end and I had to mention my camera. They wanted to take a look at it. Earlier, while I was waiting in the car, I had made another quick decision to delete those two dummy pictures on the camera. I didn't want them to see those pics and decide to confiscate my camera. I showed them that the camera contained no pictures. "See, no pictures. I thought that I would get in trouble if I took any pictures so I deleted all of them." They all kind of looked at each other and came to a consensus that I wasn't a serious threat to the security of Bahrain.

As I looked them in the eye I noticed that all five of the guards looked pretty fresh. They were all about my age. I guess there's not usually too much happening in this remote outpost in the Bahraini desert at 1:30am on a Monday night, so when an American tourist comes in and runs to the top of a mountain they had a good reason to get a little excited. It was probably the most excitement they've had in a long time.

"Ok, you may go," they said, and returned my passport. I hastily stuffed my gear into my backpack and tried to divert their attention from my GPS. They might not have liked me recording the coordinates of their outpost. We got back in the taxi and sped off back to the airport. I think the taxi driver was relieved too because he turned on some loud American 80's music on the radio and sang along.

I tried to get some sleep back at the airport but I tossed and turned for the rest of the night. They always say that the hardest part in climbing a mountain is the descent. I have discovered that this is especially true in Bahrain

EUROPE: HVANNADALSHNUKUR

ICELAND

6,592ft

Date climbed: June 25, 2010

Author: Matthew

520 miles bicycled
10 miles hiked
126,000 calories burned

The trailhead for the tallest mountain in Iceland is easy to get to by car, but we found that it's actually a lot of work to reach it by bicycle. If you have a car, the drive to Hvannadalshnúkur's trailhead at Skaftafell National Park is a cinch, but the "12-16 hour" round-trip glacier hike to the summit is a significant endeavor. But if you're on a bicycle instead of a car, we found that the 380km ride from Keflavik through brutal weather and rough roads makes the hike seem like a stroll along the beach.

We naïvely flew into Keflavik International Airport (if you fly into Reykjavik you land here) on June 21st with our bikes after a four-hour flight from Halifax. It's nice how easy it is to get to Iceland from the East Coast. Once we landed it was exciting to see everything suddenly written in Icelandic, which seemed so foreign to us. Luckily everyone spoke excellent English. The immigration officer was a little confused at first because we came on a one-way flight to Iceland and were going to leave on a one-way flight to Finland in a week. "Let me see your flight back to the US," he requested. "I haven't bought my return flight yet because we're going to buy it later on in the summer when we know where we'll be," I answered. He frowned at first but after seeing the bike box he seemed to relax a little and let us pass. "Welcome to Iceland," he said.

The most stunning aspect of the scenery was the lack of trees. Eric and I suspected that stealth camping might be difficult. But it was only 8am and we had a whole day of biking to find a good spot.

The most annoying part of the journey was putting the bikes back together. The bike boxes had been handled violently along the way and had some major rips. But luckily I had used a rope to tie together all the components inside the box so nothing would fall out. I learned this the hard way when the TSA inconveniently lost my seat post on the way to Alaska in 2008. We spent about an hour and a half putting the bikes back together.

This time we were going to try four panniers instead of the BOB trailers we had towed through western Canada. This would save us about 25 pounds and eliminate a few moving parts. We had a rack on the front and the back. Since we had glacier gear and boots our bikes were heavily loaded down and steering felt like maneuvering a big slow boat. We couldn't quite fit everything in the four panniers so we each had a big 70L drybag with backpack straps and hip strap that we strapped to the back rack. This backpack turned out to be extremely convenient the entire trip because we could put it on and carry our day hiking gear when we were climbing mountains. With 2L of water and three days of food the net weight of our bikes was probably 125lbs.

A couple of other long-distance cyclists had arrived on the same flight and were assembling their bikes next to us. They seemed surprised that we had so much gear. Their plan was to bike around the island and stay in hotels each night. I thought to myself, it would really lighten your load if you didn't need to carry food or camping gear and instead just carried a big fat credit card in your pocket so you could eat at restaurants and stay at hotels every night. To us it felt much more fulfilling to be less connected with civilization. Eric and I knew that there would be plenty of nice little "stealth" campgrounds along our route, awaiting our business.

This was the first real developed country we had been to besides the US and Canada, so at first it was strange riding through downtown Keflavik and seeing nice buildings and nice cars all around. We went to the gas station and filled up our fuel bottle for our MSR XGK International Stove. "Gotta love that stove," I said to Eric. It is one of the few stoves that can burn unleaded and diesel, among many other types of fuels, making it super-convenient for international travel, where Coleman Fuel might be scarce.

We already had three days of food so we hit the road and headed east. For a moment I felt like a dog free from its leash. I wanted to go faster and faster. This was our first day of cycling and I was hungry for the miles. But then at that moment Iceland decided that it was time to properly introduce itself to us. It started drizzling and a headwind picked up. About five miles later I heard that agonizing whoosh of air from my back tire that indicated I already had a flat. Having a flat tire can really destroy your momentum. I threw my bike to the ground in disgust and hastily put in a new tube. The rain was getting harder.

We saw on the map a shorter-looking road that passed through Grindavik ("vik" means bay) so we went for it. As we turned south an ugly 20km/h headwind full of rain pushed against us. It was too warm to wear a rain jacket without sweating so we just got soaked. Yuck. Welcome to Iceland.

Eventually the road turned to gravel. Great. We were getting farther and farther from Reykjavik, where most people live, and we were on what we called a "Billy-bob road" so it was no surprise that the condition was bad. But back on Alaska's Dalton Highway in 2008 we had biked through 500 miles of what we thought was the toughest gravel road and our bikes had worked perfectly so we thought Icelandic gravel would probably be no big deal. Unfortunately though the road became softer and softer and a few times we even had to walk the bikes. Surely, we thought, the road should improve once we meet up with a main road again.

Since there weren't any trees it was very tough to locate the nearest AAA-approved stealth campsite. But we eventually found a big sheep pasture and pushed the bikes far off the road, avoiding deep crevices, lava tunnels, and mounds of bizarre gray moss until we found a good spot.

The next day we had fun trying to pronounce the strange new Icelandic characters. We passed through towns like Strandarkirkja, Þorlákshöfn, Hvolsvöllur, and lake Hlíðarvatn. Quick guide: 'Þ' and 'ð' are pronounced kind of like 'th,' while 'hv' is like 'kw,' and 'j' is always like a 'y.' When we found out we were on the road "Þjóðvegur" we tried to see who could come up with the smoothest pronunciation but I bet a local could probably still tell we were foreigners.

We stopped at a picnic table in Hvolsvöllur for lunch. A fierce southeast headwind had been lashing us all morning. We had alternated drafting but were still worn out. We hoped that at least the wind would still be there in a few days so we could get a tailwind on the way back. (It didn't.) While we sat down a gardener dude came over to us and started speaking Icelandic. We asked politely if he spoke English. Turns out he moved to Iceland from Germany twenty years ago. We talked with him about the recent volcanic eruption that had been all over the news. He said that the volcano was no longer erupting but it had dropped quite a bit of black ash in town. He was hopeful that the ash would act as a fertilizer and help his grass grow. He pointed out the location of the Eyjafjallajökull volcano on our map, about 30 miles away. Good, we thought, we would pass right by it. We secretly hoped we could see a little lava along the way.

216

A few miles out of town we came upon some of the destruction that the volcano had wrought. The huge volume of erupting lava had flowed onto the glacier and instantly turned the ice into water. Flash floods had raced down the Markarfljót river and torn out two or three massive bridges on our road, the primary southern highway linking the east and west halves of Iceland. Luckily, that had been more than two months ago and road crews had already repaired most of the road. We just had to ride through a little bit of soft gravel.

Now we were getting into the mountainous region of Iceland. Our road, the "Ring Road," stayed between the mountains and ocean and fortunately remained almost completely flat. But the closer the mountains squeezed us to the ocean the more ferocious the wind became. At times we were battling a 20 mph headwind. There wasn't a tree or hill around to block the wind so we just kept pushing through it. We hoped that once we turned northeast at Vik we might get a little tailwind.

At least the scenery was spectacular. To our right, off in the distance beyond bright green hayfields, was the North Atlantic. To our left, somewhere high up in the clouds, was the volcano. 800ft cliffs towered above us with dozens of waterfalls. The biggest waterfall we passed by was Seljalandsfoss, about 200ft tall. A bright green radius of vegetation grew within its spray. If that waterfall were in the US there would at least be a state park dedicated to it. In Iceland waterfalls were so common that this one was merely a picnic ground. The Icelandic word for "waterfall" is the monosyllabic word "foss" which is so much less cumbersome to pronounce than "waterfall" probably because they're so common in Iceland.

Once we reached the 100-mile mark it was time to start searching for a "campground." The nice thing about miles instead of kilometers is that 100 miles is a good amount to ride in a day and it also feels psychologically fulfilling to reach such a nice round number. 100km on the other hand is pretty wimpy. I guess you could aim for 160km, but that number is pretty inelegant and would leave a bad taste in your mouth at the end of the day. So we always relaxed a little when cracked the 100-mile mark and decided it was time to be in campsite-finding mode. Thankfully at the century mark today we came across our first grove of trees of the day near another spectacular waterfall at Skógar. When nobody was looking we plunged our bikes into the neat rows of human-planted bushes/trees and vanished from the world's radar. We were unfindable once again.

A centimeter-thick layer of black volcanic ash covered everything. Luckily the ash had fallen at the beginning of the growing season so the plants would have the rest of the summer to recover.

The next day the landscape became even more spectacular. We passed by ranch after ranch and soon reached the southern cape of Iceland, at Vik. We walked on the black sandy beach and headed to the nearest Kjar Vall for some groceries. Not a whole lot was happening in downtown Vik (population ~300) on this bleak rainy June day. The temp was only about 55 degrees, but we figured that's probably as warm as it ever gets around here.

A young blond-haired kid, probably thirteen, came out of the store to get his bike. "Nice mountain bike," I said slowly and clearly to him, not knowing if he spoke English. "Thanks, yes I like this bike," he said like a native English speaker. I was surprised. He was the first local we had really spoken to and his English was impeccable. We started talking about soccer and we asked him if the US was still in the World Cup. "Yes," he answered, "but probably not for much longer." We laughed. I was impressed that a young kid here in the boondocks of Iceland would speak such fluent English and be that up-to-date on current events in soccer.

East of Vik we began heading into a vast expanse of nothing. Twenty-five miles of pancake-flat terrain spread out in front of us with dark purple lupines as far as we could see. Far to the north we could see the lower reaches of a glacier protruding from the clouds. It looked like the whole area had been created by some epic lava flow thousands of years ago. We had never seen anything like it.

Pretty soon we reached our favorite village of the trip, good old Kirkjubæjarklaustur, population 160. We rehearsed our pronunciations for miles before we got into town. The town had a couple of gas stations, a grocery store, apartments, churches, city hall—a surprising amount of infrastructure for such a small town. We grabbed a liter of Mjúkís Súkkulaði ice cream at the grocery store and replenished some calories. From the pronunciation, we guessed that "Súkkulaði" had something to do with chocolate, but we could only hope that "Mjúkís" didn't have anything to do with "mucous."

As soon as we left town, Iceland decided it was time to teach us another lesson in respect. A digital weather sign next to the road that read "Vindur: NA7" indicated that the wind would be coming from the northeast at 7km/hr for the next stretch of road. At first I thought "wow, that's pretty cool they would have technology like that," but then I realized with dismay that we wanted to head northwest so we would have a headwind. Argh. The wind picked up and a cold rain began to fall. Double argh.

It's amazing how something as simple as the wind can shape your morale when you're cycling. If you've got a strong tailwind on level ground you might be able to push 25mph. Sheer exhilaration. But a strong headwind could keep you below 10mph. Plain drudgery. Just a simple 180 degree difference in the wind direction or your own direction can mean the difference between pleasure and pain. It seems so arbitrary. On a bike you pay as much attention to the wind as a sailor.

Sprinkle some cold rain into a headwind and it's no longer fun to be on a bicycle. But there was nothing else we could do but ride. We were pedaling through the desolate Skeiðarasandur, a 30-mile wide, Kansas-flat sand plain. Through the rain we could see about three miles around us and there wasn't a feature in sight. Not a tree, a boulder, a house, a plant, just black sand and gray lichen. We saw one car every ten minutes. Our odometer read 105 miles but there wasn't a campsite in sight. True, probably nobody would care if we camped a hundred feet from the road, but we preferred more secluded campsites, especially for wind protection. We needed to keep moving.

Suddenly my fuel tank became empty. I couldn't pedal another rotation. I started shivering. I needed some quick energy. I'm not quite sure how, but cycling has the ability to physically drain you deeper than any other activity. I've found that when I'm backpacking my energy slowly fades out and eventually a little alarm goes off that says "ok, it's time to eat," and then you stop and eat and feel better. I always feel like I've got a little bit left when I'm backpacking or running, no matter how hungry I am. But when I'm cycling, by the time my body says "stop and eat" I'm completely spent. It's like I've hit a brick wall. Maybe it's related to momentum—as long as you've got a little energy left you want to keep your bike cruising because it takes a lot of work to get it back up to speed. When you're hiking, on the other hand, you can stop whenever you want because you're moving slowly anyhow.

I attacked my hunger with two Clif bars and my last-resort Gu packet. Within ten minutes the furnace was roaring once again and I was hungry for more miles. It's amazing how efficiently the body can perform when you need it to.

Fifteen miles later we made it to the abandoned farm at Sandfell in Skaftafell National Park which marked the trailhead of our route up Hvannadalshnúkur, Iceland's high point. We had printed off the SummitPost description of the route which had gotten us to this point, but unfortunately we were on our own now because the webpage did not include a route description. The only thing we had to work with was a painting of the mountain at the trailhead on which someone had hand-drawn the route. The image wasn't too helpful but we photographed it in case we needed to refer to it during the climb tomorrow. Luckily we were armed with the GPS track of another person who had climbed the route, which turned out to be helpful.

But the first priority was sleep. We found a good boulder and pitched the tent behind it. We had cycled 200km and were zapped. I looked at my watch and, holy mackerel, it was midnight. The daylight at this latitude had been extremely forgiving.

After a not-so-alpine start at 10am we reactivated our walking muscles. It had been four days since we had walked more than 100ft. The fog grew dense as we climbed but nice tall cairns marked the route. We hadn't seen any other people yet but knew that plenty of guiding services take people up the mountain, and it was possible that we were behind one. A sign at the trailhead had recommended hiring a guide for their expertise in avoiding "fissures" but we felt pretty comfortable in our skills from Denali. It also advised that each rope team should have 5-6 people, but we didn't see anyone else around so it would just be the two of us.

We had 30m of rope between us and each had a small ice axe. We each had a deadman anchor in case someone fell in, which isn't as effective as a picket, but is much nicer to carry on a bike. We had brought the minimum gear to keep us safe, but we felt we could still be safe. We carried it in our handy bright yellow drybags. After a few hours of climbing we suited up and started walking on the glacier. A nice packed trail led the way.

We wound around some pretty impressive crevasses. A few times the route crossed a thinning snowbridge that we were skeptical would even hold our weight. While I crossed Eric would hold his ice axe and be ready to self arrest at a moment's notice. The threat of falling in here was much more real than it had been on Denali. It was getting late in the season and the route was melting away. Without the footprints of a dozen people in front of us we might have turned around.

We reached the edge of the danger zone and thick clouds immediately rolled in. Pretty soon we could only see about fifty feet, it was white in every direction. But from the route drawing we photographed at the trailhead it looked like it was mostly level to the top from here. At that point we suddenly heard some talking coming towards us. It was an eight-person guided group returning from the top. They were roped up about six feet apart and looked like a giant centipede. To us it seemed ridiculous that they would be roped so close together, because if one person fell in the last person would have very little time to self arrest. But from what we had seen on Denali this seemed to be the European way.

As they got close their guide gave us a few tips: "careful, the ice will be very soft on the way down" (we thought: yes thanks, we know that, but we slept in this morning because we got to sleep at 1am and had an epic day yesterday), and "you should tie a knot in the middle of your rope so it catches if you fall in" (we thought: that might be a good idea, but that could make it tougher to climb out). We thanked him for the suggestions and continued hiking. He probably thought we were dufuses. But he was also probably jealous that we could move twice as fast as him because we weren't towing six old people behind us.

Eric and I were dressed in shorts and a t-shirt, little boots, and mini crampons. By contrast the clients all wore thick pants and jackets along with winter boots. "Geez, you'd think they'd hot in all that," I told Eric.

An hour later during our final little climb a massive hump of rock and glaciers suddenly materialized out of the fog in front of us. It looked like a gigantic pirate ship emerging silently from a cloud. We climbed out of a sea of clouds and for the first time in Iceland there was blue sky above us. As far as we could see in every direction was a uniform white sea of cloud tops. Undercast! Just a few hundred feet more and we would be on the roof of Iceland. The route steeply crossed a few very suspicious-looking crevasses that we crossed quickly. We even had to jump over one crevasse.

A minute later we were standing on the summit, the roof of the country. We could see nothing but cloud tops for fifty miles in every direction. "Well there's not a whole lot to see," I said, "but at least we can see that there aren't any taller mountains around." We were pretty darn lucky. If Hvannadalshnúkur had been just 200 feet lower we would be swimming in the sea of clouds, not able to see anything. Up on the summit it was like a little tropical island. The sun blazed down on us without a puff of wind. I'm surprised nobody had planted a palm tree up there yet.

We captured the customary summit pictures: me and Eric posing with and without shirts, me and Eric jumping, and Eric juggling. I even sent a couple of text messages from the top. Too bad we couldn't just camp on the top, we thought, because it's way nicer up here than in the rain down below. But we needed to get down before the route melted out any further. It was nice that we had been following a fresh eight-person trail on the way up; hopefully it would still be intact on the way down.

We made it down without any incidents around 8pm. The climb had taken us ten hours, including an hour of fooling around at the top. We knew there wasn't a boulder to hide behind for the next thirty miles so we decided to camp one more night at the current spot.

In the morning it was time to start heading back to Keflavik. We had given ourselves nine days in Iceland and had four remaining. We were originally hoping to take a different road back, like one of the gravel roads through the rugged interior of the island, but we had discovered that our bikes weren't well-suited for Icelandic gravel. You would need a good mountain bike to pass through the center of Iceland. So, with a little dismay, we decided that we would take the same road back that we had arrived on. We hoped that at least the headwinds would turn into tailwinds.

A little after Kirkjubæjarklaustur in the late afternoon, or shall we say "K-town," we picked up the most spectacular tailwind we had ever experienced. We were getting closer and closer to the southern tip of Iceland and it seemed the air really wanted to move from east to west. It was exhilarating. We could comfortably reach 27-28mph. While not pedaling my GPS speedometer read 17mph.

We rode the tailwind like a surfer on a tsunami and by 6pm it was time to find a place to camp. Even though, from a sunlight perspective, it didn't really matter what time of day we pedaled, we wanted to keep an early-to-bed/early-to-rise schedule in Iceland so we could pass through towns when stores were actually open. So, with a little agony because we didn't like to waste the tailwind, we pulled off the road and began to look for a campsite. It was a pity that we couldn't somehow deposit in a bank the tailwind that would surely prevail tonight in order to withdraw it at a later date when we needed it. It was tempting to keep riding the tailwind later into the night but we had just found a potentially awesome place to camp.

We had pulled off the road near an awesome rock formation called Hjörleifshöfði (look it up in a Google image search). It looks like a big grass-covered island in a sea of flat black sand. Tall cliffs guard nearly every side. We figured we could find a sheltered area at the base of a cliff. On the south side we discovered a gigantic natural cave. You could probably have driven a bus into the cave if it weren't for the boulders in the front. That's where our bikes came in handy. We pedaled into the cave and officially had a campsite that was protected from rain and wind. It turned out to be our proudest campsite in Iceland. (Here are the coordinates for future travelers: 63.413601,-18.754098).

When we pulled onto the road the next morning we couldn't believe it. The tailwind had actually intensified overnight. We were in business. As we stood there clouds of black sand came roaring in from the east and sandblasted our bare skin. It felt like taking a shower under water that's at too high of a pressure. The black clouds cut visibility down to a mile. A few rain drops made the weather downright nasty. Thank goodness we wouldn't be riding straight into that, we thought.

We turned to the west and it felt like we were wearing jet packs. We estimated that at times we had a 30mph gust of tailwind. For the first time I reached 38mph on flat ground. All you had to do was stand up and make yourself big like a sail. It was the only time we were glad to have all that frontal area on our bike. We barreled into Vik like a runaway freight train. If the wind kept up like that all day we could cover 150 miles. Unfortunately, though, soon after we turned northwest and skirted the cape we found ourselves pushing through a headwind.

Further down the road we reached an area that had been smothered by volcanic ash. Black ash was drifting across the road like snow and cut visibility down to a few hundred feet. During one big gust I had to stop my bike and close my eyes to protect myself from the ash. My bike and I emerged covered in black. It was pretty cool.

Stealth camping was shaping up to be tricky this evening. We knew that there weren't any trees for at least the next 40 miles so we would need to find a boulder to hide behind. We decided maybe we could ride up the road towards the volcano that erupted and maybe we'd find something cool. But the road soon turned to genuine, fist-sized, Icelandic gravel that was no fun to ride on with our bikes. We turned around, disgusted. We knew there was a campground at the Seljalandsfoss waterfall, but that meant we would have to pay. Paying to camp, what an agonizing thought indeed. With no other option we pulled into the official campground, defeated.

At least it was an awesome place. We set up the tent next to a magnificent waterfall that had sliced a narrow gap into the cliff. I could imagine, one thousand years ago, a Viking walking through this meadow and looking with excitement upon this waterfall. I'm sure he would have stood underneath it. Just when we wanted to cook it began to pour. Not a day had gone by yet without us getting soaked. But we found a small cave and cooked inside it. "You can't get us in here," I yelled to the rain.

In the evening we waited for someone to come by and collect the ISK 1500 ($8) campground fee but nobody showed up. In the morning I walked around searching for a campground host or ranger but the office was closed. There was no box to put the money in either. "If it's gonna be this hard to pay them $16 then they must not want it," I told Eric. We pedaled away and nobody chased after us.

The most critical module of our exit strategy from Iceland was getting another bike box so we could pack our bikes for the flight to Finland. So the goal was to stay in the big city of Reykjavik at a hostel the next night so we could be near bikes stores that would have a bike box.

The closer we got to Reykjavik the crazier the traffic became. Even though there are only 300,000 people in the country the road into the capital is as busy as an interstate. An interstate, that is, without a dang shoulder. Huge double-trailer trucks and extra-wide Super Jeeps roared by us. I would have taken the roughest Billy-bob road over this racetrack except that it was the only road that went in the right direction.

By 5pm we had gotten within spitting distance of Reykjavik and knew that it was going to be slim pickings for stealth campsites if we went any farther. Without a tree or a cliff in sight we headed up a road into a gravel quarry. It didn't look promising but it was our only shot. We escorted our bikes down a little four wheeler trail and finally came upon a gate. Uh-oh, Eric said, we're probably not supposed to pass through the gate. But as it turned out the DO NOT ENTER sort of sign was actually facing the other way on the gate, and indicated that we had just emerged from restricted area. "Oh, what do you know, we came from a DO NOT ENTER area," I said. "Well then what kind of area are we in now? Are we allowed to be in this area?" "I think that as long as we don't get caught we're now in a permissible area," Eric replied.

It turned out to be a half-mile from the end of an active runway but luckily none of the planes flying overhead called the Icelandic authorities on us. We had a pleasant sleep. It turns out that if we had gone a few miles farther we would have probably had to pay $45 each to stay in a hostel.

The next day would be an errand day. We had to find a bike box and pack the bikes, mail our glacier gear home because we wouldn't need it anymore, buy another five days of food for Finland, locate a place to sleep, and send some emails. It took one sentence to list our errands. In the end it took thirteen hours to accomplish all of them.

We took a bus early the following morning to the Keflavik airport. We had cycled 520 miles over 9 days to climb Hvannadalshnúkur, the highest point in Iceland, but that was only the beginning of summer of adventure. Finland was next . . .

North America: La Soufriere

St Vincent and the Grenadines

4,055ft

Date climbed: March 24, 2012

Author: Matthew

"So tell us about your hike today; which mountain did you guys climb?" The reporter tilted the microphone towards me and the video camera zoomed in.

"We climbed to the top of La Soufrière," I replied, not sure whether to look at the reporter or the camera. Obviously the news team from Saint Vincent and the Grenadines TV (SVGTV) knew full well which mountain we had just climbed—we were standing here at the trailhead for La Soufrière, the highest mountain in this tiny Caribbean island nation. They just wanted to orient viewers at home.

"And how was your hike?"

"It wasn't easy," I answered. My gaze descended slowly past my bloody, lacerated arms, past the muddy, gruesome gashes on my legs and settled onto my feet.
"And you hiked in those?" she asked, referring to the foam crocs (slippers) I was wearing.
"I had to because LIAT [the airline] lost my backpack, which had my shoes, pants, food, and rain jacket."

The camera slowly ascended and focused in on my arms. They wanted the viewers on their couches at home to get a good look at the damage inflicted by their country's tallest peak. Oh if they could only know how hard it had been . . .

*   *   *

GETTING TO ST VINCENT

La Soufrière would be country high point number three of the trip for me and Eric. We had just come off successful ascents of Trinidad and Tobago's Cerro del Aripo and Grenada's Mt St Catherine the previous two days and were hoping to be three-for-three after St Vincent and the Grenadines. It was Spring Break for us and we wanted to knock off a few country high points, with Barbados, Antigua, and Dominica next on the list.

Just like the other two mountains, hours of internet searching in Cambridge had yielded precious little information about La Soufrière. We knew simply that it started at the "Rabacca" trailhead in the northern part of the island. We also had a GPS track from another hiker but were uncertain of its accuracy. We realized then that we might have to gather some info from locals when we landed.

The few trip reports we found all said that either "you are required to hire a guide" or "you darn well better hire a guide." But based on Google Maps terrain research the route looked pretty straightforward, so we figured we'd be able to figure things out ourselves without a guide. The only question would be which peak was highest—Google Earth's topo data showed that a few nearby peaks were all within ten feet elevation of each other. To make things even harder, in every single satellite photo (Google Maps, Bing Maps, and Garmin Satellite Imagery) the true summit of La Soufrière was socked in with clouds and thus invisible. We could find no hiker photos of the true summit either. But we just assumed that enough people probably climb the mountain that the true summit and trail would be pretty obvious. (Boy were we wrong about that.)

The original plan had been to sneak in La Soufrière during an eleven-hour window between Grenada and Barbados. We'd fly into St Vincent 11am, clear customs, pick up a rental car and hit the road, reaching the trailhead at 1pm. We'd finish the (apparently) four hour hike by 5pm, be back at the airport by 7pm and have 3 hours until our 10pm flight to Barbados. Somehow, though, we managed to finish Mt St Catherine in Grenada in record time and miraculously caught an earlier flight to St Vincent, which landed at 5pm, which meant we'd have an extra three-fourths of a day for La Soufrière. That move would turn out to be crucial to our success.

THE CHECKBOX

The first indication that La Soufrière would not be easily defeated came shortly after we landed. "So where are you guys staying tonight?" the immigration officer asked. "We're on a big hike tomorrow so we'll just sleep in our rental car at the trailhead." On the customs form, in the little box that said "YOUR INTENDED ADDRESS IN ST VINCENT:" we had just written "Airport," figuring it'd be an acceptable response, as it had been in Trinidad and Grenada. We explained the situation.

The immigration officer thought about it for a while then summoned her superior. "That's fine if you want to camp, but I can't let you into the country without a hotel address on this form," the superior said. "I'd suggest talking to our travel agent over here; she will let you know which hotels were available."

With disdain we walked over to the travel agent. By this point we had the attention of all three of the immigration officers in the entire country. Everyone in the room knew that no matter which hotel room we reserved we wouldn't be staying in a hotel tonight. But they would be satisfied if they could simply check off the box that said they had an address for us. I talked to one hotel and made quick reservation, then scribbled their address in the correct box. Trying to keep a straight face, the immigration officer looked once more at our immigration forms, then gave a nod of approval. Welcome to Saint Vincent and the Grenadines.

"Please proceed to customs next," she said. Which brings us to Snafu #2 of the trip.

OUR FRIENDS AT LIAT

We waited patiently at the conveyor belt as the luggage went around and people claimed their suitcases. Lest the reader overestimates the size of the SVD airport, I'll set the record straight: the baggage claim conveyor belt loop cycle time is about seven seconds. Our flight was one of probably only four that day. There's one immigration officer booth, and I believe that most of the airport staff was napping before we arrived. Before long all of the luggage was claimed, but my backpack was nowhere to be found.

"Dang it," I said to Eric. Earlier we had read online about LIAT's dismal record with lost luggage and had sworn to check no bags during our trip. Our schedule was so tight that we couldn't afford to waste two hours waiting for a bag. Hours earlier in Grenada, however, we had to move very quickly as soon as we arrived at the ticket counter and realized that we had only minutes before the earlier flight departed. The LIAT rep weighed my bag and said it was 20lbs—too heavy for carry-on luggage on these tiny Caribbean planes. Ten of those pounds was probably the mud and swamp water from

Mt St Catherine that had saturated my shoes and clothes. I had traded out the muddy outfit in favor of my clean clothes and crocs for the flight.

"We're going to have to check this bag," he said. We were in such a hurry to catch the earlier flight that I hastily removed my electronics (GPS, cell phone, and camera) from the backpack and reluctantly handed the backpack over without arguing. The pack contained my ultra-thin sleeping bag, rain jacket, air mattress, bug net shelter, international driver's permit, and sunscreen. I remember thinking, "Wow, I'll be in trouble if they lose that bag. I can't hike in the outfit I'm wearing. But there's no way they'd lose *my* backpack." Little did I know that the bag also contained my glasses, contact solution, spare contacts, Android phone, food, and the precious route descriptions which we had spent countless hours compiling.

Well lo and behold we were here in Kingstown, St. Vincent and the backpack was nowhere to be found. "Crap," I said. We headed straight over to the LIAT ticket counter to sort things out. They said the next flight wouldn't arrive for another three hours. We weighed our options. "Is there any place in town where I could buy some shoes, pants, and contact solution? We're hiking up La Soufrière tomorrow and would like to leave tonight." I didn't want to be bushwhacking through no Caribbean jungle wearing little more than beach attire.

"No, I'm sorry" the LIAT rep replied, "everything closes early here on Friday night. The stores won't open again until Monday."

"Crap." Eric and I began to deliberate. We could either 1) wait three hours until the next flight—but what's the likelihood my backpack will be on that one? or 2) stay in a hotel tonight and see if we can find some store in the morning to buy shoes or 3) hit the road tonight and suck it up tomorrow without long pants, shoes, or a rest for my weary eyes.

We didn't want to blow our lead. "When the bag arrives," I said, "please hold it at the front desk and we'll pick it up tomorrow. We'd like to start hiking tonight."

"As you wish," she replied. "I hope you enjoy your time here in St. Vincent and this incident doesn't put a damper on your hike to La Soufrière."

With frustration we stormed out of the airport. Well at least once we get the rental car things will be in our hands, I remember thinking. I can tolerate one night without taking out my contacts, along with some light bush whacking with less-than-ideal footwear, if it means that we'll be able to finish this mountain. I mean, the backpack will surely arrive before we leave tomorrow night, right? We walked over to the Avis parking lot to pick up our rental car, which brings us to Snafu #3.

OUR FRIEND MR. CURTIS

Our actual rental car reservation was for the following day at 11am, but since we'd read that Avis was open until 9pm and there seemed to be quite a few cars in the parking lot, we figured we'd walk over there and easily pick one up early. We knocked on the door to the office. No answer. Wait a few minutes, knock again, still no answer. Hmm. "This isn't looking good," I said, "let's call one of those numbers written on the Avis sign." But in order to use a payphone I'd first need some St Vincent cash.

I walked over to some taxi drivers at the airport. "Do you know where I could exchange some currency?" I asked. "Sorry," one man answered, "the banks close early on Fridays, you'll have to wait until Monday, what's the problem mon?" We were starting to notice a theme here. "Here's the situation," I said, "we'd like to rent a car from Avis, and they're supposed to be open now, but there's nobody in the office."

One taxi driver, who later introduced himself as Peech, stepped forward. "I know the owner of Avis, let's give him a call." He dialed the numbers on his phone, but still no answer. "Well I know where he lives; I can give you a ride over there." We hopped into his taxi and sped off into the hills above Kingstown. "This is Cane Gardens," Peech said, "it's where all the rich people live." We continued climbing up the hill until we arrived at a car dealership. "That's Curtis right there, he owns Avis, catch him quick." Curtis had just opened his car door and was getting ready to leave when we approached him.

With a smile he said "you're just in time, come in here and I'll get you a car." Turns out Curtis owns a car dealership too. We stepped into his office and I immediately had a little uneasy feeling about Mr. Curtis. It was hard to put my finger on it, but he and his employees seemed a little bit slick. Maybe it just came from being a used car salesman, I thought. I tried to push it out of my mind. We had been lucky to catch him before he left for the evening.

The paperwork went smoothly, especially because Eric already had already gotten an International Drivers Permit from AAA in Boston, which meant that we wouldn't need to pay a visit to the already-closed Kingstown Police Station for a local permit. "We've got a four-door Suzuki jeep for you," he said as he showed us to the door. Perfect! we thought. We wouldn't need to worry about rough roads with that vehicle. "And in St Vincent we drive on the . . ." Curtis said. "Left," Eric responded. The past few days Eric had had a decent bit of experience with left-side-driving so he figured that he could handle St Vincent too. With a grin Curtis waved us goodbye. But there was something subtle in his grin that made me feel uneasy.

Somehow Curtis had managed to provide us with fuel tank that read sub-empty so we knew we'd have to gas up ASAP before the two-hour drive to the trailhead. We stopped at Shell where I picked up some ice cream then made another stop to get some spoons at a local restaurant. I triumphantly returned to the car with the plastic spoons. With a half-gallon of ice cream we were equipped for the journey ahead. Eric inserted the keys into the ignition, which brought us to Snafu #4 for the trip.

THANK YOU MR. PEECH

Eric rotated the keys but the car would not respond. "Uh that's not good," he said. Try again. We could hear the spinning of what we figured was the starter motor, but engine wouldn't start. Soon the starter stopped spinning and the car was silent. "Uh-oh, that probably means the battery is dead," I said. We waited another few minutes and tried again. Nothing. "Let's go talk to Peech, see what we can do," I said.

Once again we walked down the little hill to the airport and consulted our friend Mr. Peech. He tried dialing all the phone numbers for Curtis, the car's owner, but couldn't get through. We also tried the number on top of the rental agreement, which should theoretically get you through to a person 24 hours a day in case of emergency. Nothing. "Let's go to Cane Gardens and see if we can catch him," Peech said. Once again we hopped into his taxi and sped up the hill. But when we arrived at Curtis's car dealership it was deserted. "OK, let's drive to Curtis's house." We drove a little farther down the road to his house but still it was also empty. "OK, let's drive to his pharmacy—he owns a pharmacy downtown." But big surprise the Curtis Lewis Pharmacy was also closed. We tried the phone numbers once again. Nothing. Our options were running low.

"Where's this car parked? Let's take a look at it," Peech said. We drove over and he parked his taxi van alongside our Suzuki. He popped the hood and looked at the battery. He listened while we tried to start it. "Yes, your battery is dead," he said. He grabbed some jumper cables from his car. We stepped back while he went to work. By this time a small crowd had gathered around us, offering suggestions. We were the entertainment in Kingstown for the night.

He started his van, we started our jeep, and after about ten minutes of work we finally had a car that would start. "Thank you so much Peech!" we said.

"Keep in mind though that this doesn't fix the problem," he replied. "We can't be sure that the battery will start tomorrow morning. You don't want to find yourselves at Rabacca with a car that won't start. It's a lonely place and not many people go there, so it would be hard to find help. I really think you should stay in town tonight and talk to Curtis in the morning."

He could tell that we weren't too excited about doing that.

"If you really insist on starting your hike tonight, I think the only option for you would be to drive towards Rabacca, but stop along the main road at the turnoff for the trailhead. Park the car there. You'll have to hike about forty minutes up the road to the trailhead but you guys are strong, you'll probably be faster. And if the car doesn't start in the morning you'll be along the main road and you can flag someone down to jump start your car. People are nice here, someone will help you."

Eric and I were surprised. Peech seemed to sense our determination to get started tonight. I looked at Eric. "Ok, we'll do that," Eric said.

"Just be sure you don't use the air conditioning or the radio," Peech warned, "you don't want to drain that battery." And with a hearty handshake and generous tip we bid farewell to our little welcoming party and pit crew and headed north.

THE MACHETE DUDE

"So, basically, what we gained this evening was simply the knowledge that the car might not start in the morning," I said. We wound through the dark, curving, mountainous roads and after two hours finally arrived at a road sign that read "<– La Soufrière Trail." "It must be a forty-minute hike from here to the trailhead I guess," I said.

With the car still running we contemplated our options once again. It was like we were in the movie Speed where bus couldn't go slower than 55mph or it would blow up. It was ten pm and we were both completely exhausted. We had woken up that morning at 2:30am in Trinidad, flown to

Grenada, climbed the Grenada high point, then flown here. It was exceedingly tempting to just drive to the trailhead and park there. But we also wanted to be able to get a jump start in the morning if our car wouldn't start.

"How about this," I proposed, "we drive up to the trailhead tonight, drop off our water and camping gear. Then we drive back down and park here. Then we hike back up that road with minimal gear." I didn't have a backpack and didn't want to have to carry a ten-pound water jug in my hand. "Ok, that works," Eric answered.

We turned onto the (indeed very lonely) little road and headed up the hills and into the darkness. We passed through what appeared to be banana plantations with small mysterious little cinder block homes. About half-way up we had to slam on the brakes as a shirtless dude wielding a machete leaped out of the road. Apparently he had been sleeping in the road after a long day of work. I dreaded the point during our hike up that we'd have to pass that dude again without the protection of our car.

At long last we pulled into a parking lot that proclaimed itself as the trailhead for La Soufrière. We ditched our heavy stuff in the bushes and reluctantly dragged ourselves back into the car. We paused for a moment. "Man, it's awfully tempting to just turn the car off right now, isn't it?" I said. "Yep," Eric answered. We sat there with the car running, staring off into the jungle. With a sigh, we came back to reality. "Well we don't want to be stuck here, do we?" I said. "Let's get this over with."

In twenty minutes we were back at the bottom and with some momentary hesitation we finally turned the car off. We grabbed what few possessions we had left and began our painful trudge up that same road by the light of headlamp. I should have enjoyed the pleasant little night hike through the palm trees, with the sound of the crashing waves of the Atlantic in the distance, but the thought of the machete-wielding dude made me uneasy. If that dude had nefarious intentions we were sitting ducks. He could be waiting in the bushes, ready to spring upon us. I picked up a small palm frond and held it tightly in my hand. It obviously wouldn't be any match for a machete, but at least it had the shape of one, so perhaps in the darkness the machete dude might mistakenly think we were armed.

Halfway up the road a quick flash caught the corner of my eye. I immediately froze, clenching the palm frond tightly. All my muscles tensed. I waited for the sound of footsteps and the whoosh of a machete. Silence. I slowly turned my gaze in the direction of the flash and saw two big eyes looking at me from ten feet away, illuminated by the reflection of my headlamp. Gulp. But something in the eyes seemed a little strange. They were spaced awfully wide for a person. No, that can't be a person, I thought. Soon I could see the outline of some stubby horns and I knew what type of creature I was facing: it was the abominable jungle cow.

"Why'd you stop," Eric asked. "Well there's a cow here," I answered with a voluminous sigh of relief. We nodded to the cow and kept walking.

A CONCRETE MATTRESS

At last we arrived at the La Soufrière trailhead at 11:15pm. Now things were once again under our control. It was us versus the mountain, with no people or machines between us. But before the big battle we needed a good rest. In Trinidad and Grenada, with such tiny backpacks our sleeping gear had already been absolutely minimal. Now, without my backpack, our gear was as bare-bones as you could get. But with a rainless sky and air temperature of 65F our margin for error was generously large. We found a nice little picnic pavilion and rolled out our tarp onto the concrete. I wrapped up in Eric's spare poncho for warmth and fell asleep within minutes. The hard concrete wasn't exactly comfortable but we were just so dang tired that it didn't matter.

THE CLIMB

Now we've finally arrived at part of this story where we climb the mountain.

We knew that we had a long day ahead of us, we just didn't know at the time how long it would be. So we got up with the rest of the avian jungle wildlife at 6:30am and scarfed down a quick breakfast of bagels and granola bars. We stashed in the bushes what little spare gear we had and hit the trail. It was so hot and humid that we took off our shirts within minutes. I felt like I was missing something. My only gear consisted of the thin swimming trunks and crocs I was wearing along with a little black stuff sack that contained my GPS, camera, and cell phone. It was the most ultra light I had ever hiked. Meanwhile Eric carried a little food and water in his backpack.

We'd read a trip report from some Coloradans that the hike had taken them just two hours round-trip. We already knew that our hike would be longer because we figured that they probably stopped just short of the actual high point, which of course was our destination. La Soufrière is a huge volcano that forms the entire northern half of the island. At the top of the volcano is a massive one-mile wide caldera. Meanwhile our research showed that the La Soufrière's highest point was located about a half-mile from the crater rim. For our intended route, on the GPS we'd simply drawn a straight line from the crater to the summit, and assumed that the going would be easy.

As we climbed, the trees became shorter and shorter and the fog grew denser. After an hour the GPS indicated we were nearing the crater rim. The trail began to level out and suddenly I noticed that fifty feet in front of me the trail vanished into fog. I got the impression that we were close to the edge of the world. As I drew closer to the edge I inched forward more slowly and all of a sudden a thousand foot drop-off materialized. I gasped at the enormity of the sight below me.

LA SOUFRIÈRE

In front of and below us was La Soufrière's gaping, smoldering, mile wide caldera. I turned my head left and right as far as it would go and the caldera was so gigantic that I still couldn't see the whole thing. From the crater rim it was a thousand-foot drop to the crater's floor and it appeared that there was no easy way down. In the bottom of the crater was an annular lush valley surrounding a gigantic, black, smoldering pile of rock that was probably only a few decades old (the last eruption was in 1979). There was even a small lake at the bottom. We could only speculate how the water drained out.

We had read descriptions and seen photos of this crater but no 2D representation could justly capture the magnitude and magnificence of the scene before us. We guessed now why so many people get to this point and turn around, claiming they've been to the "summit" of La Soufrière: 1) the view at this point is probably the best view of the mountain you'll get on a cloudy day and 2) lots of people are probably acrophobic and don't want to hike any farther.

We could also begin to guess why everyone else hires a guide. We had heard that there was only one "easy" way down into the crater, and you reached it by hiking clockwise along the crater from our location. We'd heard that the route down was steep but there's a thick rope you can grab onto. If you're afraid of heights the prospect of walking ten feet away from a thousand foot drop might be intimidating. Also, we figured that the descent point on the ridge might be hard to find. So it might indeed be reasonable to hire a guide. But not for us. We didn't need a guide to tell us to stay away from the edge, and we could probably find the rope on our own.

For now, we would stick with the plan to hit the high point first, then on the way back maybe we'd try to find the way down into the crater if time permitted. It was just 8am so we figured we still had plenty of time. According to the GPS we were just 1.3 miles line-of-sight (LOS) from the summit. Piece of cake, right? The trees seemed short enough that even if there wasn't a trail the bushwhacking would probably be no big deal.

TO THE SUMMIT

We turned right and headed counterclockwise along the crater rim towards the high point. The trail gradually petered out and brought us to the shore of a small and unexpected lake. "That's weird, this wasn't visible in any satellite photo," I said. We had gotten a brand new Garmin GPS two weeks earlier that was capable of storing satellite photos and even our own custom maps. So in most places (in the US as we later found out) the resolution is so good that you can zoom in and see individual trees. But as we zoomed in our location it was completely white—all clouds. "I bet so few people are interested in satellite photos of this area and it's always so cloudy that nobody's able to get a clear shot of this mountain," I said.

We skirted the lake and walked up to a low rise in the bushy hills. "Hmm, there should be a big old mountain behind those clouds," I said. The GPS indicated we were just a half-mile LOS from the top. We watched as the clouds wafted through the high plateau. Soon we noticed a small gap coming and looked intently towards the mountain, ready to take photos.

The cloud gap passed slowly by, revealing the giant sleeping behind it. Our jaws dropped. For a moment we were speechless. "Uh, well one thing I can tell you is that we ain't going straight up that," I said. From this side the mountain appeared as an insurmountable fortress. As we gazed from bottom to top the steep jungle slopes blended into dark, sheer volcanic cliffs. As our astonishment abated we got to work. We knew this could potentially be one of our only clear views of the mountain that day. This could be our only chance to plan a route so we had better get a good look at that mountain, we thought.

We snapped a bunch of photos then began our discussion. It was obvious that from here on out that there wouldn't be any trail. We were completely on our own. It was at this point that our excursion transformed from a simple day hike into a full-fledged mountain adventure. It was actually kind of thrilling. For a moment we felt like we were back in the California Sierra Nevada, planning a route up some 14'er. Here in St Vincent, however, there wasn't snow and talus to navigate around, it was jungle and waterfalls.

"See that little gulley there, next to that cliff and above those trees?" I said to Eric, "I think that'll go." "I don't know," he replied, "that's pretty steep, what about down there?" "I don't think so, those trees are probably pretty dense," I answered. After some back and forth we soon we had a plan worked out. There weren't too many features to refer to, so it wasn't even clear that we were both talking about the same route, but with mixed feelings of excitement and uncertainty we set out towards the first obstacle.

THE BARBED WIRE JUNGLE

We were entering uncharted territory. We could very well be the first people who've ever taken this route, we thought. Judging by the tree top heights the terrain seemed pretty flat so we made a beeline toward the beginning of the route. We began walking through dense waist-deep bushes, unable see what our feet were stepping on. After just a few steps though, to my horror the ground all of a sudden vanished from below me. I plunged into the bushes, falling about six feet before coming to a stop in some dense trees. I looked back and realized that I had just stepped into a little gulley. I yelled back to Eric, cautioning him to watch out for this trap.

I extricated myself from the bushes, thankful that at least I had my shirt on. My legs and arms were already getting cut up and I worried about what kinds of interesting little jungle plants awaited us higher up (like Grenada's razor grass). We realized that this was going to be much harder that we thought. Soon we were thrashing through super-dense bushes, not sure if we were stepping onto rock or branch or thin air.

"Bushwhacking" is a relative term. There's the easy kind of bushwhacking, where the trees are spread apart, there's no undergrowth, and you can walk without worrying about your eye getting poked out or your clothes or skin getting shredded. You can see many feet in front of you and can easily plan your route. It's basically like hiking on a trail. I'll call that Grade 1 bushwhacking. On the other end of the spectrum is Grade 10 bushwhacking, à La Soufrière. It can sort of be likened to swimming. Sometimes you're standing, other times you're on your belly, slithering through trees, not sure how far you are above the ground. It's dark, wet, and you're always getting tangled up with the fallen trees and dead bushes. You need to protect your eyes from branches with sunglasses, but with all the exertion and moisture they fog up quickly and you can see almost nothing. You come out of a dense thicket with uncountable slashes on your legs, and you recall feeling so many sharp pricks that it's impossible to remember where each slash came from. It's a veritable jungle of barbed wire. You're worried that you might have to turn around, and your anxiety causes you to stop taking pictures. These are the moments that don't get documented, the moments where you're giving it 100% but still not sure that it will be good enough. You measure your speed in feet per minute, not miles per hour.

Once in a while we could crawl on top of some bushes and get a bit of a view where we were headed. We decided to aim for a gully where maybe the trees wouldn't be growing so thickly. As we looked back on the route we had taken we realized that just by looking at the treetop heights the route appeared flat, when in reality the terrain was super rugged. The vegetation had effectively smoothed out the topography. Once in a while I'd take a step and realize that I was barefoot, that one of my crocs had fallen off. I'd dig desperately through the trees and finally locate it. This would definitely not be the place to lose your footwear. Each time I would reaffirm my condemnation of LIAT's baggage handling.

Unfortunately the gulley presented its own challenges. We'd be walking up rocks and then would suddenly encounter a ten-foot waterfall and have to start bushwhacking again. It was excruciatingly slow going. But inch by inch we climbed.

THE CRUX

Eventually a big black rock emerged above us, and this was our cue to head right. I wasn't sure, but I think I remembered that the apparent crux—the hardest part of the route—was nearby. I rounded the corner and there it was—the slope that we had been worried about. The thick jungle grass couldn't mask its verticality. From afar it hadn't seemed so vertical; we figured that if it had grass it must still be a gentle slope. But from up close it presented quite the obstacle. I began to second-guess our path. Had we turned too early? Maybe we should have followed that gulley a little farther? Maybe it's less steep farther around that corner? Or maybe we should go back down that gulley and over to the easier route we had seen?

But at this point the prospect of turning back, of giving up a single one of our hard-earned inches, was as repugnant as the smell of my filthy jungle-mud/swamp-water pants. No, we weren't turning around at this point. If we can just make it up this steep pitch, the promised land of easy terrain will be just beyond it, right?

With my muscles twitching I approached the wall. My adrenaline was pumping and I had somehow become a rock climber. From this perspective it was pretty obvious that we had fifteen feet of solid vertical climbing. I grasped the first tuft of thick jungle grass as close to the roots as I could get and pulled myself up. As I climbed, each grass clump started out as a handhold and then became a foothold. With a firm tug I tested each plant before entrusting any weight to it, but still I felt that at any moment one of the clumps would pull out of the thin soil. Fortunately the trees and bushes and grass below were so dense that a fall probably wouldn't be a big deal, just a thrill and an inconvenience. Nevertheless I clenched the grass tightly. I dug my hand in as deep as it would go and tried to grab each clump by the deepest roots.

With my pulse sky high and fight-or-flight response activated I wriggled up through the grass and with a final pull I was at the top. Even though the slope above was still probably a 45 degree angle it felt pretty darn flat. With plenty of branches to hold onto I anchored myself in place and waited for Eric. "I'm at the top!" I yelled, "and it looks like this route will go!"

Finally, Eric emerged over the lip and we paused to catch our breaths. I tried to peek over the pitch we had just climbed but couldn't see over the grass. We had just free-soloed a fifteen-foot vertical pitch by holding onto jungle grass. We looked back on our route in the valley below. It had taken us an hour to cover just a quarter-mile. But at this point we felt like we could practically spit on the summit because the ridge was in sight and it didn't look like there was any funny business in between. "Well I can tell you one thing," Eric said, "we're not taking the same route down."

THE SUMMIT RIDGE

After another five minutes of moderate Grade 5 bushwhacking we had gained the ridge. To our amazement (and delight) we discovered an overgrown user trail along the ridge. Normally we'd have been disappointed to see this sign of man so near the top after so much of our own hard work. Normally we'd be disappointed that someone else had been here before. But today our only emotion was relief. This meant that not only was there a trail to the top, but moreover there was a trail down. If the trail was followable at the summit it'd certainly be followable farther down the mountain. Who knows where it led but it's surely be easier and safer than the route we had taken up.

With victory in sight we turned right on the ridge and headed east. As I mentioned before, there had been some uncertainty in the actual summit location and elevation. Several points along the ridge all seemed to be within a few feet of elevation of each other [reference: Google Earth]. But with a trail to follow we'd have the liberty of visiting all the candidate summits and could determine which one was the actual high point.

We reached the top of the first local maximum (4032ft) but it was obvious that the next one was taller. When we gained the second summit (4056ft) we noticed that the trail fizzled out. Now it certainly seemed that this was tallest but we couldn't be sure about the third summit. To make it official, we headed towards the third summit. After some Grade 4 bushwhacking we reached the third local maximum, elevation 4007ft. Beyond the third summit the ridge kept dropping. So we turned around, backtracked to the second local maximum (well I guess you could call it a global maximum then, for the country at least), and found ourselves, for the second time, on the roof of St. Vincent and the Grenadines.

At that moment, if you don't count people in airplanes, and you assume that nobody was hiking up the high points in Guadeloupe, Martinique, and Dominica, the closest higher people were probably in Venezuela, 275 miles away. Not quite as good as on Denali, we thought, but pretty good nonetheless.

Now it was time for the summit rituals. We had a well-established routine on the state high points: photos of both of us with raised arms, juggling photos, jumping photos, and the collection of a small rock; but for country high points the customs had not yet been established. In addition to the photos we made it the new ritual of scarfing down some food on the summit because we were pretty darn exhausted. Surprisingly the time was only 10:57am, an elapsed time of just 3h57m. It felt like it was already late afternoon.

We lingered on top for a few more minutes, but surrounded by the foggy, viewless sky and with a lingering cloud of uncertainty about the route ahead of us we decided it was time to go. We couldn't find a summit rock so I grabbed a little stick instead.

CRUISE CONTROL

Now the tide was beginning to reverse. Before, we had been climbing through the brush, working against gravity, defying the trees that tried to hold us back, getting farther away from civilization. Now we were on a trail, where people had walked before, gravity was helping us go down, getting closer to the trailhead. With a trail to follow we were almost on cruise control. Now it wasn't exactly what many people would consider to be a "trail" but compared with what we had climbed through it was basically a road. With a trail to follow, the uncertainty in the route was almost completely erased. We just had to follow the trail and we'd get back to where we started.

The trail followed the ridge, passing a few sketchy no-fall zones, before leveling out at sort of a little col. Eric and I were starting to believe that maybe this trail kept going to the west side of the island, which was definitely not the side we wanted to end up on, so we decided it was time to leave the trail and resume our bushwhacking. We spotted a dry riverbed a quarter-mile away and knew that the going would be much easier down there. We looked for the shortest way down, held our breath, and plunged into the bushes. It was tough, but nothing compared with what we'd climbed through. Half an hour later we spotted the riverbed in front of us. "We made it!" I yelled. "Whoa, wait a minute," Eric said, "it's a ten foot drop to get down there."

We did a little scouting back and forth and finally found a suitable route down that ended in a doable five-foot drop. At last we found ourselves in the middle of a huge dry riverbed. There were large boulders everywhere but with plenty of hard sand to walk on it was easy going. If the trail had been a "road" then this riverbed was an interstate. With all the wet vegetation we couldn't figure out why the river bed was dry, but we sure appreciated it. Maybe it only fills up when there's a hurricane, or a big storm? We knew we wouldn't want to be down there during a flash flood.

CLIFFED OUT

Now at this point, just to make things interesting, it began to rain. Hard. Fortunately we found a little cave underneath a cliff and hunkered down inside it for some shelter. From the coziness of our cave we observed fifteen minutes of torrential downpour and noticed some trickles starting to form in the riverbed. I was expecting at any minute to see a big wall of water come roaring down the riverbed, but fortunately the rain eased up. We continued our little trek down the "interstate" and I soon noticed a curious topographic feature in front of me. It appeared that the riverbed, along with a small trickle of water, vanished into thin air. "Uh-oh, I think I know what that means," I told Eric. We walked a little farther and found ourselves standing on the threshold of a 30ft waterfall/cliff.

"Well that's just great," I said to Eric. "Ain't no way we're downclimbing that." We looked to the right side and saw a steep, but potentially downclimbable slope. We put our game faces on. It was bushwhacking time again. And this time it was back to the old Grade 10 junk we had swam through on the way up. But descending this stuff was whole different ball game.

As I slowly descended I went to plant my left foot on what I thought was level ground, but to my dismay there was nothing but air beneath it. Luckily I had been holding onto a strong tree, so in a split second I found myself swinging in thin air. "Eric, watch out for this," I yelled back, "it's a ten foot slope." Unfortunately one of my crocs had fallen off and preceded me into the little abyss. So carefully I lowered myself into the bushes, trying not to put weight onto the bare foot, and was reunited with my little slipper. Most of the time the vegetation was a total nuisance, but on this occasion, I could hold onto some of the jungle grass to slow my descent. We made it past that obstacle and pushed on. Well, that's ten feet down, we've got twenty to go before we're back at the riverbed, I thought.

We descended a few feet more. I remember thinking, "I wonder what those last fifteen feet are going to look like, it's getting pretty steep," and all of a sudden air materialized once again beneath my feet. The brush was so dense that I wasn't able to fall more than a few inches. Those fifteen feet were indeed very steep, but with the super dense brush we were able to ease ourselves down it safely. Finally we were at the base of the little waterfall. It was pretty much vertical and definitely not down-climbable.

We brushed ourselves off and kept walking. After a little boulder scrambling the riverbed began to widen out even more. "Wow, this is just too easy," I said to Eric. "It's about the only easy hiking we've done today." We began to congratulate ourselves on finishing all the hard stuff. We just had to descend a little farther along the riverbed, then climb up to the crater rim, where there'd be a trail, and it'd be easy going again.

But a short while later we rounded a corner and found another little topographic feature to greet us: another waterfall. Fortunately there was only a little trickle of water in the riverbed so we could safely approach it closely to see what we were up against. But this wasn't an ordinary little waterfall, this was a full-fledged cliff that dropped about sixty feet. We didn't dare walk close enough to peek over.

Neither of us was too surprised, one more obstacle like this just seemed par for the course. "Well that's too bad," I said, "I don't know how we're getting out of this one. There's cliffs on every side of us. There's no way we're walking around this one."

BACK ON CRUISE CONTROL

"Why don't we backtrack a little; it seemed like there was a little hill we could climb up back there," Eric said. "Maybe we're close enough to the crater that we can just walk up to it?"

With little optimism I agreed and we headed back up the riverbed. We came to the base of a steep—but doable—hill and started climbing. "Hmm, that's weird," Eric said, "this almost looks like a trail." We climbed a little higher and lo and behold the trail opened up before us. Salvation! We noticed some discarded shoes and some trash on the trail and knew things would be getting easier. It's not often that you rejoice at the sight of trash, but when it means that your life is about to get a lot easier it's something to celebrate.

After another hundred feet of climbing we were back on the crater rim and back in business. We were now on the opposite side of the crater from this morning, so we'd need to hike halfway around it, but with a nice trail to follow it was almost trivial. Once again, just to make things interesting, it began to pour. This time it was very hard.

Eric and I threw on our meager rain gear and plodded on. Luckily it was still in the upper 60F's so even though we were already completely saturated we were still warm. I looked down and began to contemplate the crocs that I was wearing. The most treacherous part wasn't the lack of foot protection from branches, it was the lack of friction. The foot/croc friction and croc/ground friction coefficients were both pretty dismal, meaning that (especially on steep climbs) I was at risk for my crocs slipping with respect to the rocks and also my foot slipping out of my crocs. It was particularly treacherous during this torrential downpour.

HUMAN CONTACT

Eventually we spotted a curious sight in front of us. Other people! They were probably just as surprised as we were. We talked with the lead dude and found out they were part of a big group headed from one side of the island to the other. They had started at the same trailhead as us, were walking along the rim of the crater, and were planning to take another trail down to the leeward (west) side of the island. Everyone greeted us with a look of surprise. Maybe they were surprised we didn't have a guide. Maybe they just didn't expect to see anyone else trudging through this rainstorm high on this volcano. When we reached the end of their group we noticed three guide-looking dudes each carrying a big bucket. They gave us each a nod of approval. I figured that if anyone ever asked why we didn't have a guide I'd just tell them that Eric was my guide and he'd say that I was his guide. We were guiding each other, I suppose.

Sometime while we were passing their group we noticed the big rope leading all the way down to the crater floor. It was steep, but not unreasonable. We were tempted to do it, but we had already attained our objective today and didn't feel like pushing our luck any further.

For the rest of the hike our minds were on cruise control. True, the wind was howling, driving the torrential rain into our faces. I had to hold my hood on my head and at one point I finally brought my arm down; with it drained a full cup of water that had accumulated in the elbow area. But this was the easy part. We just needed to follow the trail in front of us and didn't need to think too hard about much else.

BACK ON THE REAL TRAIL

We made it back to our starting point on the crater rim, completing a big loop. With my mind still on cruise control and with super-dense fog, we almost didn't recognize the spot and nearly kept going. We took one last look into the crater and noticed twenty brand new waterfalls that had just formed. Some cascaded all the way from the crater rim, a thousand feet down to the floor. It was amazing to think that somehow all that water drained out underground.

We turned back onto the main trail and began the one-hour descent back to the Rabacca Trailhead. The tiny little trickles we had barely noticed on the way up turned into full-blown creeks on the way down. You could still jump over them but we couldn't help but wonder what our "dry" riverbed looked like right about now.

The rain soon let up. After passing a few hikers near the bottom we suddenly heard a bunch of people talking up ahead and after climbing one last hill we were finally back at the start. As we emerged into the parking lot a news-reporter-looking-dude was pointing a video camera at us. I gave him a big thumbs-up.

237

"WE SAW IT ON WIKIPEDIA"

A woman with a microphone pulled Eric aside and began to interview him about the hike. Turns out they were interviewing everyone who had "climbed the mountain" that day. When it was my turn they asked me the standard questions about what mountain I had climbed. When we told them how difficult it had been and showed them the scars on our arms and legs they probably wondered "which mountain did they climb?" They probably couldn't figure out just why our bodies were so torn up on such an easy trail. I'm not sure they understood the distinction I tried to make between "where the trail stops" and "where the highest point is."

At the end they asked me how we had heard about this mountain. "We're trying to climb several Caribbean country high points this week," I said, "and we heard about La Soufière on Wikipedia." I could tell that wasn't the answer they were expecting.

But our hike wasn't exactly over yet. We still had another three miles back to our car with a potentially-dead battery. We mingled with the people in the parking lot, trying to make friends, in the hopes that someone would give us a ride down, but it appeared that everyone was pretty comfortable hanging around and wasn't prepared to leave anytime soon.

FINISHING WITH HONOR

"Fine, let's just get out of here," I said to Eric, "at least we can control what time we make it back to the car." We packed up our meager belongings and trudged down the mountain. As we passed through a grove of palm and banana trees I noticed something yellow in the grass ahead of us. Bananas! We looked around to make sure nobody was looking and scarfed down the ripe ones. It was our first dose of fruit in the past three days. The clouds thinned and soon the sun came out. Our sunscreen was still in my lost backpack, but at this point I didn't even care if I got sunburned, it would only be a minor discomfort compared with the gashes on my arms and legs.

We heard some cars speeding down the mountain and stuck out our hands and waved, hoping that they could drive us down the last mile of road. But the drivers simply waved back and kept going. "Maybe we should have stuck out our thumbs," I said to Eric, "I wonder what the gesture for hitchhiking is down here?"

Finally at 3pm we arrived back at the car, finishing honorably under our own power. "What do you think the chances are that it'll start?" I asked Eric, "I say it starts." "I'll say it starts," Eric said. And indeed it started. "Now how do you like them apples?" he asked.

Along the two-hour drive back to the airport we got our little tour of St Vincent that we had missed in the darkness last night. As we drove along the spectacular coastline it was pretty clear that very few tourists come to this part of the island because there wasn't a single hotel in sight.

We were back at the SVD airport by 5pm and knocked on the Avis door, ready to give Curtis a piece of our mind. Of course the door was locked. "Well it's nice we flew in yesterday," Eric said, "because there's no way we could have done this mountain in eleven hours, especially with all this hassle with the rental car."

VICTORY

After we got done unpacking we sat down next to our Suzuki and talked about what to do next. Mysteriously my backpack still hadn't been found yet, but the LIAT reps said they were still looking for it. With five more hours before our flight to Barbados we still had plenty of time to see the sights and sounds of Kingstown. But we couldn't muster the energy to stand up. We both sat there, in the parking lot, silent, with absolutely no desire to do anything. We were exhausted.

I thought about my contacts and rubbed my dry, red eyes and reluctantly came to the conclusion that I ought to find some contact solution before we left. My eyes couldn't take much more of this. I summoned a taxi and we embarked on wild goose chase to pharmacies in downtown Kingstown that eventually came back fruitless. It appears that nobody in the country wears contacts.

We dragged our stuff into the airport, slumped down onto the benches, and awaited our flight. La Soufrière had taken a lot out of us, but today we had won. It had been at the expense of some blood, some sleep, and perhaps my backpack but we had won. We hoped that our next mountain, Mt Hillaby in Barbados, would fall more easily . . .

(Note: the backpack was finally located and repatriated two weeks later. I think US customs abandoned their inspection of its contents after they got a whiff of the one-gallon of two week old Grenadan jungle mud and swamp water infused into my clothes and shoes.)

SOUTH AMERICA:
CERRO TRES KANDU

PARAGUAY

2,762ft

Date climbed: June 30, 2012

Author: Eric

I slowed my car to a stop and leaned forward for a better look. The road I saw ahead of me did not look appealing. An old bridge had apparently washed out and been hastily repaired. Dirt had been bulldozed or shoveled on top of a big concrete pipe, but the bridge width was only just barely as wide as the car, and there were 15-foot drops on each side. The road was rough too—enough so that I suspected my little car might bottom out and get stuck on the bridge even if I managed to keep it from slipping off the edge.

I stepped out to investigate closer, bringing my headlamp because the sun had long-since set. It didn't look quite as impossible up close, so I got back in the car and drove up a little closer. I started inching the front wheels over the first big bump. I couldn't tell exactly where the wheels were by looking out the front, and I desperately wished I had a spotter to help out. I rolled down the window and stuck my head out for a better view.

I glanced from the road ahead down to the 15-ft drop and immediately slammed on the brakes. "This is crazy," I thought. I pulled back into reverse and got back off the road, looking for a place on the side to pull over. Road-walking would add several hours to my hike up Cerro Tres Kandu, the tallest mountain in Paraguay, I figured, but at least my car wouldn't fall into a river.

Then I saw a light in the road behind me, and noticed a lone man biking quickly towards me on the rough dirt road.

"Uh oh," I thought, "he must have seen me sneaking through that gate a few miles back."

I could definitely outrun this guy in my car, but now I was trapped with an impassable road ahead of me, and nowhere to turn. I nervously awaited my fate.

Earlier that morning I had successfully climbed the highest mountain in Uruguay, Cerro Catedral, and made it back to Montevideo just in time for my 11am flight to Asuncion, Paraguay. But of course in South America, as I was beginning to learn, flying was not quite as reliable as back in the US.

"You do know, sir, that the airport is currently closed," the ticketing agent told me as I checked in in Montevideo. "No flights are departing or arriving. I will let you go to the boarding room, though, and maybe you will fly out today still."

I quietly nodded and took my ticket. At first I was sure she meant the Asuncion airport was closed, because the Montevideo airport certainly had a lot of activity. I knew that just the previous week the president of Paraguay had been impeached in what some newspapers were calling a coup d'etat, and I had heard there were street protests in Asuncion. Could that be causing the airport to close? It didn't matter, though—I had only given myself 20 hours on the ground in Paraguay, and if I didn't fly out today there would be no hope of summiting Cerro Tres Kandu.

I passed through security and noticed the boarding room was packed. The departure monitors said "Retrasado" [Delayed] for every single flight. I looked out the window and the whole airport was engulfed in dense fog. Now it made sense: the *Montevideo* airport was closed due to weather.

I took a seat and began reading a Spanish newspaper. One by one the flights on the screen started changing from "retrasado" to "cancelado." I was nervously watching the cancelados crawl down the screen wishing I could build some sort of force field around Asuncion. At 12:30 pm I glanced outside, and for the first time all morning started seeing some high-rise buildings of Montevideo. The fog had cleared!

Now the retrasados started changing to embarques [boarding], and Asuncion jumped up to a 13:30 embarque. I happily hopped on the plane, and promptly went to sleep. I've learned when traveling like this to take advantage of any time window possible to put some sleep in the bank, just in case I might need it later. That would turn out to be a wise decision today.

Two hours later we touched down in Asuncion, and with no checked bags I quickly made it through customs and to the Hertz car rental counter. I handed over my printed out reservation form and said I had a reservation for today for un "carro automatico."

"Donde vas?"[where are you going] the woman behind the desk asked, apparently to get an idea of how many kilometers/day to charge me.

"Voy a la cima del Cerro Tres Kandu, la montana mas alta en el Paraguay. Es cerca de Numi." [I'm going to the top of Cerro Tres Kandu, the tallest mountain in Paraguay. It's close to Numi] I replied.

She raised her eyebrows. "Numi?? En el interior del pais?" [Numi?? In the middle of the country?]

I pulled out a map printout and pointed out the location. I guess she was expecting me to say I'd just drive around Asuncion looking at museums or something. She turned around and consulted with another guy behind the counter. They started discussing how far away Numi was and whether my highlighted route would even be possible given road conditions. Eventually she accepted my plan and started filling out some paperwork.

"Cual es el nombre de tu hotel?" [what is the name of your hotel?] she asked, needing to fill that line in on some form.

"No tengo hotel. Voy a hacer de camping." [I don't have a hotel. I'm going to camp] I replied. She looked confused, not sure how to fill in that line. After a little bit of thought she just wrote Numi, and then handed it to me to sign.

I was getting a fancy white Pasat with automatic transmission. I think that was the only automatic transmission car out of all the rental cars at the airport and I was the lucky one to drive it for the next day. I could probably handle a manual if needed, but was unsure how crazy the driving would be in Paraguay and didn't want to worry about anything except where to drive.

I stepped inside, pulled open the sunroof, and started powering up both my GPS units. It was currently 3:15pm and Google maps said I had a 3.5 hour drive to the start of the hiking. However, that didn't account for any traffic, bad roads, or getting lost as I would soon find out.

The car GPS turned on fine, but for some reason couldn't acquire any satellites. I waited around for 15 minutes with no luck. My hiking GPS worked fine and I had loaded satellite images of Asuncion on it, but none of the streets on there were labeled. I finally decided to navigate the old fashioned way and rely on my printed out map.

I headed out of the airport and soon realized that absolutely no roads are labeled in Paraguay. I thought Boston was bad, but I've now found a new first place city on the impossible-to-navigate-through list. I started following the first big road I found that looked like it went in the generally-correct direction, then after 10 minutes at a traffic light checked my hiking GPS. This road was taking me right into downtown Asuncion, where I definitely didn't want to be! Turning around was nearly impossible, and it took me another 10 minutes to finally find a spot.

I headed back toward the airport, and turned right on the first big road I came to. I saw a sign for San Luis, which happened to be on my intended route, and started relaxing that I was finally on the correct road. After I passed through San Luis I looked at the GPS again, and I was somehow almost to the Argentina border south of Asuncion! Could the GPS be wrong? Or maybe the San Luis sign was wrong?

I started heading east on a different road back into Paraguay, but the road soon deteriorated to dirt. This had gone far enough. I tried playing around with the car GPS again and it finally acquired satellites, but could only highlight my route in a "walking mode" which didn't help too much when I was driving. I probably could have figured it out, but was too anxious at this point to just get out of Asuncion that I accepted that level of performance of the GPS. I finally got on a road heading toward my intended destination and started making real progress. I figure I probably lost an hour driving around Asuncion, and by now it was getting dark.

I cruised down [unlabeled] highway 1 through Ita, Paraguari, and Villarica, then turned east just past Numi onto an unnamed road. I had marked waypoints on the GPS where to turn once the road started getting rough, and I pulled over in the little village of General-Eugenio-Alejandrino-Garay to assess my position. I had somehow chosen to stop exactly at the next turnoff, though it was hard to tell there was even a turnoff there. I started following an indescript dirt path (I wouldn't even call it a road, more of a patch of grass worn down to dirt by a couple cars) on what was supposedly Camino al 3 Kandu. I had actually just marked the way-points based on a satellite image of what looked like a road, so there were no guarantees this would route would even work.

Camino al 3 Kandu Obstacle Uno

I continued on this path for a minute until the GPS indicated I should turn left. I pulled the car left, and saw the remnants of an old decrepit wooden bridge in front of me. Someone had stuck huge branches up in front of it indicating not to try to cross.

This didn't look good. This was sort of a residential area with a few houses, so I figured there had to be another way around that bridge. I turned around and drove back down the path, then took a right turn following another road, and eventually ended up on the other side of the bridge. Piece of cake! Now I was back on my intended route. Somehow the path looked more traveled now and I'd actually call it a road. But it was super rough and I came close to bottoming out in a few places.

Camino al 3 Kandu Obstacle Dos

I kept following the dirt road, making turns every once in a while to follow my waypoints but then I ran into more trouble. There was a big wooden gate in front of the road, and it was closed. I stopped the car and looked at my GPS, but there was no apparent way around this one. I was on the outskirts of the village and this was the only road up to Cerro Tres Kandu.

I had learned, however, from my adventures over the years that gates over roads are almost never actually locked. The gate might indicate you're not *allowed* to pass through, but it seldom actually *prevents* you from passing through. That was true in the US, at least. I was hoping that would be the case in Paraguay as well.

I stopped the car, jumped out, and pulled on the gate. It swung open with ease. I looked around to gleefully boast "Look! I told you so!" to someone, but luckily I was still alone. I drove the car through, closed the gate behind me, and continued up the road.

Camino al 3 Kandu Obstacle Tres

Before long I reached my third obstacle of Camino al 3 Kandu—the sketchy narrow impassable bridge. And then I saw that biker racing towards me from behind. He must have seen me sneak through that gate . . .

I stepped out of the car and tried to smile and be friendly.

"Buenos noches!" I tried.

The man stopped and got off his bike. He started talking in some language that definitely wasn't Spanish, but somehow he didn't seem mad. Then he stuck his hand out as if to shake hands. I couldn't understand a word he said, but shook his hand and tried to see if he spoke Spanish.

"Hola, me llamo Eric. Y usted? Mucho Gusto." [Hi, my name is Eric. What's your name? Nice to meet you], I tried.

He obviously didn't understand, but kept smiling and talking and pointing toward the bridge. He had to have some name, though, so I thought of him as Pedro.

I kept trying to speak in Spanish using hand gestures, and Pedro kept talking in his language and using hand gestures, and then he brought me over to the bridge. He was motioning like the bridge was good and trying to say my car could make it over. I shook my head and motioned that it was not wide enough, but Pedro whipped out a little flashlight and started showing me more of the bridge. I got the impression he might have been one of the people who constructed it and had a sense of pride that I could indeed make it over.

Pedro walked over to the other side and motioned for me to drive over. I was actually getting more confident with all his persuasion, and he could even be my spotter, so I got back in the car and slowly started inching my way over. He kept nodding and waving me forward and I soon cleared the last bump and was safe on the other side! Pedro greeted me with a huge smile and waved me on. I later learned from my dad's Paraguayan student Fatima that the language "Pedro" spoke is Guarani and is very common in all of Paraguay.

It was another 1.5 miles to the end of the road and some vegetation in the middle of the road started scrapping the underside of the car, but as long as rocks weren't scrapping I figured the car would be fine. At 8:30pm I rounded the final corner, drove through one more gate (this one was already open), and reached the end of the road. Amazingly there was a trailhead sign and even an outhouse! The sign had a huge topo map with a trail drawn and the summit of Cerro Tres Kandu labeled. I didn't even know there was a trail to the summit! There was basically zero information online about this mountain, so I had had no idea what to expect.

I parked the car and started scarfing down some food. It had taken me five hours to drive to the trailhead, and the trailhead sign claimed the round-trip hike to Tres Kandu was 3.5 hours. I started doing the math: I had an 11am flight tomorrow so needed to be back to Asuncion by 9am, which meant leave the trailhead by 4am. But at 3.5 hours of hiking I'd get done by between midnight and 1am. My conclusion: I'd just have to be faster than 3.5 hours for the hiking and then earn myself some sleep.

By 9pm I'd packed my bag and started heading up the trail. I wish Paraguay would have put as much effort into the access road as they'd put into this trail. It was very well-maintained, had check steps, wooden benches every kilometer, and even signs every few hundred meters noting how far I'd come, how much farther to the summit, and what my current elevation was. It was amazing! The one fault I can find, though, is that the trail had zero switchbacks. Apparently that technology hasn't reached Paraguay yet.

Instead they tied metal cables between trees on the really steep sections, and I certainly used these cables for balance. By 10pm the trail started leveling out, and I reached a big sign proclaiming "Bienvenido al punto mass alto del Paraguay" [Welcome to the highest point in Paraguay]. That was the summit! I was still in the middle of the jungle so there wasn't really any view, but I suppose there wouldn't have been much of a view at night anyways. At least I could see the summit, unlike Uruguay the day before.

I took a bunch of pictures, including my very important juggling picture. I couldn't find five rocks here like I normally do, but three sticks seemed good enough. After 10 minutes of fooling around I turned back and started my descent. It was tricky descending the steep sections but I still managed to get back to the car by 11pm for a 2-hour round trip. I quickly hopped in the car and went to sleep, knowing that I'd need every minute I could get for the drive in the morning.

My alarm jolted me awake at 4am and I quickly got behind the wheel and started moving. I was surprised to have never seen Pedro again, but figured he must have a hut somewhere back in the woods there that I didn't notice. I carefully drove over the sketchy bridge again and luckily had no trouble.

The drive back to Asuncion was straightforward except for two minor little incidents. First, at 5:30am just before the sun rose I came upon a tractor driving on the shoulder on my side, and an oncoming car in my lane coming straight at me. Apparently he was either drunk, thought the tractor was actually in the opposing lane instead of the shoulder, or some combination of the two. I was alert though and swerved out safely behind the tractor before the car could get too close.

The second little incident happened just outside the town of Ita, and I don't think a certain chicken will ever be crossing any roads again anytime soon. The stupid bird was pecking away on the opposite shoulder, but got scared by an oncoming car and flew right in front of my car.

I made it back to the airport well-ahead of schedule (I didn't get lost this time), and successfully got on my plane to my conference in Rio. The highest points in both Uruguay and Paraguay made for quite a fun weekend adventure.

OCEANIA: AORAKI/MT COOK

NEW ZEALAND

2,762ft

Date climbed: November 5, 2012

Author: Eric

"NOOOO MOOOORE ROOOPE" Matthew yelled across the icy ridge to me as the lines tied to my harness went taut.

I cursed loudly, but the wind blew the words out of my mouth before they could reach Matthew.

"CAN I HAVE JUST 15 MORE FEET?" I yelled hopefully, louder this time. I was perched precariously, balancing on the four front-points of my crampons each poked a half-inch into the steep ice, with my two ice tools hooked over the top of the knife-edge ice ridge I was traversing. I looked down at the 5,000ft of mountain falling away beneath my feet. It was not the place to build an anchor and start belaying.

I twisted another screw into the ice and clipped it to the rope. The summit of Mount Cook was literally close enough to throw a snowball at, if not for the wind that would have blown the snowball away.

"NOOOO MOOOORE ROOOPE" Matthew yelled back again.

Day 0

"Nobody's been up Cook yet this season," the ranger on the other end of the phone warned me. It was Saturday, November 3, and I had just called up the Mt Cook ranger station to check in before heading up to the mountains. "We've had a snowy winter, and the weather hasn't been clear for the past 5 weeks. A crew just went up to Plateau Hut last weekend to check up on it after the winter. Do you know the avy conditions up there?"

"Yes," I replied, "I saw today was forecasted to be considerable above 2000m."

"Well, we'd really like to talk to you in person before you head up, but it's not required."

"I'll try to make it to the station in person," I replied, before giving him the details of my itinerary, planned return day, and emergency contact information. The ranger's response was a little surprising to me. I thought November was the standard start of the climbing season for Mount Cook, and that there'd already be all kinds of climbers up there. Over the phone he had seemed concerned that we knew what we were getting ourselves into, and I hoped to dispel his concerns when we met in person.

I had found myself in New Zealand for a conference and decided to tag the highest mountain in the country, Mt Cook, before returning to the US. Mount Cook is not a trivial mountain. The altitude may be modest (12,316ft), but the easiest way up involves significant glacier travel, several pitches of rock and ice climbing, and a traverse of the famously corniced and icy knife-edge summit ridge. I'd read reports of the summit "day" taking from 15-30 hours round trip. On top of all this, the weather in the Mt Cook region is notoriously bad, and climbers have reported waiting out weather for a week or more before getting a summit window or giving up. Matthew and I had given ourselves a one-week summit window, and hoped that would be sufficient.

In Christchurch on Saturday I met up with Ian, a good friend from Kentucky now living in New Zealand, and we spent most of the day running errands to prepare for the climb. I bought 14 person-days of food, maps, a new headlamp (to replace the one I'd given to a kid in Fiji the previous weekend), and checked in with the rangers over the phone. Ian very generously offered to let us borrow his car for the drive, so I also practiced my left-side-of-road driving, and practiced navigating from Ian's house to the airport to the road towards Mt Cook.

Day 1

On Sunday morning I drove to the airport and met Matthew just as he landed at 9:10am, 37 hours after he had left Boston. We immediately jumped in the car and took off towards Mt Cook village. The prudent thing to do after 37 hours of travel to a new time zone 17 hours ahead of Eastern Time would probably have been to take a rest day to recover. However, a high pressure system was just starting to bring a good weather window to the Mt Cook region, and we didn't want to risk the weather turning bad again before we had a chance to summit. We had also arranged a 2:30pm flight onto the glacier that day, and would have just enough time to make the 4.5-hour drive from Christchurch to Mt Cook village.

I navigated the roads of Christchurch as I'd practiced with Ian, and soon reached the open countryside on Route 1. We cruised past innumerable sheep farms, with huge snowy mountains always looming in the distance to the west. We passed through Ashburton, Geraldine, and Fairlie before turning up the Mt Cook road at Lake Pukaki.

Here we got the first view of our objective. Mount Cook was hard to miss—it was the only mountain with a lenticular cloud forming above it, and was obviously the tallest object around. Other than near Mt Cook, the sky was completely sunny, and we noticed patches of fresh snow on the ground in the shade. The snow Saturday must have reached all the way down to the valley floor, and Mt Cook had undoubtedly been hammered by yet another storm.

We continued up the valley and reached the Mt Cook Village airport at 1:30pm. With an hour to spare before our scheduled departure, we kept driving into the village, and pulled off at the visitor center to officially check in with the rangers.

"Hi, we're planning to climb Mt Cook and wanted to check in," I said to the ranger behind the desk.

"Oh yes, I know you two. Gilbertson, right?" the ranger asked, flipping through a registration book. "The weather actually looks good for the next few days, and there's a group of three from Aspiring Guides already at Plateau Hut. Looks like I have all your information so you're all set."

We thanked him and headed back to the car.

"That's reassuring," Matthew said as we drove back to the airport. "If a guide is willing to take his clients up there, the conditions must not be that bad."

We walked into the little airport at 2pm and talked to Trish at the counter. She had two items of good news: there were two other climbers that would split the ride up with us to lower the price, and we'd get to ride in a helicopter. We quickly paid and ran back to the car to pack our gear. Everything was thrown out on the gravel lot then crammed back into backpacks. We lifted the packs, decided they were too heavy, and threw out a couple pounds of food and some extra climbing cams back into the car. Satisfied, we brought our gear around to the loading dock and heaved it on an enormous trolley with the other climbers' gear.

The helicopter started revving its engine and a group of hunters in orange camouflage began loading up gear. Five men climbed on board and the helicopter took off up into the mountains. They were apparently hunting Tahr, an invasive mountain goat from the Himalayas that produces tasty meat.

As the helicopter made several rounds ferrying gear up for the hunters, Matthew and I hung out in the airport lounge talking to the two other climbers, Geoff Wayatt and Philip Somerville, both from New Zealand. Geoff is a seasoned guide and local legend with many ascents of Mt Cook under his belt. As we learned over the next few days, Geoff was the first person to ski-descend from the summit of Mt Cook (1982) and has climbed Cook 24 times and Mt Aspiring 87 times. His friend Philip, a reporter for the Otago Daily Times (NZ), was aspiring for his first ascent. They had the luxury of being locals, and had decided to give Cook a go based on the good weather forecast. Matthew and I had decided over a month ago to fly up to Cook on this particular day, and had merely gotten lucky with the weather.

By 3:30pm it was our turn for a ride. We pushed the big metal trolley over to the helicopter and crammed the backpacks and duffle bags into a little box on the helicopter's leg. We hopped inside, put on our earphones, and buckled up.

The next 15 minutes were spectacular. We took off high above the Tasman glacier, passing over Tasman Lake and all kinds of rugged mountains on the side. At the foot of the Boys Glacier we started climbing straight up, and then angled forward towards a big red building perched on a rock overlooking the Grand Plateau—Plateau Hut.

We slowly touched down on a flat mound of snow 100ft from the hut, and quickly got out to unload the gear. We threw all the packs onto the snow, held them down solidly, and then the chopper flew away.

Plateau Hut was much more luxurious than anything we had imagined. It had bunks for around 30 people, with soft cushions and blankets at each bunk. Bunks were partitioned into five rooms, so it almost felt like a luxurious hostel. There was a huge kitchen with picnic tables, pots, pans, bowls, spoons, and even gas-powered burners. Huge black bins outside were full of liquid water so we didn't need to melt snow, and a nice two-seater outhouse was positioned just outside the hut. There were even solar-charged lights in the hut. We now realized we had brought much more gear than we needed. The two stoves and fuel bottles, pots, pads, zero-degree sleeping bags, and more were all unnecessary.

Matthew only had one thing on his mind, though—sleep. It was currently the middle of the night Boston Time, and since Matthew hadn't had any time to adjust to New Zealand time he was exhausted. He immediately found a bunk, crawled into his sleeping bag, and tried to go to sleep.

I threw my gear on a bunk and started cooking a fresh pound of pasta. There were three other climbers there part of the Aspiring Guides group. They had flown in that morning and decided to hike up the route a ways to check out conditions. They hadn't brought snowshoes, but managed to make it up to the Linda Shelf before turning back. Apparently the snow was quite soft and made for difficult walking without snowshoes. They decided to make Monday a rest day to recover and give a summit bid on Tuesday.

Luckily Matthew, I, Geoff, and Philip had all brought snowshoes so were prepared for these early-season conditions.

At 7pm the radio in the hut came to life with a ranger down in the village giving a weather update. The forecast for Monday was sunny in the morning with afternoon snow, winds 60kph on the summits, and considerable avalanche danger. Tuesday had a similar forecast.

Geoff said the conditions sounded marginal but he'd give it a go, and Matthew and I decided to go for it as well. These might be the best conditions Mt Cook ever sees, we reasoned, so why wait? I think we all realized that a group of four was much safer than a group of two on this mountain, so we coordinated to all leave at the same time, 2am. This time was a bit of a compromise—I'd read many groups leave earlier, like midnight, to try to get back to the hut before the heat of the day when snow bridges start melting. But Matthew also needed all the sleep he could get to be at full strength, so we agreed to sleep in a little.

We all went to bed by 8pm with alarms set.

Day 2

Monday morning 1am. It was game time. Matthew and I got out of our sleeping bags and quickly started some water boiling. We scarfed down some cereal, packed up our bags, and were out the door by 2am. I made the decision, based on Geoff's advice, to pare down my rock rack even more in anticipation of a mostly icy climb. I left my set of nuts, bringing only 4 cams, 6 ice screws, and a bunch of slings. Extra weight would only make the climbing more difficult.

The sky was perfectly clear at 2am, with millions of stars and a half moon illuminating our path so as to almost not need headlamps. Geoff and Phillip started out first as Matthew and I sorted out our rope system, but we soon caught up and volunteered to take the lead breaking trail. We were mostly following the tracks of the Italians from the previous day, but they were often drifted over from blowing snow.

We started out descending onto the Grand Plateau, then climbed up onto the Linda Glacier. I headed towards an obvious snow gully on the left, but after consulting with Geoff I got back on the right track and continued up the Linda. I think our team of four worked well—Geoff and Philip kept us going in the right direction and Matthew and I broke trail.

I had seen pictures of this section of the Linda riddled with a labyrinth of crevasses, but this early in the season we hardly noticed we were even on a glacier. Most of the crevasses were covered with snow bridges, and we could be reasonably confident that, in snowshoes, we probably wouldn't poke through. The biggest crevasses still remained open, though, and these required special caution to avoid. We soon passed the highpoint of the Italians and were blazing our own trail. It's thrilling walking across a glacier where you're not following anyone else's tracks and aren't sure whether you're walking on solid snow or a thin snow bridge.

Matthew and I alternated leads as the glacier got steeper. Occasionally the leader would yell out "CREVASSE!" as he approached a particularly questionable gap, and the follower got ready to catch a fall. We even had to jump over a few small ones.

Around 5am we hooked left onto the Linda Shelf just as the alpenglow started forming on the horizon. By now we were well ahead of Geoff and Philip and were pretty confident we could find the route on our own. We ditched our snowshoes at a bergschrund just before the shelf, sticking them in the snow to retrieve on the way back. On top of the shelf we traversed a steep snowy slope, and climbed up to a bigger bergschrund at the top of the Linda Glacier.

This bergschrund marked the beginning of the fun part of the climb, where many parties start pitching out the route. Matthew struggled over the bergschrund first, then marched straight up a snow/ice gully above it. I soon squirmed over the bergschrund as well and started up the gully. The climbing was easy enough that we felt comfortable without placing gear or belaying for the next two rope-lengths.

Matthew soon reached the top of the gully, clipped an old sling, and belayed me up the rest of the way. We had reached the ridgeline at the base of the summit rocks. To our right was a short rock cliff, to our left the snow ridge continued down gently, and in front of us was a 2,000ft drop straight back down to the Grand Plateau. The sky was still clear in all directions as predicted, and the wind was hardly noticeable.

"Looks like we might need all this climbing stuff we lugged up here after all," Matthew said, looking up at the cliff.

I took out my screws and cams, and Matthew started flaking out our second rope. We'd been using one of the double ropes on the glacier, and now needed both of them connecting us for the steeper climbing. As we prepared for the climb, both physically and mentally, Matthew queued up "Born to Be Wild" followed by "We Will Rock You" on his phone and set the volume to maximum. "This might drain the batteries, but it'll be well worth it," he said.

As Matthew hit play, I soon started climbing up the rocks. It was probably only moderate 5th class climbing, but in crampons, with a big pack on, with snow-covered rocks and big gloves on it felt considerably more difficult. I struggled for a few minutes, stuck a cam in, clipped it, then downclimbed back to the snow to rest.

"We'll never make it up at this rate," Matthew lamented.

"Yeah, there's got to be an easier way up this," I replied. I looked to the right, but was deterred by the smooth down-sloping snow-covered rocks. To the left, though, was a steep rock ramp covered in deeper snow. It looked like it would go.

I climbed back up to retrieve my cam, then wound around left. After mantling up a boulder I managed to angle right and get to the top of the original cliff. I clipped a cam and continued climbing.

"That's how you do it!" I yelled down to Matthew.

Just for fun, we had decided to bring walkie-talkies to enhance our communication during the climb. They actually turned out to be invaluably helpful on the Summit Rocks—when I built an anchor I'd radio in to Matthew "take me off belay, Matthew" and then pretty soon I'd hear "ok, Eric, you're off belay" crackle over the radio. Without them, it would have been next to impossible to hear each other with fifty meters of rope and rock in between us.

Geoff had told us the summit rocks are usually all iced over this time of year, but this must have been an unusual year. I was climbing on lightly snow-covered rock for the most part, with only the occasional icy bit I could sink an ice ax pick into. I clipped an old sling, then at the end of a rope length found a solid steel cable wrapped around a rock. I clipped this and belayed Matthew up the first pitch.

We continued inch-worming up this way with me in the lead for two or three more pitches of mixed rock, ice, and snow, until the ridge leveled out and the rocks disappeared. I built a solid ice-screw anchor this time and belayed Matthew up to meet me.

"That was the crux, right?" Matthew asked. "So it should be a cake walk from here."

"Um, not exactly," I replied, looking up at how much mountain we had left. I think I could see the summit, but we still had a thousand vertical feet to climb on narrow ice and snow ridges. The ridge we were standing on was, in fact, particularly sketchy. It was mostly firm snow, but fist-size solid-rime-ice feathers stuck out intermittently, and would break off if stepped on, acting like ball bearings propelling anything above them down the mountain. The slope wasn't particularly steep near the top of the ridge, but it still felt better to have the protection of the rope here.

We decided to pitch out one more rope-length to be safe. I carefully traversed the ridge, placing an ice screw along the way, then cut around a rock outcrop and front-pointed using my ice axes up another ice gully. The snow conditions were better at the top of this gully, so I dug down with my adz to the ice underneath, built another anchor, and belayed Matthew up.

Now we decided to simul-climb to speed up the ascent. I climbed first up the snow ridge, and at the end of a rope length pounded a picket in. Matthew then unclipped from the anchor and we started walking in unison. This way we were making progress at twice the rate as before, and if someone fell there was always at least one piece of gear between us to catch the fall.

The snow soon turned very deep—first shin deep, then knee, then mid-thigh, until I reached another huge overhanging bergschrund. The left end was a 15-foot tall overhanging ice cliff, shrinking to the right to a more manageable five-foot gap. I wallowed over to the 5-foot gap, and started testing the snow on the edge. The top was firm snow, but the bottom was fluffy powder that I struggled to get a firm foothold in. I eventually jammed both ice axe shafts into the firm snow above the gap, leaned forward, and pulled my body over the gap. It wasn't elegant, but it worked.

The slope steepened above this bergschrund and changed to ice, so I continued frontpointing up, placing ice screws more liberally. Matthew had no problem with the bergschrund, and we simul-climbed up the steep ice/snow slope.

I reached the top of the slope and was immediately blasted by a gust of wind. There was apparently no more mountain remaining to provide shelter. Did this mean I was at the top? I looked around, but it was apparent I had merely reached the edge of the summit ridge. I spied a local maximum about 200ft down the ridge that was definitely at least 20ft taller than the spot I was at. Come to think of it, this location did look awfully familiar from the pictures I'd seen. There was one picture taken right here of two climbers congratulating each other for reaching the summit, even though there was an obviously higher part of the mountain in the background.

I pounded in a picket and an ice screw and belayed Matthew up to my perch.

"Yep, that's definitely the true summit out there," Matthew agreed, his voice trailing off.

"Well, the summit rocks weren't the crux of the route, then, that's for sure," I responded, still staring at the ridge. The elevation change wasn't the problem—it was the sharpness and shininess of the ridge that made it intimidating. Here in front of us was the true definition of "knife-edge ridge." I'm not talking like the Knife-Edge Ridge Trail on Katahdin in the US—this one was literally sharp enough to cut you. If you took the ridge, and shrunk it down to something that could fit in the palm your hand, you could shave with it. The middle section of the ridge was solid blue ice, almost completely vertical on the left side dropping 5,000ft down to the Grand Plateau, and probably a 60-70 degree slope on the right dropping the same distance. There was no way to walk on top of it—the only hope was to traverse.

"We could always respect the Maori beliefs to not hold our heads above the summit and turn around here, or we could do what we've already climbed 5,000ft to do, and stand on the roof of New Zealand," Matthew said.

"Let's do it!" I replied.

The wind had been blowing relentlessly and I was anxious to get moving. Matthew handed back all the gear he'd accumulated, put me on belay, and I was off. I carefully walked along the top of the ridge at the beginning, tiptoeing along the 1-foot wide snow section between solid ice on the right and cornices on the left. As the gap narrowed I started crawling on all fours, and then put an ice screw in. At least the ice was solid enough for bomber ice screw placements, even if that made the climbing harder.

Now the gap was narrow enough that I could no longer crawl—I had to traverse. I planted my ice tools in the snow and carefully kicked my crampons into the ice beneath the screw. The ice was very hard, and I could only get my points in maybe half an inch, but that was sufficient. I started traversing sideways—kick right foot in far to the right, plant right ice tool in, kick left foot in farther right, move left ice tool right, repeat. The snow on the top of the ridge got thinner until my ice tool poked through to clear sky on the other side. There was a 1-foot cornice now on top of the sharp ice ridge.

I tried a few times to swing my tool into the ice, but then discovered it was much easier to merely hook the top of the ridge with the pick, since the top was so sharp anyways. I continued delicately traversing across this way, putting a few more screws in until I was just about off the icy section.

"NO MOOORE ROOOOPE!" I heard Matthew yell. But the summit was so close! There was no way I was building an anchor and hanging out in such a precarious position. By now the walkie-talkie batteries had succumbed to the cold and communication would have to be self-powered from here on out.

"SIMULCLIMB!" I yelled back.

Matthew quickly broke down the anchor and started climbing. On a traverse like this it was actually almost equally safe to simul-climb or pitch out the climb, since there was no real vertical component. It was thus an easy decision to switch into simul mode.

I continued off the icy section onto a more snowy knife-edge, marched up the next local maximum, and found myself the highest person in New Zealand.

"WHOOOOOOOOO" I yelled, waving my ice ax in the air. I could just see Geoff and Philip making the final push up the ridge, and they probably saw me on the top too. I pounded an ice ax into the snow, clipped in, and belayed Matthew over.

But it wasn't quite that simple. The wind had been relentlessly blowing our climbing rope over the ridge, and now a large section was looped over a cornice. Matthew passed the last ice screw, stepped onto the snow section, but was then stopped when the ropes plummeted onto the other side of the ridge. We tried in vain to swing them back over, but it was no use. The wind was too strong. Matthew was a mere snowball's throw from the summit, but couldn't make it there because of the dang cornice!

"Let's just saw the dang cornice off!" I suggested as a last resort.

We pulled back and forth on the ropes and it actually started to work. The ropes gradually worked their way through the snow until—plop—the cornice fell off and the ropes were free. I belayed Matthew up the final few feet and we both basked in the glory of the summit of Mt Cook.

We both snapped a few pictures, and ate a little snow from the summit, but it wasn't actually very pleasant there. I was starting to shiver from the cold—it was 5F that morning down on the Linda, and probably similar now but very windy. Also, some pesky clouds were rolling in from the East straight into the summit, obscuring half our view. Matthew claimed he could see the Tasman Sea off to the other side, and indeed there were amazing mountains in all directions, but we couldn't really afford to enjoy the view for long.

"I'm cold—let's get outta here," I suggested after about 90 seconds on the summit.

"Yes sir," Matthew replied.

I started back across the ridge, placing a few extra snow pickets this time to try to save the ropes from getting blown over the cornices. The icy traverse was as sketchy as before, but this time I knew what to expect and made it across with ease. We started simul-climbing shortly after I left the ice, and were soon both reunited on the flatter side of the ridge.

Now the entire route below us was enshrouded in clouds. I looked at my watch—1:30pm. The rangers had predicted afternoon snow, and it looked like we would indeed be getting afternoon snow.

We downclimbed the ice/snow slope, placing protection between us just in case as before. The bergschrund was much easier jumping down, especially into the soft fluffy snow.

At the top of the summit rocks we caught back up to Geoff and Philip, just as they were getting ready to rappel. "You guys could just rappel on our ropes if you want," I offered. We had two 60m ropes for full-length rappels, while they had only single 50m rope. They gladly agreed, so we set up the first rappel at a big steel cable wrapped around a rock. I descended first, with the undesirable job of untangling the ropes as I went. At near 60m down I found another steel cable rappel station and clipped in. By now it was starting to snow and the visibility dropped considerably.

Philip, Geoff, and Matthew all came down to my station, and then we repeated the process. The second rappel brought back to the base of the summit rocks, and now the situation got a little bit trickier. We didn't really trust the ratty old slings at the base of the summit rocks to rappel off, but didn't want to downclimb the steep gully.

Geoff said there were some better slings at another gully along the ridge, so we all climbed down there. I found a set of slings that looked a little bit better, so added a caribbeaner to the anchor and rappelled down. I was fully expecting to need to leave gear and build my own anchor for the next rappel, but somehow I stumbled across another steel cable around a rock about 50m down. It was in a terrible position—there were no foot placements below it so I just had to clip in and hang from it—but it seemed solid and meant I wouldn't have to leave gear.

Matthew followed down to the anchor, while Geoff and Philip decided to take a different route down. We pulled the rope, set up one final rappel, and were finally back onto the snow slope of the Linda Shelf.

By now the conditions were basically whiteout, and we could only barely make out our tracks from the morning. The snow had stopped but dense fog had rolled in. Matthew and I roped back up for glacier-travel mode and continued over the bergschrund and across the shelf. The snow definitely seemed deeper now. It was probably a combination of afternoon softening in the hotter part of the day, wind loading, and new snow.

I struggled to follow the tracks and eventually gave up. As I was traversing up high I luckily spotted a black object down below—the snowshoes! I diverted back to the right course and reunited us with our snowshoes.

The terrain was still too steep to allow snowshoes on the descent, so we strapped them to our packs and hiked down in crampons. The snow momentarily abated and a gap in the clouds rolled over us. We felt confident now that Geoff and Philip would have no trouble following our tracks down if our groups got separated, so we quickened our pace down the glacier.

Our tracks from the morning were almost completely wiped out, but we managed to follow a similar course through the crevasses. However, the navigation soon got much more difficult as the gap in the clouds disappeared and it started snowing again.

It was 7:15pm now and starting to get dark, and we were only just approaching the Grand Plateau. There was no way we'd find our way back to the hut in this whiteout with no tracks to follow. I could barely even see Matthew on the end of the rope. However, we had brought a secret weapon: a GPS with satellite photos of the area loaded and a waypoint marked for Plateau Hut. I whipped out the GPS, handed it to Matthew in the lead, and we continued on.

"1.25 miles to the Hut, as the crow flies," Matthew yelled out.

"Awesome!" I replied, "but I think that you mean '1.25 miles as the kea flies.' We are in New Zealand after all." We had picked up this phrase from Geoff, a reference to the beloved New Zealand parrot. Anyhow, we should be there in less than an hour, I thought.

But that 1.25 miles didn't include navigating around crevasses. Matthew initially tried to avoid several huge crevasses that showed up on our satellite image, but we instead ran into even more crevasses. We eventually agreed that the crevasses must have moved since that image was taken, and instead made a direct bee-line for the hut.

Our progress felt agonizingly slow. We were just walking in one direction, with nothing to see in any direction, blindly following our GPS. After an hour we stumbled across some ski tracks which were heading in relatively the same direction, and we decided to follow them. In all likelihood they would lead to the hut, and they provided a solid backup for our GPS navigation.

At 8:45pm we finally saw a dark shape in the distance, and had reached Plateau Hut. It had been an 18+ hour day and we were exhausted. We were also extremely dehydrated and famished. Somehow I had managed to drink only one liter of water all day, and had eaten half a bagel. Matthew was similar. I guess the technical terrain had made it inconvenient for us to eat and thus we just didn't eat, though we definitely should have.

After heaving our gear off into a big pile we started some water boiling and some pasta cooking. We could finally take a well-earned rest.

Geoff and Philip made it back an hour later, after following our tracks across the plateau, and short-cutting around some of our glacier wandering. By 10:30pm we were all sound asleep.

Day 3

By 7:30am the next morning we were all up and Matthew radioed down to the airport.

"Hi, we're two hikers at Plateau Hut looking for a ride back down—are there any rides available?" he asked into the speaker. There was no response. Matthew tried again twice at 10 minute intervals but still there was no response.

"Here, let me try," Geoff suggested after the last one. "Plateau Hut to base, over" he said in his New Zealand accent.

"Base to Plateau, good morning," the radio replied.

"You see, sometimes they respond better to a local accent," Geoff said with a grin. Perhaps Matthew's American accent had been too intimidating to the Kiwi on the other end.

They said they had a helicopter coming up at 9:30am with a group of sightseers and we could split the cost for the ride down. We agreed and quickly threw our gear in our backpacks and put them outside next to the landing area.

We waited around inside but then heard another message over the radio. The sightseers had never shown up, and the flight was canceled. The next available ride would be at 5pm.

"That's too late," Matthew said. "Let's just hike down." "I'm down for hiking out," I agreed. The hike out would involve descending the Boys Glacier, then climbing down a big scree slope, traversing the moraine at the base of the Tasman glacier, and hiking 6 miles of trails down to a road, where we could potentially hitch-hike back to the airport. Geoff and Philip graciously offered to take some of our extra gear back with them when they flew out the next morning, and we gladly took them up on the offer.

We removed all unnecessary items from our packs—including, as we'd later regret, our sleeping bags—and headed out the door at 11am moving fast and light. The clouds had crept back up to the hut level and we were yet again walking in a white-out. A pair of skiers had hiked into the hut the previous day, though, and we at least had their tracks to follow. We soon found the ski tracks and descended onto the Grand Plateau, then traversed across the glacier to Cinerama Col.

By the time we reached the col the clouds had burned off, and we could again see where we were going. We dropped down the opposite side of the col, traversed over to the top of the Boys glacier, and started a steep descent. The terrain soon became too steep for snowshoes, so we switched to crampons and plunge-stepped our way down. We tried to walk quickly through several recent avalanches, still following the ski tracks from the previous day.

By 3pm we stepped off the last bit of snow onto the large scree slope. Finally, we could take of the glacier rope and crampons and go back to normal hiking. Not that we didn't like the security of the rope on the glacier. It just constrained us to hike at exactly the same speed the whole time, which got a little old.

We dropped down the scree slope to the moraine of the Tasman Glacier below, and then started hiking down the valley. Matthew found enough time to take a quick swim in a little glacial meltwater pool that was probably 32F, but I chickened out. I'd had enough of being cold for today. The talus and scree covering the glacier were extremely unstable, and forced us to continue the hike in our heavy mountaineering boots.

Following Geoff's directions, we soon climbed back up a boulder slope to a big terrace on the edge of the moraine, and met up with the remnants of an old trail. Apparently the Tasman glacier used to extend much farther down the valley, but in recent years it has melted considerably, and this melting caused the terrace holding the trail to slide several hundred feet down the side of the mountain. There used to be a hut in this area, but it was destroyed by the slide.

We followed the old trail for about a mile, hiking through several rough areas, until we passed the last of the slide zone. Now the trail changed to a rough 4wd road, which we cruised down. Six miles later, at 6pm, we reached a parking lot with several cars in it. Luckily two Swiss hikers were just returning from the mountains and offered to give me a ride back to the airport. I'd have to come back for Matthew and the packs since they only had a little bit of room, but that was no problem.

I rode down to the airport, and then drove back up to meet Matthew at 6:30pm. We threw the gear into the car and made it back to Mt Cook village in time to have a celebratory pizza dinner at the Old Mountaineer Café.

After a chilly night camping out with no sleeping bags we met Geoff and Philip the next morning at the airport to pick up our extra gear. It was certainly nice of them to fly that down for us! We all four checked in at the ranger station that we had made it down safely. The rangers confirmed that we were indeed the first ones to summit this season, and they anxiously asked about conditions higher up on the mountain. Apparently the icy traverse we climbed on the summit ridge is usually an easier snow traverse, and the rangers guessed it may have been exceptionally windy over the winter to blow all the snow off.

Matthew and I still had six days left in New Zealand, so we called up Ian to coordinate the next leg of our adventure—a backpacking trip in Fiordland National Park.

Stay tuned for many more adventure stories!

ABOUT THE AUTHORS

ERIC GILBERTSON
AND
MATTHEW GILBERTSON

According to the USA State Highpointers Club, they are the first twins to climb all fifty state highpoints and the second team to climb all of them unguided. As of 2012 there are fewer than 250 people who have climbed all fifty state highpoints.

They were born in Berea, KY in 1986 and started hiking with their Dad in the nearby hills and hollers of Kentucky as soon as they could walk. Before that, their parents carried them in backpacks. As they grew older and became faster, they started hiking and backpacking at the Pigg House, the Pinnacle, and Anglin Falls near Berea, the Smoky Mountains in Tennessee, and Philmont Scout Ranch in New Mexico

Eric and Matthew started college in the fall of 2004 at the Massachusetts Institute of Technology (MIT) in Cambridge, Mass, and there they discovered the MIT Outing Club. They both graduated in 2008 and again in 2010 with Bachelor's and Master's degrees. Since fall 2010, they have been at MIT working on their mechanical engineering PhDs and squeezing in state highpoints whenever they can.

In February 2012 they finished the final state highpoint—Guadalupe Peak in Texas. Now they are busy working to finish PhD degrees: Matthew is designing an improved handheld force-controlled ultrasound probe and Eric is working with autonomous kayaks.